Tim Hector

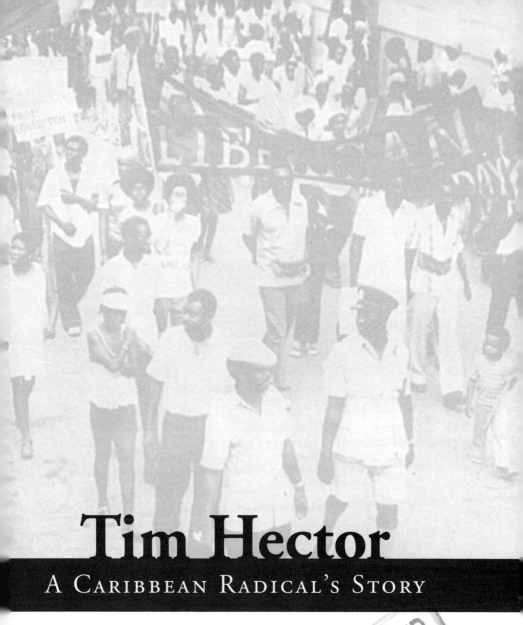

Tim Hector
A Caribbean Radical's Story

PAUL BUHLE

UNIVERSITY PRESS OF MISSISSIPPI / JACKSON

www.upress.state.ms.us

The University Press of Mississippi is a member of the
Association of American University Presses.

Photographs courtesy of the Leonard Tim Hector Memorial
Society

Copyright © 2006 by Paul Buhle
All rights reserved
Manufactured in the United States of America

First Edition 2006
∞
Library of Congress Cataloging-in-Publication Data

Buhle, Paul, 1944–
Tim Hector : a Caribbean radical's story / Paul Buhle.— 1st ed.
p. cm.
Includes bibliographical references and index.
ISBN 1-57806-851-7 (cloth : alk. paper)
1. Hector, Tim. 2. Caribbean Area—History—20th century.
3. Antigua and Barbuda—History—20th century. I. Title.
F2183.H43B84 2006
972.905'2—dc22
                                            2006002050

British Library Cataloging-in-Publication Data available

To Richard Hart,
a Founding Figure of the Caribbean Left

Contents

Contents

Chapter Five

Beyond Tragedy

Afterword

Tim Hector, Humanist, Political Values,

and National Reconstruction

Tim Hector

Introduction

In the Sunlight, in the Shadow

The Caribbean is not an American lake. It is the estuary of the Americas.

—Edward Glissant, *Caribbean Discourse: Selected Essays*

In my continuing and never-ending challenge to White Power, I am the bete noire of both parties, and even the nonparty supporters. "And all the congregation shall stone him" (me). They all claim they do not know where I am, even though that it is pellucid. I am against, inalterably against, white minority economic control . . . and for a new system of social ownership and control. . . . Clear? Very clear.

—Tim Hector, "The Black Condition, Here and Now"

An audience from across the Caribbean, representing most of the heads of state, gathered on October 20, 2002, to bid farewell to Tim Hector, editor of the socialistic weekly *Outlet* and a leading personality in sports and culture so beloved novelist Jamaica Kincaid vowed to repatriate to Antigua and Barbuda if he ever became prime minister. In permanent opposition during life—fired, jailed, his wife murdered, and his press torched—Hector suddenly seemed respectable in death. It was an illusion. But an illusion that drew out of Prime Minister Lester Bird, among others, paeans about Tim as the political intellectual of the island par excellence. No one would deny him that in death. Nor his determination, right to the very end, to do what standing politicians would not do, to look unflinchingly in the face of regional catastrophe.

"Globalization," Tim Hector had observed in one of his typically incisive and widely read columns, is "unrelentingly hostile" to its Third World victims, contrary to the mainstream media images of peoples held back from entering the modern cornucopia only by their own ignorance and by corrupt rulers. The problem is also, contrary to the rest of the current hype, locked in a relationship of development to underdevelopment at least a half-millennium old.[1] Both sides of the equation merit close examination.

The essential nature of the modernizing as well as the modern world, ultimate motive force behind the contemporary thrust, can be grasped in the tale of the Caribbean. Today's rivalries of clashing powers seem to leave the region completely behind in world events, a backwater of tiny islands whose very existence may be in doubt with the effects of global warming potentially raising sea levels. But this would be looking at things upside-down, not only because crucial origins of the modern era lie here, and not only because descendents of the Caribbean Basin (including Mexicans) bid fair in the coming generations to become the largest population group in the world's leading power. There is another reason: people of the Caribbean are in many ways quite special. They can have a singular effect on the project of redemption that has become by now a do-or-die proposition for civilization and the planet Earth.

The path from that now distant past of conquest and contest—depopulation and repopulation, slavery and its world-changing profits, the creation of colonial institutions and popular uprising against them, independence and the penetration of neocolonialism into the very fabric of Caribbean being—is the background of this short book. The life of one utterly remarkable intellectual, a former Shakespeare teacher until fired and jailed by his own government, a New Left/Black Power intellectual, a political organizer, and a newspaper editor with advanced ideas on issues ranging from ecology to feminism, combines in itself the currents sweeping the islands like seasonal tides.

But Leonard Tim Hector offers both voice and template. If the bane of Caribbean politics and labor movements has been the division of the middle-class leaders from the rank and file, no one of his generation—that is, who came of age during the final struggle for independence—worked so consistently or wrote so eloquently for the participation of ordinary people in their own unified Caribbean government and economy.[2] No one had more day-to-day contact with them, casual as well as formal, or likely took so much pleasure in it. Shunning alike the appeals of Stalinism and neocolonialism, he pointed to the possibilities for a different way out of the mess of the postindependence era.

Nor could anyone in the region so accurately take the measure of the successes and failures of the region and grasp the vast tragedy when global power mongering and the absence of regional political will conspired to bring the Caribbean people down from their high potential. No one better understood the living historical legacies of black and brown self-contempt and of little worth that plunged people back from hope into apathy and violence, mirroring the dog-eat-dog behavior of the politicians coming to state power and its perquisites. No one better saw moments of reversal, political or cultural, where ordinary West Indians gave signs that they could do better than their leaders.

Over thirty years, as the saga was played out, Hector offered up a vision to his readers and listeners as a gift. The passing of regional giants supplied a decisive moment for reflection and interpretation. He looked centuries backward at the slave past, fast forward to vapid consumerism and reacceptance of the status of third-rate citizens, no longer of Mother England, but of an extended American imperium. The hopes and bitter disappointments of Pan-Africanism and the Third World at large stood revealed in Hector's columns as nowhere else.

The secret to his accomplishment was no secret at all. He chose early to return and stay put, not out of a sense of self-sacrifice but because Antigua and Barbuda were where this magnum intellectual belonged. He combined so many sides of regional culture, historical and current, literature, art, scholarship, music, and dance into so brilliant a synthesis. His own status, intimate observer of the cultural history of the region, had been underlined by his aggressive participation in the amateur sports of his own island microculture. Readers of the *Outlet* across the diaspora, Canada and the United States to the United Kingdom and beyond, knew this secret and treasured it. Many of them would be fortunate enough to see him in person, in his travels; some were fortunate enough to hear him at the United Nations, or more intimately at Pan-African gatherings from the Middle East to Africa to Caribbean home turf.

His committed life, political and artistic, egalitarian and multiracial, is also a saga unto itself, a beacon for the socialistic visions that many millions died seeking in the nineteenth and twentieth centuries. It was a cause repeatedly betrayed, but never entirely lost. To quote Calypsonian Destroyer Sr., who speaks for Hector to a bereaved people:

I heard the tributes
Pouring through the land
On every radio
And TV programme
I saw you crying at my funeral
The whole nation mourning
A great man is gone.
But when I was alive
I was demonized
Banded and maligned
As a communist
Arrested and jailed
Tear gas in me tail
I forgive but I can't forget
You for this.

[Chorus]
So don't cry for me
Don't cry for me
My work on earth is done
I am now at a better place.
Don't cry for me
Don't cry for me.
Tell all Antiguans
To wipe de tears from their face
Because every election
I offer you my service
But you reject my plan I ever lost me deposit.
But today I am so happy

I am in much better company.
Don't cry for me, don't cry for me
I am happy with Garvey, don't cry for me
CLR James and Manley, don't cry for me
Antiguans weep not for me
But for your children and your country
Don't cry for me, don't cry for me.

I try to feed you intellectually
You refuse my menu
For years you scorn me.
We try to raise de level
Of your consciousness
To elevate my people
Was my sole interest.
As I close my eyes
I was surprised
To hear the great things
They say about me.
****
I am your Freedom Fighter
I am your Journalist
Teacher, commentator
Politician and activist
Fought to end apartheid
And colonialism
All my life I am fighting
To liberate all people
Now I am dead and gone
I am so shocked to learn
My works must be recorded in history.[3]

These days, when black sports and film stars make millions of dollars and capture headlines, it is easy (especially for those eager to do so) to forget the extremity of history's weight. Many wish to put the burden back in the slavery period, long ago, growing steadily more distant and irrelevant with the benevolent and inevitable arrival of meritocracy, the victory of transrace individualism. Hector's friends, searching the Colonial Office records, came across a secret communication by three white leaders of

Antigua in 1937, inadvertently providing keener insight than most official histories. In answer to the emerging cries for freedom against a background of fascist threat and the American New Deal, the colonial leaders stood firm by their own conception of historical ground: the "Negroes in these Leeward Islands are not an indigenous native race and have no claim to self-government." Very simple, very clear. The homeland and "white settlers" had a "trusteeship toward the Immigrant Negro race," best met by a combination of charity and recognition of "those individuals of the black race who fit themselves" with "character, balance and education" to help carry the "responsibilities and position of the white race."[4] How well put! And how little changed, in a global sense, from that day to this.

Hector's home island of Antigua, a mere nine miles by twelve miles, joined politically to the even smaller island of Barbuda, is poor, water-scarce, and tyrannized, a favorite of the garrisoned American military, of casino gamblers and off-shore operators who leave little behind for the native employees but environmental damage and wasted resources. It would therefore seem an unlikely setting for a great story. The entire Eastern Caribbean, rarely in its modern history a hub of activity like Cuba and Puerto Rico, indeed hardly appears in the popular literature of Europeans or North Americans except as a tourist destination for fun in the sun and (for those who so choose) sex in the shade. The literary phenomenon of Antiguan native Jamaica Kincaid and the sheer contrary individualism of her famed semifictional writings seem to underline the impossibility of a coherent narrative here. Kari Levitt and Lloyd Best, among foremost regional analysts, might as well have confirmed for Antigua and Barbuda as they did for the region that backwardness is inscribed in the heart of historic colonial relationships even after the colonizer is gone.[5]

But these conclusions would miss much. Hector, moving through a life of furious activity into middle age and just beyond, toward a tragically early end, often reminded the reader that he stood upon the shoulders of others, including a few giants. The first of these, the one closest to him personally and politically, is C.L.R. James. Emphatically a world figure increasingly recognized by younger scholars as such, James (1901–89) summed up an age in his thinking and his actions. He left behind not only a large view of Caribbean history and life but also a large view of the seemingly hopeless dilemmas in which humanity finds itself. More important than diagnoses were James's prescriptions for cure, no simple Rx substituting one hierarchical system for another (as communism, capitalism, and national- or religious-based exclusionism have posed against each other) but a wholesale replacement based upon the participation of ordinary people in all the decisions, economic as well as political and also ecological, that face them. That vision, as old as the dream of the Golden Day before the existence of hierarchies, fared badly in a bitterly disappointing twentieth century. But the dream outlives the century, and its last words have not been uttered.

James's vision upon which Hector largely built his own was never devoted to leveling down. Contrary to utterly false charges of "Russianism" against it by Caribbean politicians (and notably by his fellow Trinidadian V. S. Naipaul, who invented in *A Way in the World* a brutal and dishonest caricature of James so as to attack the reputation of the original a few years after his death and no longer able to defend himself), it had a distinctly different purpose.[6] Achievement of great things depended, in James's wide view, very much upon the role of individual genius, not of the genius individual in a vacuum but the ways in which the writer, poet, musician, filmmaker, and the political revolutionary could articulate the sensations and perceptions of the ordinary crowd.

James had been trained for this perception by a childhood and youth in seemingly backward colonial society, absorbing as much of British culture and the gifts of Greek antiquity as any precocious youngster might anywhere in the Commonwealth (and more likely than at home). He had also been trained by his close observation of the society around him, and as he grew to maturity, by the unfairness of the rules that seemed to place the graceful black cricketer outside the bounds of formal aesthetics and even sporting history, the last a particularly informative passion of the young man. Cricket helped him understand the disastrous effects of racism upon an entire society and (on a larger stage) how the uplifting of sport might also uplift a people.

Cricket gave Hector, like James before him, a certainty that the Caribbean was a single region in desperate need of a unifying confederation that could overcome the miniscule island size, economic backwardness, and otherwise permanent disadvantage of West Indian peoples in world society. Hector commented glumly, late in life, that the long-awaited common market and common interests of the region had finally arrived—not, as hoped, independent and proud, but imposed as baneful commercialization. The fat and listless society of consumers made West Indians into nothing better than the lowest of Americans or Europeans, with dramatically fewer life chances, more deadly diseases, more frantic pursuit of life's little corruptions hiding more complete despair. He returned to the subject frequently, examining the stages of this sorry outcome, analyzing the moments of political truth during the 1940s and after when things in the Caribbean might have gone a different way.

One of Hector's chief antagonists was nevertheless, for his genuine accomplishments, also somewhat of a personal hero. Vere Cornwall Bird, the labor leader and politician who stood courageously against the British for decades, later capitulated to the corruption of postcolonialism, grabbing a share of it for himself and his descendents. Like Vere Bird, others—such as C.L.R. James's protégé Eric Williams, genius historian and longtime premier and prime minister of Trinidad and Tobago; Guyana's Cheddi Jagan; Jamaica's Michael Manley; and Grenada's Maurice Bishop—all could rightly be described as martyrs, in one way or another, to the ruthlessness of neocolonialism. This is not to level the differences between them. Hector knew, and carefully analyzed for his readers, the strengths and weaknesses of each leader. But they did share a vast disadvantage of the island economy and society within a world of imperial giants. James once quipped that if he had stayed rather than leaving, he might have become a prime minister and spent his time in office explaining why he could not accomplish the goals he set out, and this was indeed their common fate. Hector crossed paths with them personally, seeing them, knowing them as intimately as a West Indian of intellect and taste knows another.

Two radical leaders of his own generation, Walter Rodney and Maurice Bishop, inevitably had special meaning for him. All three younger martyrs—including Hector himself—were part of a cohort that moved more easily abroad, many of them into waiting academic positions, joining hundreds of thousands of their fellow Anglophone Caribbean émigrés in London, New York, Toronto, and elsewhere. These three made the difficult and ultimately fatal choice to return, renewing the familiar lamentation that long life and enduring satisfaction all but demand a fatalistic acceptance of exile. Their fate was an ominous indication if not final judgment for island life, island culture; they sacrificed so others could hope to live better, more productively, more free, more proud, more meaningfully.

"We know that we are nourished by the past," Wilson Harris reflects, "but we know that the past also needs us, and that unless we can create an original role for ourselves in the present we will destroy our connections with the past."[7] No one in the region responded more deeply, more continuously, to that appeal than Hector, for whom the lessons and the enigmas of the past bear lessons for today.[8]

In James's exceedingly wide view, as he came to maturity, the Caribbean had vital contributions to make to the reconstruction of a wounded and self-destructive global society. Harris, urging West Indians to take advantage of what he called the "open state of consciousness" latent in the regional experience, insisted similarly that the "true capacity of marginal and disadvantaged cultures resides in their genius to tilt the field of civilization," making possible a "different apprehension of reality" and a different reality itself.[9]

Stated one way or another, this is a view that Hector absorbed from James at close range and transformed in his own distinct way as the salvation of the region in a transformation of the world. To understand the real meanings of a culture based on extermination and on slavery, denied its own language and religion but triumphant in survival, is to see the hidden potential beneath the rubble. No one from the region except the master himself, not even such activist-scholars as Rodney, has seen the history, the rubble, or the surviving potential as well as Hector. None but Rodney lived it more fully, with so many comrades and admirers, amid the pain and the promise.

Like any political intellectual deeply ill in the last months of life, Hector ruminated about all that he could not do and hoped that others would do, above all for the Caribbean and his own Antigua and Barbuda. Having experienced so much personal tragedy, he nevertheless determinedly counted himself as "lucky" for the opportunities that life had given him, his family, his friends, and his one very special mentor, C.L.R. James.[10] Thus in declaring, in June 2002, that a "definitive biography of C.L.R. [is] urgently required," he confessed that just once, contemplating a possible fellowship to Simon Fraser University, he had imagined himself taking on the task. But "I preferred the exchanges we were developing in ACLM and around Outlet to the research halls and the dust of academia."[11]

He had other reasons as well for this difficult choice. His son Amilcar—named for freedom fighter Amilcar Cabral—had just been born, and as a father, he had personally grown to the point where not staying to share the burden (and not merely "helping out" Arah Hector at home) had become unthinkable. No doubt the absence of his own father from his childhood home was an important consideration. Hector, at any rate, dropped the notion of the great work to be done in Canadian exile, never to pick it up again.[12] Subjected not long before his intensifying heart problems to what he called laconically "Rafter Worship," that is, counting the rafters above him, while in excruciating back pain and unable to move, he had been mentally tormented by memories of that May, in 1989, when Arah had been murdered. Nevertheless, he could still be amused at the suggestion of a visitor that he would have been better off, in so many respects, in academia. Summoning up the strength of his badly weakened spine, so to speak,

> I replied that since 1966 I had turned my back against an academic career. And firmly so. I was an island boy. I believed then and believe now that there are certain qualities which island people have which are critical to the emancipation of humankind—one of them being the capacity to produce a regional state of City States in which the sheer scope and range of human achievement would make the ancient city-states pale in comparison. I would die trying. It is in that sense I was an island boy. The continents were not my métier or home.[13]

This was a most revealing observation, if (as usual) too modest by half.

Hector, as we shall see, knew his fellow islanders, their strengths and their failings, their histories frequently intertwined with his own at close range, as only a lifelong islander possibly can. He had danced to their music, organized their sports leagues, knew personalities by the hundreds or thousands. No one, it is safe to say, his written more intimate eulogies to ordinary West Indians who might otherwise surely have been forgotten musicians, teachers, sportsmen or women, ministers, or unionists, but who were treated, in his writings, as the best that civilization had to offer. But Hector had also made himself an international figure, far more than most intellectuals ever manage. In an age when George Lamming declared that Caribbean intellectuals after Eric Williams had fallen back into intellectual insularity and careerism, Hector was the veritable opposite.

Hector traveled widely, carrying the gospel of Caribbean unity and Pan-Africanism globally, without hope of financial reward or career advancement, delivering impassioned addresses and meeting privately in endless sessions with older and newer comrades, from Toronto to Dar Es Salaam. *Outlet*, and especially his "Fan the Flame" column (not to take anything away from the rest of the paper), was read across the African diaspora, but especially in Canada, the United States, the United Kingdom, and throughout the English-speaking Caribbean. With the disappearance of the church-based *Caribbean Contact*, no other Anglophone regional newspaper tilted leftward against the pressure of the International Monetary Fund (IMF) and the deep roots (not merely the particular manifestations) of corruption. After his death, *Outlet* failed, and no such regional paper remained to connect older struggles with those at hand and those to come. If Pan-Africanism had badly flagged, with the disappointments in personalities like Kwame Nkrumah, Julius Kambarage Nyerere, and Jomo Kenyatta, along with institutions like the Organization of African Unity, the necessity for a Pan-Africanism had never diminished.

Other islands and mainland Guyana saw the brilliant individual Marxist of his generation—most of them working intermittently in U.S. or Canadian universities—such as Brian Meeks in Jamaica, Hilary Beckels in Barbados, Walton Looklai in Trinidad, and Hector's closest counterpart, Eusi Kwayana in Guyana. At the high tide of Pan-Caribbean sentiment, during the 1970s, larger islands and outright socialist experiments (that is, Grenada) attracted more interest. Hector gained all the greater prominence afterward, as scattered left-wingers looked to him and to the *Outlet* to uphold the Red flag and to dissociate socialism from IMF-corrupted social democracy, demagogic racial populism, or

Soviet-style party rule (which, despite Cuba, was practically extinct but was still an intellectual force in anti-imperialist circles). As Paget Henry commented, Hector's "Fan the Flame" column was also unique in all Caribbean literature for the range and depth of issues tackled and the border-crossing between journalism and scholarship.[14]

Hector's unique politics, depending far more on his writing than upon the implements of power, could not possibly be so successful. One of the great tragedies of his passing is that the newest challenges to U.S. hemispheric domination, the leftist currents moving through Latin America—sweeping up indigenous communities, working people, and intellectuals alike; taking up new ideological forms not classifiable in traditional terms but closer to anarcho-syndicalism than to Leninism—had not yet found Hector and his messages for the Caribbean Basin. Nor did he live long enough to find them.

What sense might he have made of recent Bolivarism, when Venezuela's Hugo Chavez reached out in 2005 to offer Caribbean leaders discounted oil and the usually servile prime ministers actually rejected the warnings of the U.S. State Department against any such arrangement? What of Bolivia and its rebellious movements rejecting corporate theft of natural resources? What of Mexico, Brazil, and so many other places where brave minorities stood against vast ongoing ecological degradation, conducted hand in glove with the corrupt existing governments? Surely, Hector would have had much to say, and his fellow islanders every need to listen.

Toward the end of a hyperactive political life and entering a new century without any notable rebellious movements at large in the region or hemisphere, Hector took the turn, curious to some and outrageous to others, of moving toward détente with old enemies. He had sought, by shifting his forces into the United Progressive Party (UPP) in 1995, to create a successful coalition of uncorrupted Antiguans, democratic nationalists, and radicals to overturn the Bird machine. It was a remarkable effort. But as the 2000 elections approached, UPP leader Baldwin Spencer as much as ordered Hector to stand down as a candidate, pushing him aside so as to bring bourgeois (or more properly, petite-bourgeois) respectability to the coalition. As widely expected, the opportunistic UPP lost anyway, or lost all the more because it had disgraced itself with all-too-typical maneuvers. When Hector then accepted an official government request to serve on a regional sports committee, UPP leaders seized the pretext and expelled him. He responded by proposing something that he had never previously aired, not even suggested privately outside a small circle of friends: a power-sharing arrangement with the Bird government, not unlike the coalition governments created during crisis periods in various parts of the world.

It was a stunning turnaround, and an occasional writer in the *Outlet* itself cast doubt on his judgment and his activity. (That they did so in the paper while he was alive and writing for it was another mark of the commitment to open discussion, no-holds-barred.) Could the revolutionary leopard change its spots? Only weeks before his death, Hector assayed Prime Minister Lester Bird's *Antigua Vision: Caribbean Reality* and judged it both a miserable literary failure and an outright political deception. The Antigua Labor Party (ALP), whatever its origins, had become (and the UPP to boot) "bureaucratic political formations for self-perpetuation of a lower middle class elite and sordid adventurers in or out of power, without substance or achievement."[15] No compromise here.

Then, suddenly, Hector was dead, and the same Lester Bird was heaping praise and quoting poetry over Tim's bier, insisting that Hector was the truest Caribbean patriot—very nearly an admission of Bird's own guilt. Perhaps, as a hotel clerk in Antigua once remarked to me in a commonplace of the island, Tim would "be prime minister someday," but the time had not yet come. Not because Hector himself wasn't already prepared, of course, but because the islanders weren't ready for him. Perhaps this phantom, decades in the making and ended only by Tim's demise, is no more real than writer Jamaica Kincaid's occasional threat to return and repatriate under Hector's imagined island premiership. We will never know. What we can say is that Tim Hector remained to the last an intrepid intellect and activist, seeking fresh roads to Caribbean unity almost literally until the hour that he died. In recounting his life, this volume is also intended to add something to the effort ahead.

The belated victory of the UPP in the 2004 elections seems to have added very little than a depressing footnote to the larger story. Baldwin Spencer, lining up for the rewards of office, even bore a suspicious sonlike physical resemblance to old Vere Bird, as the gossipmongers were quick to point out. The departing Bird family machine meanwhile sequestered and successfully "vanished" official documents by the thousands, but no matter. As Baldwin Spencer soon demonstrated, daily life and misgovernment went on as normal.

And yet something had changed in the region to restore to Hector's life and work a relevance that similar activities had lost, at least in the eyes of many, just a decade earlier. Brian Meeks observes, in the introduction to the important volume *New Caribbean Thought: A Reader*, that after the shock of Maurice Bishop's murder and the accompanying collapse of the revolutionary government in Grenada, followed by the collapse of the Eastern Bloc and the drama of the Berlin Wall's destruction, the entire project of Caribbean Marxism seemed to fade. With it went the notion that any small nation could carve out a decent place for itself in the global system—as Hector had written most eloquently—and that anything, thought or deed, collective or personal, could escape the maw of the world market's greedy claims.[16]

Then swiftly came the disproof of the vaunted "End of History," with the Balkans out of control, the blatant theft of the world's most important elected leadership in a farce of democracy, the World Trade Center bombing on September 11, 2001, and a sudden return to what looked very much like old-fashioned neocolonial behavior. The dot.com crash, wildly spiraling oil prices, and unprecedented American debts dashed all confident predictions of "progress" under business rules. Popular rage at U.S. leadership from every corner of the world made actual terrorism and the accompanying religious fanaticism an epiphenomenon, something highlighted to justify the bullying but unconvincing either as logical world management or as Judeo-Christian morality.

Meeks noted that a younger generation of Caribbean intellectuals and activists had already begun gathering informally during the later 1990s, both in their home islands and abroad, looking toward the new challenges ahead.[17] The C.L.R. James Centennial Conference in Trinidad during 2001, with Hector very much the man of the hour, was one of the key forums in which the discussion moved forward. Tim had not missed the morning hours of the newer day after all.

In this volume I link Hector differently to C.L.R. James than, I am sure, any other author would have done. My afterword to the massive compilation *C.L.R. James: His Intellectual Legacies* (1995), an essay subtitled "From a Biographer's Notebook, the Field of C.L.R. James Research," noted that the very "field" had barely emerged before it veered away from social history and outright political claims, heading toward literary criticism and cultural studies.[18] Thanks no doubt to the depressing political climate, interest in James the revolutionary thinker lagged badly. Only here and there, especially in the conversations of Caribbean specialists with a background in the radical politics of earlier decades, did the real James remain. Mostly, he seemed as a prophet neglected if not scorned.

Not that the resulting literary and cultural studies have been lacking in value—far from it.[19] But there can be no doubt that the passing of so many older comrades who shared Hector's political relations with James threatened to push the issues still farther away from politics and into the discursive postmodern.[20] Tim Hector, a disciple reaching the apex of his political and literary talent, would not get much sympathetic attention here. Meanwhile, Naipaulesque accounts of James's engagement with West Indian radicals from the 1950s to the 1980s caricatured his very persona as silly and destructive, a masquerade of Black Power posturing, altogether the monkey in the dress-up suit of Western civilization spouting communism and black racism. All the hopes and dreams for a different kind of society had evidently been a mistake. To believe the leading publications and many of the highly regarded regional-minded novelists of Britain or the United States, colonialism turned out to have been no worse and probably better than its successors after all, and for the Caribbean, the only kind of regional identity ever to be expected.[21]

Yet I am convinced, as the reader will gather, that shifting political tides will bring back the political questions in a less melancholy way. When that happens, it will be seen that no one was more important in extending and developing James's traditions further than Leonard Tim Hector.

Only a fellow native Antiguan could likely know, with deepest personal insight, the person who was Hector, his life, his family, and his place in island society. No one who did not share his decades of effort in the regional unity and Pan-African movements, or even the organized sports of the Caribbean, could offer an equal degree of intimacy into the full complications of his politics.

I am thus admittedly an outsider several times over. But what I shared with Tim, apart from the many connections of Caribbean and U.S. New Lefts and their successors, was the larger trajectory of James's influence, decisive in itself and equally decisive for each of our lives, notwithstanding assorted differences of background, culture, political styles, and so on. Tim and I "discovered" James at almost the same age in our lives, and in many ways we have lived, written, and acted according to what we learned in the extended engagement with the aging savant. I took it upon myself from 1968 onward to introduce James to the New Left at large. Those *Radical America* issues that I published, especially the 1970 "James Anthology," the first selection of his writings, reached beyond the U.S. boundaries to Canada, the United Kingdom, France, Germany, Italy, and, of course, the Caribbean and, in particular, Tim.

Hector had already become a recognized lieutenant of the old revolutionary general by this time, while I was mainly a publicist and scholar. Had things gone differently and Hector become James's activist arm in the Sixth Pan-African Congress and after, I would have had the joy of using *Radical America* to broadcast the good news of accomplishment. There weren't many of us in the work, at any rate, and we felt ourselves as part of a global community of his faithful.

Most of our erstwhile comrades fell away in time. But those who remained naturally developed a feeling of being all the closer, so that when Hector and I finally met in 1993, it was as if we had known each other for a large part of our lives. As Tim might say, risking a mystical turn: destiny, even. That I should write articles and books about James (or other subjects of deep concern to James, such as the labor bureaucracy, the promise of popular culture, Caribbean literature, and so forth) and that Tim should carry the banner into politics and journalism, the two of us meeting mainly via the pages of the *C.L.R. James Journal* or *Outlet*, offered evidence of a congruence in life tasks that we chose or, we sometimes reflected with bittersweet irony, tasks that pitilessly chose us.

I hope the reader will not resent my detailing one deeply personal part of the saga. The political collapse of the American New Left and the physical collapse of James found me editing a first collection of essays about the aging giant, reprinted in revised form as *C.L.R. James: His Life and Work* in 1986.[22] I made a point of visiting him in the middle 1980s, just above the *Race Today* office of Brixton, London, of his grand-nephew Darcus Howe's headquarters, where the weakened but still voluble and distinctly witty old man resided.[23] I learned that the memoir he had announced more than a decade earlier had not advanced further than a few very rough, repetitive chapters dictated over the years, and that it was not, realistically, going to advance further. I offered myself as biographer, and the *eminence grise* readily agreed. Within a year, it was finished, an authorized if desperately hurried effort based on available sources, interviews, phone calls, and an extended visit with James.[24] I had not traveled to the Caribbean—with the exception of a trip to Barbados to see George Lamming—to interview old-timers or devotees, or found the way to track James's fast-disappearing British friends of the 1930s. Still, James pronounced it a good job, and just in time: he slipped away only weeks after the book's appearance in March 1989.

Several years then passed. Thanks to the friendship and collaboration of Paget Henry, who had been Tim's student in Fifth Form, I quickly made the *Outlet* my much-awaited weekly window on Tim's world, and I never missed an issue afterward. We two colleagues in another small, picturesque, and notably corrupt island (Rhode Island, that is) put together the award-winning volume *C.L.R. James's Caribbean*, with a very distinguished cast of scholars, critics, and novelist George Lamming. Tim did not himself contribute, but Henry offered in an eloquent major essay, "C.L.R. James and the Antiguan Left," that amounted to an indispensable overview of Tim's political career.[25] The particulars of Henry's burning insights were new to me, as new as *Outlet*, its pages stunning in their prose as much as in Tim's political acuity.

Meanwhile, Henry and I also worked together in the C.L.R. James Society, planning its biannual award banquets (Hector, in the last year of his life, was the third awardee and the first one too young to have been in James's old 1940s political group) and the *C.L.R. James Journal*, which has appeared more or less annually since the end of the 1990s.[26] The two of us, plus Anthony Bogues, made the selection for the "Tim Hector

Anthology," appearing as the winter 2000/2001 issue of the *Journal*. The *Outlet*'s coverage of the event, published on the occasion of Hector receiving the James Society award, was titled modestly, "National Gets an Award—and a Book."[27] Henry put it best later when he wrote, "we knew not the lateness of the hour, we never suspected how soon the light of this powerful flame would dim. It would have been nice to have seen Tim in the winter years of his life."[28] Of course, "nice" is a drastic understatement: Tim would still have been *guiding* us in important ways, so long as we lived.

It is a consolation to know, especially after Tim's death, how much that little plaque and all it symbolized meant to him, along with the opportunity for readers to see a small selection of his best essays reprinted. Without the comradeship of Paget Henry, none of this would have happened, indeed nothing of my work on James or the Caribbean Left subsequent to *The Artist as Revolutionary*, could have taken place. The same applies, to a lesser degree, to Anthony Bogues, the co-organizer with Henry of so many things around James's legacy.

I've also been fortunate, for a very long time, to have the attention of other followers and scholars of James, and they have directly or indirectly been important to this volume, too. The older ones are almost all gone now, and I wish they had lived long enough to see this book in publication: Martin Glaberman, who knew Tim especially well; Conrad Lynn, James Boggs, George Rawick, Stan Weir and Jim Murray, to name only a few. Happily, George Lamming, Wilson Harris, Sylvia Winter, John LaRose, James Young, Stuart Hall, Selwyn Cudjoe, and Grace Lee Boggs are still with us. Among those my age and younger, I can count Margaret Busby, Anna Grimshaw, Walton Look Lai, Tony Bogues, Scott McLemee, Selwyn Cudjoe, Noel Ignatiev, David Roediger, Kent Worcester, Neil Lazarus, Cedric Robinson, William E. Cain, Robin Blackburn, Robert Hill, Matthew Quest, Derek Seidman, and surely more to come among still younger generations. Indeed, as I write these words, some of my most intellectually and politically active students formed a sort of James study circle without informing me, Among these last, Matthew Quest, Derek Seidman, Yesenia Barragan, and Eric D. Larson have all given me renewed inspiration to finish this text.

Richard Hart, one of the pioneers of the Jamaican Left during the 1930s and the 1940s, has supplied me with documents, including his own writings, that make the picture look different and fuller than it could have been otherwise. Of all these colleagues, comrades, and friends, Tony Bogues, Paget Henry, and Brian Meeks among others—and George Lamming, after all the rest—have most thoroughly gone over my work here, borrowing against their own busy schedules to give me thoughtful and constructive criticism. I am also grateful to an anonymous reviewer for the University Press of Mississippi and to Seetha Srinivasan, director of the press, and Walter Biggins and especially Robert Burchfield for seeing the book through to publication.

It is important for me to say, finally, that this book is by no means intended as a day-to-day accounting of Tim Hector's life or of politics in Antigua. That would take an extensive oral history as well as pursuit in various archives unavailable to me. Rather, it is the political and cultural world of the Caribbean and beyond through Tim Hector's eyes, as close as I can attempt this daunting feat.

I do this at a certain risk because of the importance of the subject, but also because the two of us envisioned decades of collaboration ahead, working together at a distance. Occasionally, in a side comment that must have mystified readers of "Fan the Flame," Tim lamented that he had not been able to stay in touch with his good friend Paul Buhle; I felt the same way, of course. That future collaboration won't happen, and as so often, writing helps to fill in part an emotional void that cannot truly be filled. At any rate, so very much remains to be known about the Caribbean radicals that this volume is only a beginning; but like work on James, work on Tim Hector has an independent value that can only grow. As Tim himself reported of his life and companions, so I consider myself "lucky" and a great deal more to have known him, worked with him in common cause even at a distance, and read closely and learned much from his writings, his bearing, his integrity, and his sense of humor.

CHAPTER ONE

The Caribbean Context

The not so ancient histories of the Caribbean region have expanded in recent accounts to include the evidence of earliest human habitation earlier than 3000 B.C. Remarkably, the indications point to the very Antigua where Tim Hector was born. It's not a densely recorded history compared to the Egyptian dynasties or to the species origins in deeper Mother Africa, where Antigua's modern population can trace its direct ethnographic roots. But this is the New World, where nature seems to have had almost unimaginable stretches to itself with light or intermittent intrusion of the human foot tread.

Who these inhabitants were and what they were doing in Antigua, among other nearby islands, remain in doubt. The Arawaks, spreading their culture south of Antigua to the coast of South America, were still on hand on some islands (and many traces of them survive on the continent). But they had meanwhile been displaced, during the immediate precolonial centuries in Antigua and elsewhere in the eastern Caribbean, by the Caribs, from whom the region and its sea earned the name.

Fierce warriors, hunters, and gatherers but also agriculturists, these Arawaks and Caribs had made pottery, utilized dug-out canoes, and in some places had developed arrows. They apparently knew nothing of the nearby Mayan advances—if the rise of imperial splendor may be called an advance—such as palaces, organized sports, and choreographed ritual murder in Mexico and parts of the archipelago. As early explorers and later anthropologists discovered to their amazement, Mayan high culture had subsequently retreated, its grand ruling classes wiped out, probably from the mixed effects of war, pestilence, and ecological malpractice. The jungle had overgrown the remnants centuries before the arrival of Columbus, leaving the island tribal cultures virtually untouched.

Still, the European intrusion constituted a rude shock from which many small surviving cultures and some not so small would never recover. In Eric Williams's classic account, the European invasion of the distant East and beginning conquest of Africa achieved what the Crusades had failed to accomplish, thanks to technologies hitherto unavailable. The nation-state was emerging, at once exacerbating and exacerbated by discontent and violent uprisings. Times out of joint for royalty meant new woes for ordinary folk, new hopes for a different kind of society (perhaps one "remembered" from a mythic past), new needs for the emerging and increasingly commercial powers to wield force unrestrained by "honor" and bloodlines.[1] Hector liked to add to this account, after 9/11, that the once-glorious Islamic empire was finally surpassed because it had been built upon territorial conquest rather than the forces of production.[2]

History in Black

We often forget that Columbus already designated African blacks to be the compulsory help-meets and collaborators of whites in the task of agrarian colonization. He also knew that the so-called collaboration was one way. If the category of agrarian colonization were to be broadened to include mineral and plant (notably timber) extraction, we would immediately get a fifteenth-century glimpse of the modern world system climaxing in the massive deforestation, oil drilling, and agribusiness, along with starveling peoples and the industrial and consumer debris of our own less-than-glorious age. Hieronymous Bosch, painting minimurals from a little manufacturing town in Belgium, captured the trauma and its long-term effects better than anyone else, artist or intellectual. Greed and agony were, we might say fatalistically, hard-wired into the process known as "development."

Columbus believed, of course, that he was sailing west in order to reach the East (hence the West Indies). He died certain that he was not far from the Orient. The illusions of conquest have nearly always been large ones. The actual triumph of the new rulers in the Caribbean can be summarized in one word: sugar. The subsequent creation of a productive system focusing on one global crop, organized with hitherto-unimaginable efficiency, made all the difference for the capital accumulation needed to launch the emerging capitalist system.

American Indians were quickly too reduced to serve as an adequate labor force. Welsh and Irish indentured laborers had limited terms of service and could not be rounded up in sufficient numbers. Even if the Cuban experience offers ample counterevidence, we might still suggest that most Europeans' health simply could not stand up to the demands of toil in severe climatic conditions. By contrast, West Africa was relatively close in climate, and its inhabitants had learned to survive in the blinding heat and associated diseases. On an especially productive island like Barbados, where the absence of rough territory offered no escape, poor whites had almost literally died out as a class before the end of slave importation, while slave numbers multiplied to three-quarters of the population, not counting the modest proportion of freed mixed-race.

The commonplace of scholarship, that the fifteen to fifty million Africans made into slaves and transported across the seas carried no culture with them and had nothing but brute labor to add to the creation of vast profits, has been contested with special sharpness (if by no means overturned) during the most recent several decades of scholarship. C.L.R. James himself, in order to stress the *new* experience of the Caribbean population and its role in modern production, was rather inclined to undervalue the specifically cultural tools brought along and maintained under the worst of conditions. Drawing upon the scholarship of Barry Gaspar, Robin Blackburn, Bernard Moitt, and others, and not forgetting calypso artist-historian Hollis Liverpool aka Chalkdust, Hector saw something different. Assorted rituals, including the masking (or "mas") associated with grassroots creative (and often satirical) expressions of various kinds, could be traced back to Ghana among the Coromantees people, and forward to the modern Caribbean and most definitely to little Antigua.[3]

Hector credited these historians, especially during Black History Month each year. But he criticized their work whenever he thought that they had not made the most of their data. The familiar emphasis upon the supposedly servile nature of Afro-Caribbean women provided, for him, a powerful case in point. They had never, he had suspected from his life as well as his reading, been all that servile. Reasoning analogically, he suggested that the appearance of servility, in women as in black men, was a classic strategy of the powerless. Caribbean women had acted as veritable Joan of Arcs in moments of armed conflict, not to mention the various kinds of cultural practices from growing and preparing food to child rearing, that remained to be discovered by future researchers about the daily life of slaves and its larger political significance.[4] A presumptuous opinion in the face of psychological and other arguments about female docility? In Hector's comical response, "What the hell a little fella like me, living in a fly-blown, neo-colony, hardly a dot on the world map . . . doing by challenging the real masters?"[5] The "single-mother Caribbean society" nevertheless had its own truths, little explored, and he insisted upon them.[6]

James had early and often stressed the role of skilled labor: if slaves and their descendents had actually lacked skills, the key jobs of the plantation economy could not have been performed, especially in islands where whites were few and largely indolent. The ability to acquire the necessary insight to operate within the sphere of the most sophisticated agriculture in the world presupposed a sophisticated society in the Africa unwillingly left behind, an obvious conclusion that white scholars had resisted for many generations.[7] To this important point, argued with particular relish in connection with current demands for reparations, Hector liked to lay out the figures provided by Robin Blackburn. If the British, for instance, expropriated the produce of a million slaves, each working twenty-five hundred to thirty-five hundred hours per year, then profits were almost unimaginably large, a degree of exploitation (given the sudden burst of sophistication in production, transportation, and the market) likely to outdistance, over several centuries, any other known to history, certainly up to that time.

Rhoda Reddock and others have in recent years added greatly to our knowledge about the contribution of the gender (and household) division of labor to this process.[8] Clearly, the merger of African traditions and plantation economies found women in the extraordinarily difficult situation of few concessions made to childbirth and raising children until the dawn of the nineteenth century. The subsequent turn toward maximum fecundity was always undercut by the demand for labor, emphatically including the labor of children. Forced and unforced sexual relations with white and Creole men, violence, and even murder directed at those who took (or were forced into) such chances marked other avenues of complexity and frequent tragedy. But out of this moiling social life emerged the Caribbean woman, legendarily "in charge" of the household that men had abandoned, perhaps (or not) continuing matriarchal conditions or merely responding to life chances.

Already by the first third of the eighteenth century, the West Indies took up a quarter of England's iron exports, while the African trade had become a key market for the burgeoning British weapons industry. Until competition from the industrializing North Americans, the black skin trade continued directly and indirectly to supply major markets for British manufactured cloth and clothing, making Birmingham and Manchester world cities, not to mention the various seaports risen from mere fishing villages to vast modern complexes of manufacture and transportation. *Magnum est saccharum et prevalebit* (Great is sugar and it will prevail) constituted holy writ.[9] Like the antebellum U.S. South's King Cotton, and closely linked to the cotton trade, it owed everything to the workings of black consciousness and black flesh.

No wonder Holland, for a historical moment the epicenter of world commerce and culture, strove to make the Caribbean (as Williams put it) into a Dutch canal.[10] The wars of commerce, fought only in part with bankbooks, ended with the Dutch practically excluded, the Yankees entrenched. When the North American colonies became the suppliers of Caribbean food, livestock, and lumber, likewise the buyers of West Indian sugar and molasses, shrewd observers might have concluded that another mercantile empire had already been born and was only awaiting a political movement. That movement, resulting in the American Revolution, took another century to work out fully. But the Yankees meanwhile acquired the treasure needed for revolt, independence, and ultimately the conquest of the planet. Meanwhile, parallel creation of a North American–style infrastructure definitely did not take place in the

Caribbean, at first more prosperous (or at least profit producing) than its northern neighbor.

What did take place, politically as well as economically, was a great deal more complicated. Antigua scholar Paget Henry observes about that small island that "the demands of the transition to peripheral capitalism were met by creating of a state system which contained within itself a small area of the practice of democracy." This meant democracy for the planter class, of course, and on some islands for a considerable mulatto class at a considerably lower level of rights and participation. Voting (for males at any rate) and colonial parliamentarism depended, however, upon the "high degree of militarization and institutional exclusion of the dominated classes."[11] The political transition would always be problematic, as would any significant degree of independence from the preferential rates of sugar offered by the British system, with all the implications that followed.

Britain definitely did not intend to see cities with manufactories spring up in the colonies, demanding through a variety of means an unbalanced trade of raw materials for manufactured ones—just the sort of unbalanced trade that became the American model for its own relation to commercial colonies in later centuries. The future Americans managed in various ways to get around the British scheme, finally going to war when opportune. Meanwhile, in the West Indies, the British successfully repressed the possibility largely because the colonial ruling class was more than willing to accept the current arrangement. The sugar lobby in the British parliament, amply represented by absentee planters who lived a life far from their plantations, gained the power to sway votes on many issues, and that was all that the lobby wanted. The fleshpots of empire for its favored classes suited a self-styled gentry class, even as island rulers tilted against each other for special favors.

The planters therefore had no wish to achieve anything like economic self-sufficiency. Leaving large zones of their land idle, they did not even maximize sugar production, rightly fearing the consequent drop in price. Nor did these planters wish to create anything like a human (that is, bureaucratic) infrastructure for the society around them. Establishment of schools was put off for generations: Bishop Berkeley's vision of a regional university (in Bermuda) was abandoned, schools for teachers treated in as low regard as teachers themselves. In all, public services were noticeable by their absence. Why establish anything when the white, civilized minority merely acquired wealth, imitated European fashions, and awaited a personal return from the colonies to real civilization? The considerable public works, transportation, and sanitation systems eventually operated by the British in parts of India, for instance, would have been viewed as unnecessary and impossible for small islands, whose population would never become significant consumers.

In that spirit as well as in fear of an empowered independent nonwhite population, colonial law utterly forbade nonwhites their own means of subsistence, even as modest supplement to their daily tasks. In the regional lexicon, the "Negro sector" was plantation labor and the "European sector" everything else. In some parts of the region, the very possession of coffee beans constituted a crime, as did the sale of assorted crops without slave owners' permission and definitely the acquisition of trade skills. Codes on clothing were also enacted, as if slaves or mulattos were somehow likely to wear clothes or jewelry akin to those of the whites. Meanwhile, the facts of miscegenation embraced ideological absurdities, beginning with the seventeenth-century conception that mulattos, like mules, would not be able to reproduce. Degrees of mullatohood, as infinitely complicated as those in New Orleans, ruled the lives of mixed-race descendents, with manumission discouraged (with some exception in the Spanish colonies) or virtually disallowed.

The sweeping social system was, of course, built upon an economic foundation of sand. Substitutes for cane sugar, above all the extracts of beet, were bound to derail the Caribbean locomotive of profit and dubious progress. Ultimately, rivalry from other sugar regions, first Brazil and then especially India, would have undercut the Caribbean planters in any case. Sugar as Bastard King could be maintained only through political influence, and then only under mostly deteriorating conditions of profit. But even before the competitors had their due, another event pointed in thoroughly unexpected directions.

The Haitian Revolution remains, after slavery and the holocaust of native populations, the one decisive event in Caribbean history. Indeed, C.L.R. James, who understood its importance earlier and better than anyone else, later proclaimed that following Toussaint, only Fidel Castro as individual giant had such impact or world importance. For the colonialists at home and on hand on the island, also if more ambiguously for many among the Creole populations, the uprising of slaves was the ultimate horror, constantly feared and anticipated in the ways that Hegel would explore philosophically in his famous dialogue of master and slave in *The Phenomenology of Mind*. The master is the immobile force; the slave's movement hurtles the dialectical impulse of history forward, toward freedom. Never mind that Hegel had only mental or spiritual freedom on his mind, that he regarded blacks as barbarians and the goal of happiness as unattainable: he had seen through his own racism to the essential point. Hector claimed that he could not bear to read Hegel until C.L.R. James explained the revolutionary content of the great philosopher's work, above all his quest for universality.[12]

Slave revolts had taken place across history, of course, but success was exceedingly rare except in the most distant provinces of the Roman or other empires, generally in terrain not worth reconquering. The real story of Spartacus was something different: that uprising repositioned the very empire itself and set the conditions for the success of Christianity and of empire in a new sense (with, as James often pointed out, equality proclaimed, after death, for believers if not for others).[13]

The revolutionary consolidation among the Haitians, as James learned in the Paris archives during the 1930s, decisively weakened the British in their warring against the French and almost reached out successfully to the revolutionary Jacobins, that is, the frustrated Bolshevik vanguard (so to speak) of the new global rebellion. The Haitian Revolution struck at the heart of industry that pumped wealth into Europe and allowed mercantilism to thrive. Its example might have undone modern empire before consolidation had been nearly complete. The example of the American Revolution, replacing one mercantile empire with another, would presumably also have been constrained or even undone in the process, no longer the self-proud model of an emerging bourgeois world. Then the "Marseilles" would truly have been the call to modern freedom, with the trio of Rousseau, Hegel, and Marx, not Jefferson or Adam Smith, its truest philosophers.[14]

In its own terms, the rising of the Haitians brought a new subject into history. Until this time, the shame of slavery had been described in fairly abstract humanitarian terms, a crime of whites showing the evil at the center of civilization's claims. Montesquieu said it best: blacks obviously could not be human, because if so, logically, the Europeans could not be Christian. Rousseau, Blake, Tom Paine, and the earliest of the large-scale antislavery societies made essentially the same point. Thomas Jefferson and other enlightened members of the American plantocracy wanted, characteristically, to have it both ways. Thinking as so often in the framework of the ancient republics divided into slave and free, they declared that slavery was horrible—but necessary for the great American freedom. On that basis, any solution must be postponed: the very argument or excuse utilized for endless imperial adventures and demands for global hegemony during the following centuries.

To all that, Toussaint and his followers gave the answer in advance. The turmoil of the colony of San Domingue over the meaning of the French Revolution for themselves, the victims of empire, let the genie out of the bottle. Living and working in the worst imaginable conditions, slaves and their ambivalent allies, the mulattos, arose and took power. Toussaint himself was betrayed, captured by the agents of Napoleon determined to restore the colony to France. When slavery was reintroduced to Guadeloupe, black Haitians knew that they had to fight and certainly to die in great numbers, or return to enslavement. The black legions of Dessalines and Christophe, along with the effects of yellow fever, successfully defeated the re-invaders. Traumatized by war's slaughter and the loss of the middle classes, economically isolated by the colonial powers, and ruled by their own dictators, Haitians could not seriously hope to realize the potential for a free Caribbean society. But they had made the indefinite continuation of slavery elsewhere in the region impossible. Perhaps—James suggested against the background of the events in Ethiopia—Haiti had shown that rebellious peoples across the world only awaited a signal from the Western proletariat to finish off class society once and for all.

Drawing out the example of the Haitian Revolution (and drawing upon his own intuitions as an intellectual leader of the emerging

Pan-African movement of the 1930s), James insisted that intelligent observers had seen something like that revolution coming since the early days of the Caribbean slave economy. Slaves had been taken from African peasant societies not so different from those of much of Europe and placed within a new environment. As James liked to emphasize, every race had passed through slavery, and in recent centuries, parts of Africa had seen slavery in various regions before the European invasion. But in the Americas, the color line was and would remain decisive, down to a single metaphorical drop of "Negro blood."

The response to this horror was inevitable, and not only in Haiti but in the British colonies as well: a commentary on Barbados written in the mid-seventeenth century already recorded the craving of the recent black inhabitants, exposed in their foiled plots, to make the society their own and to rid themselves of the burden imposed upon them for their skin color. But successive slave revolts were crushed one after the other, out-gunned and outmaneuvered by colonists who could count on British warships to come to the rescue, and barbaric aftermaths to teach the lessons of extreme tortures such as burning alive, quartering, and mutilations—destined for future rebels and their supporters.[15]

Emancipation arrived as political and economic inevitability, the result of the demand for free trade from above as well as the threat of black rebellion from below. In the aftermath of emancipation, therefore, the region saw adjustment rather than a real change of social relations, including (for Marx, the vital point) the social relations of production. As Hector pointed out so often and so acutely, the logic of slavery's abolition in the British colonies should have brought financial compensation to the victims for two centuries of torture and exploitation. Instead, compensation went entirely to the former slaveholders now bereft of their "property." Maroons and marronage, which played such a large role in history and folklore, were denied their existence and sometimes influential role.[16]

Freed from formal bondage, blacks were systematically denied every opportunity to become freeholders, while in Trinidad and British Guiana tens of thousands of East Indian laborers were induced to immigrate on labor contracts, the needed servile substitutes on the plantations. This grand manipulation was only successful to a degree. Despite every effort to prevent the birth of a black peasantry subsisting upon their own agriculture, thousands of freedmen dug in, working their own plots with their families in their scant free time away from wage labor. Or they set out entirely on their own, some twenty thousand in Jamaica alone, in farms of ten acres of less. Not just the production of subsistence crops but also of exports marked a modest path before the end of the nineteenth century, with arrowroot, cotton, spices, cocoa, citrus, bananas, logwood, rice (an East Indian specialty in Guyana), and of course sugar. It could have been an important beginning toward a different society.[17] But these prospects would never be allowed to turn into sound national economies.[18]

People rather than crops moved from island to island and onward to mainlands far away. Blacks used manumission to flee by the thousands, not only from Jamaica and Barbados but also from smaller islands to the banana plantations in Costa Rica, to U.S.-paid labor on the Panama Canal, to Cuba (where they resumed work on larger and more efficient if no less cruel sugar plantations), and to the United States itself. Those who remained behind, on the estates, actually produced by the later decades of the century more sugar than ever before. They received little in return for their efforts, scarce prospect of education into literacy for the following generations.

Thus flourished the secondary diaspora that sustained the revolutionary opposition in Cuba (and socialist-anarchist movements of cigar workers around Ybor City, Florida) but also established homes away from home in Harlem, Boston, and elsewhere. Incipient class divisions rapidly expanded, with highly skilled, business-minded Bajans (Barbadians) the veritable aristocrats of many a black U.S. community and its churches. So did remissions to families left behind, an increasingly important source of selective sustenance from the mid-nineteenth century forward, and of continuous contact of Caribbean peoples with U.S. social and cultural trends.

But so did outright U.S. control of the region, with all the dire implications of Manifest Destiny. The Monroe Doctrine, proclaimed in 1823, was for its first few decades more intent than insistence. The United States had to settle for a colonial status quo in the region with Britain,

France, and Spain, especially on the issue of Cuba. But American leaders were only waiting their chance, meanwhile trying out an assortment of options like the "gunboat diplomacy" of short-term invasions and occupations of Latin American capitals in response to supposed slights. The Danish monarchy offered to sell its Virgin Islands holdings to the United States in 1867 and 1870, but Congress refused. Annexation of the Dominican Republic was solemnly proposed by a government commission in 1871. As the European powers continued to slice up Africa and the United States grew more mighty in every sense, presidential appetites and their commercial counterparts were whetted for territories to fly the flag and for prospective economic expansion.[19]

The Spanish-American War provided, at little American cost, the prizes of Cuba and Puerto Rico (as well as others in the Pacific). The Platt Amendment made the former a virtual protectorate and foreshadowed the permanent colonial status of the latter. Shortly after the turn of the new century, U.S. supremacy was declared firmly and absolutely in the "American Lake."

In this light, the outright colonization of Puerto Rico, the blatant theft of land, and the creation of an altogether artificial Panama was child's play, except of course for those thousands who died in wars and thousands more laborers who died in the canal's digging. Other world powers, to say nothing of local governments, necessarily accepted regional life under permanent sufferance of Washington, knowing that nothing could halt the Americans and their marines. (Close to a century later, the frequent U.S. invasions of the Caribbean and Latin America would be cited by members of Congress as proof that preemptive wars were nothing new and therefore, in a remarkable twist of logic, could not be considered unconstitutional.) The acquisition of the formerly Dutch Virgin Islands in 1917 and the stationing of armed forces in a variety of spots simply confirmed the logic of regional occupation.

The styles of American investment in Cuba and Puerto Rico meanwhile showed the main way forward. Corporations that owned their own railway cars, their own steamer ships, and their own warehouses put the small cane farmer out of business but also put the whole British operation into the shade. Monoculture triumphed once again and absolutely over all the alternatives, apparently for a last time ruling out regional self-sustenance.

Continued British holdings into the twentieth century might, then, be regarded as a consolation to Britain slipping a huge notch downward, to a junior partner in empire. The willingness of the British to accept the assorted costs and difficulties of administration (including education) of islands regarded as economic backwaters offered to the world the final proof of "white man's burden," as the symbols of constitutional kingship and commonwealth status demonstrated. Nevertheless, the islands were steadily becoming American in a thousand subtle ways.

The Ambiguities of English-Speakers' Revolt

No Haitian-like revolt actually took place in the British West Indies, nor did these West Indians a century and more later form sustained revolutionary groups or Communist parties along the lines of rebels in the Spanish- and French-speaking islands. By the third decade of the twentieth century, Marxists as individuals or small groups exerted, at times, a very considerable influence from rhetoric to organization, sometimes even in high government circles if more often in labor movements. These efforts rarely reached institutional form in anything larger than makeshift alliances within larger forces. Garveyism, Marxism's nearly constant if generally unacknowledged companion, gained far greater popular recognition. If Wilson Harris could write that "the Marxian dialectic" provided the most successful intellectual effort of West Indians to engage a philosophy of history, it offered a dialectical process with a material basis as limited as the variety of Marxism was varied.[20]

Modern histories of the Caribbean, including popularized versions offered by Tim Hector in his columns, begin with the wrongs of slavery and colonialism, add in the slave revolts, the restrictive and race-divisive character of the Crown colony system—and then move forward decades or centuries to the labor revolts of the 1930s and beyond. It is a sensible narrative but generally fails to account for the lapses into apparent passivity or political "backwardness" often attributed to the presence of whites and Creoles in charge of political movements within these societies. The restlessness expressed from emancipation forward, in some cases intensifying around the turn of the century and in nearly every case during the First World War and the years immediately after the war, actually connected past and future, but with a subtly different content. Had Hector written from Trinidad or the Guyanas, he would have been forced to add in the conflicts between East Indians and the African diaspora, often coloring the class conflict with unpredictable hues.[21]

The problems of the nonwhite middle class would alone, in other circumstances, have prompted nationalist (and race) impulses based upon the impossibility of transcending narrowly circumscribed social as well as economic limits, and upon declining real standards shortly following emancipation. The restriction of government jobs to British citizens was felt with special sharpness, the more so as an educated, native colored class began to recognize its own superior qualifications. The decline and reorganization of the sugar industry toward the end of the nineteenth century were catastrophic for the social layers between the "masses" and the "classes," because petty merchants depended upon the poor for customers and because those poor on many islands had become suddenly riotous.[22]

And yet: to go with the black (in some places, East Indian) peasantry and the urban slum-dwellers was perceived as suicide of a different and more immediate kind. The respectable route remained the petition to the Crown's representatives, because only in that way could the privileges of lighter skin color, however limited, be maintained. With unions still outlawed, every mass action was illegal in any case, direct resistance against government policies practically and almost immediately seen as insurrectionary, no matter how mundane the demand.

The rage of protests swept from Jamaica and Guyana to Grenada, Doiminca, Belize, St. Kitts-Nevis, Monserrat, and Trinidad in the twenty years after 1884, counting at least seventeen major uprisings. In British Guyana, for instance, protests occurred as early as the 1870s among indentured (that is, East Indian) laborers, and spreading in the first years of the new century toward urban (that is, Afro-Caribbean) workers, led by the perennially dangerous sector of stevedores. Rioting in the Georgetown capital in 1896 and widening strikes during 1905 were successfully suppressed with British armed troops brought in by warships. Land and water access, taxes, and above all the misery of unemployment became burning issues as rural dwellers were forced into the cities and the population grew at large. Elites naturally met the problems of declining revenues by turning the bills over to others to pay. Police enforcing taxation became natural targets for public rage, black constables among those placed in the middle of the storm. Ordinary Belizeans thus petitioned the governor in 1892, noting that they were "the real inhabitants of this colony, by the sweat of whose brow in the forests, all its prosperity has been achieved," but were excluded from all decision making, the ruling councils being "filled with merchants and other employers," whites, and a handful of Creoles. Disdained by the merchants, told to be patient by the governor, some hundred forest workers attacked the stores in Belize City, and after an armed detachment from a British ship landed, were given a 50 percent rise in wages. It was a happy result rarely achieved elsewhere; it was also a lesson in the efficacy of mass action.[23]

Here and there, a middling strata, feeling its own resentments, began to show preliminary signs of militancy in the name of community if not of race.[24] The "Water Riot" in Trinidad of 1903, ostensibly directed at the aristocratic classes known for their wastage of precious water resources, aroused a confrontation with authorities by working-class men and, famously, working-class women, resulting in several deaths and the torching of the legislative Red House. It was a turning point in Trinidadian history, clarifying the distance between the rulers and the ruled. The failure of middle-class reform to alter the conditions of colonialism in any significant way prompted the outbreaks of mass demonstrations, whether specifically regarding economics, culture, politics, or water. Such events pointed toward a future of class-conscious and race-conscious nationalism.[25]

In the uncertain prosperity of the new century, things seemed for a time to have died down—until the approach of world war. Guyanese, Jamaicans, and Trinidadians all reacted to the simultaneous shortage of workers and the skyrocketing wartime price levels for the most ordinary commodities, like flour. Longshoremen and their fellow boat loaders and unloaders, like the coal heavers, struck for higher wages. The waterfront at Port of Spain extended out to sea—thanks to the inadequacy of the harbor itself—and the extended process required the largest concentration of workers on the island, in close contact with each other. Bukka Rennie has argued persuasively that these workers, many of them immigrants from smaller islands, were able to form a community of sorts.[26]

The major shipping interests, sensing unrest and perhaps anticipating trouble, sought to put through an ordinance forcing any male who was "habitually" absent from a job into a work camp, akin to southern U.S. chain gangs, in forced labor on agricultural estates and then turned over to private employers contracted by the state. Petition drives to block enactment created a mechanism for political mobilization (as well as three thousand signatures, putting any signer's job at risk). Part-time, casual labor, often with no special hours of work and heavy or dangerous loads, increased the sense of unfairness. Bullying by supervisors prompted calypso songs against them. Thus the strike of 1919 had not only an organized framework but also a culture. Lacking any central body (the Trinidad Workingmen's Association [TWA] was supportive, but more cultural and more petite-bourgeois), workers strategically resolved to strike at crucial moments, against the most lucrative incoming ships, using information supplied by friendly administrative clerks.

For two weeks, a skeleton crew of scabs kept the docks open. During the third week, in the final month of 1919, strikers shut down the port (a crowd of sympathizers was said to sing, "Washed in the blood of the New Jerusalem"), and the strike began to spread through the island. As a British warship sailed toward port, an agreement was reached. When the strike ended around the waterfront, it petered out elsewhere on the island. But there could be no question that the society had been shaken or that working-class self-confidence had grown and that race lines had been tightened under the stress. "Black Power" was born as a concept if not a phrase.[27]

In Trinidad as well, the first oil-field disturbances erupted. Although this future center of militant workers was intimidated back to the jobs, the TWA could claim ten thousand members between oil fields and waterfront. Attempts were made in some of the smaller islands, notably St. Kitts, to form unions. Jamaicans formed the Workingmen's Co-operative

Association, described as a "union under cover," growing into a partial if highly limited legality.

The resentment of returning members of the British West Indies Regiment (BWIR) played a notable role in all this. They were embittered at their treatment, during and after their mobilization, had faced hard fighting (although never, at the orders of the Colonial Office, against white Europeans, even as "the enemy"), made ineligible for bonuses given to white soldiers, and discriminated against at every level. Facing unemployment back at home and unintimidated by threats of force, they were naturally perceived as a dangerous element in the combustible atmosphere, likely to lead confrontations over wages and conditions, with a racial edge to their emerging self-consciousness.[28]

After 1920, with the mixture of recession and repression, all organized efforts fell apart. The colonial governments nevertheless felt able to suppress labor publications as well as banning Garvey's *Negro World*. But seeds had been planted.

Social histories are now emerging of the next and shaping wave of protests, the regionwide uprising of 1934–39.[29] The family dynasties that carried the nations into political independence and continued economic dependence were largely born here, thrown up by volcanic uprisings from below. Notwithstanding arrests and imprisonments, imperial rhetoric, and the occasional appearance of British gunboats and shock troops to overpower outbursts of disorder, the fundamentally peaceful and evolutionary, even Fabian character of emerging independence movements and postcolonial governments can be found here. This particular trajectory, however, takes us back sharply to the history and circumstances of the British Left, for Labourites could almost have been said to have negotiated Caribbean modernity, easing pressure for violent revolts while patiently prodding the Crown's representatives to end the colonial experiment.

A heated discussion among radical intellectuals of the early 1960s, centrally involving E. P. Thompson, socialist giant of British working-class history, traced out the critical thinking about Labourism in its root form. The resulting discussion has not been improved upon since.[30] If England had experienced the first truly bourgeois revolution, then why—contrary to Marx's predictions—had its citizens been so slow and plodding toward a socialist one? Thompson and his colleagues, Communists coming out of the war, nearly all of them dissident breakaways after 1956, had defended the legacy of English working-class struggles for legality and dignity. They struggled to interpret sympathetically the apparent lapse after the great Chartist Movement of the 1830s–40s, and to grapple with the ambivalent legacy of the early socialist movements, syndicalists, Fabian reformers, and British Communists in producing a polyglot but deeply class-conscious radicalism. Very much like scholars of the Caribbean, the circle around Thompson and the journal *Past and Present* offered stronger theses for the social struggles of early periods and weaker ones approaching the present.[31]

British Labourism had been a disappointment all the more because of moments when it had seemed capable of bringing about real social transformation (and not just a welfare state) both at home and abroad. In retrospect, by the second decade of the twentieth century, bourgeois hegemony depended finally upon the Americans, whose power to stabilize global capitalism overwhelmed British radicals along with all the others, and whose ultimate control of British Caribbean territory was never in real doubt. The weak support of triumphant Labour after 1946 for Caribbean independence, let alone territorial unity, had definitely been foreshadowed. But that fact did not make the letdown less bitter. So often Labourism had been understood by its popular supporters, from the coal pits to the universities, as a defiant socialism, a universal creed capable of overcoming the legacies of capitalism and colonialism, that the denouement cast doubt upon the whole history of the British Left's opposition to class rule.

Thompson's critics, ranged around the journal *New Left Review*, challenged his historical sympathies mightily, in terms that resounded unto the outward edges of the empire.[32] The Civil War of 1640 cast a shadow across British (and imperial) history for, to quote Perry Anderson, "never was the ultimate effect of a revolution more transparent, and its immediate agents more enigmatic."[33] The New Model Army, with its Levellers and Diggers, made possible the overthrow of the monarchy; then the landed officer elite destroyed the self-sacrificing revolutionaries. The most

explosive consequences took place overseas, not revolutionary but imperial, and not only in Ireland and the overthrow of Dutch and Spanish
sea supremacy but also in the taking of Jamaica. Thus the Caribbean
was part of the arrangement from the very beginning, its exploitation a
backhanded effect of failed and perverted British class struggle, akin to
Cromwell's treatment of the Irish.

The Glorious Revolution had, Anderson and others insisted, certainly overthrown royalty, but kept not only property relations but even
personnel intact. Profits and the profiteers themselves tended thereafter to disappear into the English countryside with the landed gentry
whom they craved to join, the same countryside where the successful
imperialists of the Caribbean placed themselves (and their children) after
achieving their blood-stained booty in the colonies. Moneyed and landed
interests married, in effect, with global consequences. Scarcely ever had
there been a clearer case of dialectical turns to the opposite, negations so
sharp that the synthesis no longer resembled the thesis. If further proof
were needed, the surviving Puritan dissenters set off for the New World,
founding the Massachusetts Bay Colony—and wiping out their saviors,
the local Indians, offering them blankets poisoned with smallpox.

The unresolved differences among elites for another century and a
half were mediated severely, according to this reading, by the opportunities and profits of mercantilism, the organization and plundering of the
colonies and slave inhabitants. The rising industrial bourgeoisie (again,
the world's first) might have clashed more seriously with the gentry at
the turn of the nineteenth century—but the French Revolution terrified
British rulers, as the Napoleonic wars unsettled them. As Anderson
acutely noted, the massacre of workers at Peterloo followed the victory
over Europe's would-be conqueror, a nascent war against the poor more
unnerving after victory abroad.

The ballot for the commercial classes in 1832 and the repeal of the
protective Corn Laws in 1846 both aimed at the landed classes, but never
hit them squarely. (Neither Thompson nor his critics made much of the
contemporary Sugar Acts, which protected sections of the aristocracy
almost as much as the eclipse of the Corn Laws threatened them.) The
long-arriving new middle class had by this time finally won the right to

intermarry with the aristocracy, and simultaneously exhausted, for the last time, the desire to overwhelm them.

The working class in turn—and this is the most debatable element of the argument—had been afflicted with something of the same ailment. It had, according to this narrative, attached itself to the coattails of commercial property-holders, hoping to gain admission into a modern society that had yet not evolved, and too patient (or little self-confident) to rise up against it. By being *too* English, the British proletariat had been doomed, in any collective and redemptive sense, from the start.

The burden of the argument against Thompson's view of a sturdy English socialist tradition fell most significantly, for Caribbean purposes, upon Thompson's massive biography of William Morris—and upon the weight of the poet-socialist himself. Poet laureate, utopian novelist, brilliant designer, and preservationist, Morris made himself the foremost English socialist, practically the only left-wing Britisher with a global reputation during the 1880s. He set the model for the Yiddish socialist press of the East End that shared so much, as a marginal but vital socialistic culture, with its future Caribbean counterparts.

More than anyone except the sympathetic but definitely nonparty Oscar Wilde, Morris gave socialism such a bohemian twist. The "anti-scrape" campaign against the devastation of historic architecture and the associated defense of centuries-old hedgerows were regarded by Engels with considerable suspicion as too utopian and unscientific. The romantic Morris, whose 1896 death prompted literary weeping, the tribute from across the socialist world, was definitely heterodox in his belief that socialism had to be a cultural quite as much as an economic system. He had likewise insisted that the desire to preserve older (even vanished) collective ways of life was important, and that struggle to live some part of the future existence, in every possible gesture, helped make the future possible.

Thompson, writing in terms that might well be applied to C.L.R. James or a politically irregular crowd of literary radicals including Claude McKay, among others, distanced himself from his critics when he applauded Morris's exposition of "utopia's proper and new-found space: the education of desire." This Morris was proper successor to William Blake (another great favorite of Thompson's) and in Thompson's eyes linked to C.L.R. James. "Marxism," as Thompson concluded the thought, "requires less a re-ordering of its parts than a sense of humility before those parts of culture which it can never order."[34] Just what Wilson Harris might have written, and important for that reason—though hardly an adequate explanation for the problems of transporting socialist ideas to the English-speaking Caribbean.

Thompson's conclusions have great analytic value for us, nevertheless. In Thompson's view of Morris, utopianism (including the magisterial *News from Nowhere*, the first utopia set down in precise geographical terms) leaped ahead of British working-class history for some good reasons not unrelated to the Caribbean. Despite Morris's appeals for social solidarity, the consolidation of the British labor movement came in the form of craft unions—the very model for the conservative unionism of the United States—both indifferent to political socialism and largely excluding ordinary unskilled workers, including women and nonwhites. Between these two classes of workers stood a barrier and inverse relation of lifestyles that mirrored the relation of white and nonwhite across the seas. Fabian socialism, with its inbred sense of guidance from above, was a compromise between the socialistic sections of these skilled workers and the intellectuals, with others (one might better say Others, because their otherness defined the aristocrats of labor) on the margin.

Morris himself was close in spirit to the future British syndicalists with their propaganda for massive uprising. Whatever their faults or contradictions, were fundamentally overwhelmed by the hegemony of the labor aristocrats and Fabian intellectuals for whom gradual reform through the growth and development of the state would finally place society in better hands.

Oblivious to how race submerged benevolent sentiments into imperial instincts, assuming the colonized were far from making history and best treated within the British imperium, the ruling forces of Labourism naturally chose to join the Crown in the Great War. Fabian supporters of gradualism could not have chosen otherwise, even when the enemy was Germany, the veritable home of parliamentary socialism. (The utopians of Holland, across the waters, were better prepared by interwoven traditions of anarchism and anti-imperialism, but that is another story.) The global battle for colonies and markets swept nearly all in its train, and those not swept up were quickly if not entirely suppressed.

The fate of working people in the colonies, and the irony of Fabianism transported, could usefully be put into the nutshell of the TWA experience. Formed in 1897 by skilled tradesmen and small proprietors, it aspired to include all categories of working people, and it urged a political mission of sorts. Its demands, as first formulated, included better public transportation, the opening up of public land, and reduction of taxes on key imported goods; within a decade the TWA was seeking changes in federation status, pointing (albeit cautiously) toward some kind of independence. Clearly in line with Fabian ideals, the TWA applied in 1906 for membership in the British Labour Party—and was turned down on the basis that affiliation of colonial institutions was barred by the Labour Party constitution.[35] Jamaican craft unionists were to make no better progress among the American Federation of Labor (AFL) leaders who, in practical fact if not in letter of the constitution, saw restriction of the labor market as their key strategy and therefore barred nonwhite workers along with the unskilled as unworthy of joining the aristocracy of labor.

The world war with its horrible suffering and its prompting of rapid disillusionment when the smoke lifted led to a very British Bolshevism (notably including autodidact Methodist miners and syndicalist-minded Scottish shipbuilders) and to the General Strike of 1926. But it never led to a sturdy force outside the bounds of the Labour Party, given to reformism and its own version of a benign imperialism.

Thus Sidney Webb and Beatrice Webb, admiring the new Russia, could nevertheless remain almost as imperial as the king (or Winston Churchill). Their Labour Party counterparts and the successors to Fabianism objected ardently to the heartlessness of the Tories in a thousand ways, proposing all manner of public programs and reforms that would one day uplift the common man and woman and point toward a more cooperative order. But social crisis, war, or depression could be counted on to bring them eagerly into a coalition government to uphold British capitalism and the British status in the world. Thus did they restrain themselves and set a model for their avowedly socialistic West

Indian counterparts, and successors—not always excluding Caribbean Communists by any means—followed with different arguments and alignments. The model was followed nevertheless.

One might ask whether Thompson, in his defense of the British working class, or his critics have been better vindicated by history. The issue is complicated because the critics offered up a sort of New Left Leninism, a derivative of Trotskyism with an emphasis on "scientific" ideas about radicalism, while Thompson, from the Popular Front tradition, argued for romanticism and an end to vanguards of every kind. A brief flurry of Leninism or Leninisms confined to relatively small groups (except perhaps in Guyana and Trinidad) formed a Caribbean counterpart, less cerebral but more dedicated to working-class constituencies and more "cultural" than in London or, for that matter, New York.

Neither side has won; neither side could win. Labourism, apparently swallowed up—at least for the moment—in a Blairism contrary to most of the core values of historic Labour, is steadily supine to (American) visions of global empire. But British radical romanticism, now in multicolor and with a very different working class, has become one of the centers of resistance. In regard to the English-speaking Caribbean, what we can say is that opposite impulses run simultaneous in a series of conflicts with romantic uprising (with race usually at the center, along with class) confounded by continued Fabian political maneuvering from the top. In the end, even before the collapse of the Soviet bloc, erstwhile Caribbean Fabians became as compliant as Blair in accommodating whatever policies the U.S. State Department and U.S. economic strategists chose to follow. In the name of "structural adjustments," Fabian aims seemed to disappear almost entirely. And yet, even in the shadow of crushing political failure, that "almost" contains untold possibilities, including a regional alliance with Venezuela and the "Bolivarist" Left against the American juggernaut.

The old eagerness of the British bourgeoisie to attain aristocratic pretensions at home had, historically, a vivid counterpart in colonial (and also most postcolonial) administrations, an expressed ideal of noblesse oblige rather than unembarrassed plunder. Sections of the nonwhite middle classes, black and Indian, took up the task whenever allowed, while the plantocracy itself, intent on preserving the profits that it hoped to repatriate one day, never much bothered with such high aims. Would a more aggressive and successful "native" bourgeoisie, as in the United States, have made ultimately for a more clear-cut, less beaten down nonwhite Caribbean workforce? Might it yet? This, too, remains an imponderable.

The rise of a modern Trinidadian Left, at any rate, offers a powerful case in point for this complex of traditions and possibilities. As in the United States, the shortage of labor during the First World War prompted strikes and associated actions by the most favorably placed workers, especially in transportation. Novelist and historian Michael Anthony has wonderfully re-created, in his fictional *In the Heat of the Day*, precise images of a struggle over rate paying and a waterworks bill in 1903 that turned the society upside down, in no small part reacting to colonial authorities unable to see blacks as more than beasts of burdens, intermittently threatening to rise out of control.[36] Nearly a generation later, in 1918, longshoremen struck warehouses in Port of Spain, driving out scabs, marching through the city the following year, and shutting down the port.[37] This was already Black Power (without the name) because Marcus Garvey's name was on the lips of activists, his weekly newspaper, the *Negro World* (officially banned but widely available) in their hands. Soldiers rushed in from Jamaica, too sympathetic to the Trinidadians to commit outrages against them but sufficiently powerful to quiet the nerves of the rulers and the passions of the ruled. Things returned to something like normal.

During the follow decade, Arthur A. Cipriani, swarthy horse trainer and commander of a volunteer black and brown regiment in the Great War, reorganized a dormant TWA and made into a power. Soon it was the Trinidad Labour Party, electing him to a seat on the legislative council and then as mayor. The Corsican spoke vigorously for the "barefooted man," also seeking (as some of his radical successors did not) to bring the East Indian laborers into the movement. Nothing, perhaps, frightened most whites here or in British Guiana quite so much as the prospect of black/Indian unity.

But no more perfect miniature replica of the British Labour Party could be found anywhere either: Cipriani politely, sometimes not quite politely, pressed the issues of minimum wage, shortened working day, workmen's compensation, child labor, compulsory (and improved) education, and the abolition of outright racist practices. Hardly any of these demands were adopted before the labor uprisings of the following decade, but hope for their realization no doubt kept resentful locals and especially their own professional elite in check, while turning the ordinary noncitizen toward apathy and the familiar conclusion that politics only affected, beyond the whites themselves, the brown classes after all. James remembered being asked by a prominent colonial official what would happen if Cipriani were arrested, and telling the same official that the whole island would arise. The attempt was never made: a stasis had been reached, unlike in India, unlike parts of Africa and Asia still under the British flag. "The captain," in effect, deserted the ship with the onset of the Depression, fearing a mass uprising far more than colonial rule unchanged. Cipriani, the wags suggested, was perpetually a man at the end of a rope—a rope pulled by the British Labour Party and the Trades Union Congress. Even when his every expectation was betrayed by these august bodies, he could not imagine turning elsewhere.[38]

Much of the same might be said for Jamaica and British Guiana. Agricultural and waterfront strikes had burst out intermittently from the 1880s onward; rudimentary trade unions formed among the construction trades and other crafts around the turn of the century, on the American rather than the British model. Indeed, Jamaican printers formed a local of the International Typographers Union (ITU), the oldest continuous American union and for a century the one most likely to enroll the autodidact intellectual. In Jamaica's case, the vice chair of its compositor's chapter in 1907 was none other than Marcus Garvey. Governor Sidney Olivier, a Fabian socialist, resisted legislation legalizing unions in Jamaica specifically on the grounds that it would serve to promote U.S. control, and if this were a mere rationalization, he had a point at least. AFL union leaders were often nearly as imperialistic minded as American corporations: the very claim of these virtually all-white unions to govern "Internationals" rested on a thin base of affiliates in Canada. Toward the Caribbean, real solidarity between working classes had never been suggested, save by the dangerous radicals suppressed in wartime. Worse yet: in 1917 Samuel Gompers had hatched a scheme for secret subsidies from the U.S. State Department to launch a regionwide (but U.S.-controlled) Pan American Federation of Labor dedicated to business unionism loyal to American interests.

In British Guiana, as in Jamaica, employer resistance proved overwhelming, and when it did not, the government stepped in to crush unionism. Even negotiations granting wage advances without union recognition were viewed as the stalking horses for dangerous black and brown advance. The strikes of the later 1910s, however, set the path for the future. Labor federations sprung up with assistance from some small shopkeepers, faced firings and blacklisting of their leaders, went out of existence, and left behind memories of courage under fire.

Two other closely related if often mutually hostile elements destined to play an unpredictable but vital role also showed themselves first clearly, in ideological form, during the 1920s: black nationalism and communism. Both vitally involved a second middle passage, this time as proletarians atop the deck rather than slave captives below, between New York and the Caribbean, with many stops in between. Both black nationalism and Marxism implicated Marcus Garvey, whose 1916 shift from Jamaica to Harlem signaled the rise of the Universal Negro Improvement Association (UNIA) into the largest nonreligious black organization in the world.

Black nationalism was far from new. Emigrationist efforts from the eighteenth century, the "exodus" impulse from the Old South to the West after the Civil War, Chief Sam (aka Alfred C. Sam), E. Sutton Griggs, and others had set out extravagant if little-fulfilled schemes. But with the "New Negro" and rapidly expanding Harlem, a new time had come. In and around the UNIA, peaking in its unprecedented international conventions of 1921–22, a variety different radical black nationalist personalities and plans emerged, nearly all with some kind of Caribbean connection.

Scholars have only begun treating the complexity of this and related issues crucial to the transnational Caribbean Left. But research has begun to clarify something about the major personalities. Hubert H. Harrison, born in the Virgin Islands, was one of the "New Negro" personalities lighting up Harlem between 1910 and 1920. Joining a Harlem branch of the Socialist Party in 1909, he became a familiar corner speaker. Fired from his job at the post office (at the insistence of Tuskegee officials) after criticizing Booker T. Washington's philosophy in print, he was hired on as organizer for the Socialists. He became the first black writer for the daily socialist *Call* and assistant editor of the *Masses*, but he grew disillusioned with the party's lack of enthusiasm about recruiting blacks.

Suspended in 1914 for his support of the Industrial Workers of the World (IWW)—and very likely the first black, but by no means the last, ever mistreated in this fashion by a Left movement in the United States—Harrison returned to street speaking but with a nationalist message of black history and current issues. Assessing the outbreak of white pogroms in 1917, he personally formed the Liberation League of Negro-Americans and edited its *Voice*. With the small organization's demise, he moved on to Garvey's *Negro World*, for which he served as principal editor in its last vital phase, 1920–22. He continued after Garveyism's decline to urge the formation of a separate black state, founded the International Colored Unity League (ICUL), and launched its paper, *Voice of the Negro*, before his premature death at age forty-four in 1927. Neither the ICUL nor the *Voice of the Negro* made much of an impact, but Harrison had been a pace-setting personality. He was perhaps, during the second decade of the twentieth century, the first to explore in public the mixture of Garveyism and Marxism that became Caribbean nationalist politics.

A second radical nationalist would be the Barbados-born Richard B. Moore. Only fifteen when he arrived in New York in 1909, son of a building contractor and lay preacher in the Church of the Brethren, Moore lost his parents at an early age and left with his stepmother for a fresh start in America. Intuitively drawn toward socialistic schemes, he worked in a cooperative grocery, wrote for a church publication, read widely, heard Harrison speak, and joined the Socialist Party's Harlem branch along with Wilfred Domingo. Moore, too, preached socialism from the streets, one of the stepladder innovators who helped create a political public in the black metropolis. He launched his own paper, the *Emancipator*, in 1920, at once more race conscious than A. Philip Randolph's the *Messenger* and, at the same time, more eager to launch attacks on Garvey for lack of class consciousness.

Moore was deeply influenced by yet another personality, Nevis-born Cyril Briggs. Enraged at the attacks upon African Americans during the war, Briggs formed a virtual secret society, the African Blood Brotherhood (ABB), and launched the monthly *Crusader* (1918–22) advocating a separate state and autonomous Caribbean zones set apart for American blacks. The ABB went further than the Socialist Party, Garvey, or the *Emancipator* in articulating the connections of the Caribbean and the United States, and it also drew upon the same roots as the emerging Caribbean Left, the fraternal societies that had sought to fill a vacuum in Afro-Caribbean organizational life from the emancipation onward. In a difficult political atmosphere full of spies from the new Bureau of Investigation, the ABB swiftly built dozens of branches, or "posts," evidently drawing upon local Garveyite organizations but with more militancy and considerably more sympathy for the Russian Revolution.[39]

The ABB declared itself the true organ of the Hamitic League of the World, then the African Black Brotherhood, in either case the expression of black history, black culture as congealed and reinterpreted by émigré West Indians and their multiracial allies.[40] Urging the "renaissance of Negro power and culture throughout the world," Briggs envisioned a Pan-Africanism barely considered elsewhere. Africa here became the ancient source of all civilization, while contemporary lynching, segregation, disenfranchisement, and assorted ills suffered in the United States became a mirror of the history of slavery and of the global determination to keep blacks underfoot. Openly socialist from its beginnings, the *Crusader* immediately understood the worldwide implications of the Russian Revolution: capitalism could no longer maintain its empire of whiteness.

For a few years, the *Crusader* operated effectively within the vastly larger UNIA, with Garvey's permission, and some of its writers participated in the *Negro World*, which (unlike the *Crusader*) had a wide Caribbean audience. Had Garvey not headed rightward, the ABB might actually have found a modus vivendi, given various personal connections that went all the way back to Domingo's and Garvey's days together in the National Club of Jamaica. When Garvey abandoned radicalism and met with Ku Klux Klan leaders, the fat was in the fire.

But Wilfred Domingo, another Jamaican nationalist who had come to the United States, had been the *World*'s first editor, until his class-oriented editorials made Garvey increasingly uneasy. He had actually introduced

Garvey to leading Harlem personalities, and the elder man feared Domingo's influence as well as his prestige. The leading black Socialist Party intellectual after A. Phillip Randolph, Domingo taught at the party's Rand School and made his home in the Socialist Party briefly (at a moment when the Socialist Party nearly carried the Harlem vote for Congress) until embittered at the Party's failure to reach out to blacks. W.E.B. DuBois, a Socialist Party member until the world war converted him temporarily to Wilsonianism, had earlier felt the same sense of disappointment. Domingo followed Briggs into the *Crusader's* alliance with Bolshevism, while DuBois held the Communists at arm's length for another two decades. Of this Caribbean crew only Domingo, never actually a Communist, returned to the region in the 1930s to take part in labor politics.[41]

The ABB, more a support group for the *Crusader* than a self-sustaining entity, sought to replace the UNIA in the early 1920s. It had no real chance to do so, because the persecution of Garvey by the Federal Bureau of Investigation (FBI) and the Justice Department put black nationalism itself into a corner, with Garvey's own deportation in 1927 decisive. The UNIA had a year earlier actually expelled Briggs— and all members of the Workers Party, that is, the emerging American Communist entity.

Minus the fast-ebbing surge of black nationalism, the *Crusader* and its Crusader News Service (a reporting service for local black papers) could not find a place within African American life. With a certain logic, the institutions became an entering wedge for their leaders and supporters into the Third International. Thanks to Lenin and even to Stalin, Communist leaders drawing back from their early expectations of early world revolution quickly saw anticolonial nationalism as the one great chink in the (white) imperial armor. They also believed, with a fervor that had few socialist precursors (among them Rosa Luxemburg, a syndicalist Dutch Left with talented anti-imperialist activists, and the sectarian American socialist leader Daniel DeLeon with his protégé, Louis C. Fraina, the first American Communist intellectual), in the responsibility of Marxists to support anti-imperial revolution anywhere and everywhere. One could say with some exaggeration that the road from

Curacao's DeLeon to Jamaica's Briggs had led naturally to New York and the Caribbean/Left connection. But few in either region would have recognized it at the time.[42]

Traveling to Moscow and back, a small handful of the African diaspora actually played an important role in the formulation of Comintern policy, at least in regard to the United States. The stakes of any American Marxists in the "Negro Question" were laid out as never before and the tremendous contribution of Communists and their fellow travelers to racial equality in virtually every realm prepared here. Under different conditions, the Harlem Renaissance (a largely if by no means entirely African American cultural movement) would have been mirrored by a black communism that was, especially at its leading levels, very largely a Caribbean transnational phenomenon.

That such a development would have stolen a march upon the London-based Pan-African activities of the next decade is demonstrated by the meeting of the International Congress against Colonial Oppression in Brussels, 1927, with Arthur Schomburg himself providing Richard Moore the funds to attend. Nearly two hundred delegates—including Albert Einstein, Henri Barbusse, Jawaharlal Nehru, and Madame Sun Yat-sen—urged, among other aims, Caribbean liberation from suffocating U.S. rule.

But the promise of the Caribbean Left within the United States was not to be. The "bolshevization" of the Communist Party, tightening lines of discipline by cracking down on the continuation of the familiar (often ethnic-based) decentralization of the Socialist movement, seemed to advance the case of black Communists by making the membership of the entire party starkly aware of race issues. Thanks to the positions taken by the Comintern, a handful of black Communists could become international figures, if mostly in symbolic terms by participation in Comintern congresses. But the Stalinization of the movement, a sequel of the late 1920s, closed the progress in key ways.

Democracy within Communist ranks, always limited by a factional mentality of leadership blocs launching salvos against each other, dissipated and disappeared.[43] Orders came down from above for black Communists, too. But the disillusionment with the Communists accompanying the shift toward antifascism and the consequent de-emphasis on anticolonialism was felt most sharply by Caribbean radicals, who would have been the first to know about George Padmore's break with the Comintern in 1934. By that time, a minigeneration of African American radicals bitterly resentful of Caribbean leadership formed the black administrative apparatus tightly bound to the party leadership. The apparatus did wonders in legal defense cases, as ordinary Communists would rally to the call of racial equality. But it was not black peoples' own expression.

The goal of a Black Belt in the American South, adopted and then abandoned by the Communists, derided by (black as well as white) socialists and in later years by many ex-Communists, actually had considerable support among black nationalists from Harlem to the rural South. But it was never a realistic option for African Americans, and the intermittent Communist support of if typified the substitution of slogan for serious strategy. Isolated among immigrant and nonwhite lower classes within a nation of emerging consumerism and a vibrant Ku Klux Klan, the Communists fumbled in their effort to find more realistic policies. Thus did the West Indian leftward thrust into the United States fail in an important second sense.

Before the inward collapse, the Communist outreach to the Caribbean had planted seeds. The Trade Union Unity League, established in New York in 1928 with the impossible aim of building a "Red" federation of labor outside the AFL, sent its organizers into Jamaica in 1929–31. The Negro Labor Congress, first of the post-ABB Communist "fronts" for the black community of the United States, dispatched to the same site Suriname-born Otto Huiswood, typographer and the first black Communist to actually meet Lenin. The work failed but took on new forms, more around and outside than within the Communist global apparatus.

The Great Strike Wave

We are only beginning to grasp, even after all these years, the facts much less the full effects of the 1935–39 strike wave across the Caribbean. Certain it is that the movement was largely spontaneous. The palpable failure of capitalism, including its preeminent form in the United States; the terrible shortage of work on the plantations and in town; the waning deference toward colonialism; and the greater mobility of the population may have been set off by something so distant as the Italian invasion of Ethiopia. Race-conscious blacks across the world were stunned by the energetic work of leftists and Pan-Africanists throwing their energy into the cause.

Jamaica and Trinidad again offer the models of the strike's spread and impact. Legalization of unions in 1932 had been at best partial, but unions formed. The Jamaica Workers and Tradesmen's Union (JWTU), founded in 1936 by war veteran A. G. St. Claver Coombs and master mason Hugh Clifford Buchanan, saw an important ally in the new daily *Jamaican Standard*, founded the following year with much sympathetic labor coverage. The Poor Man's Improvement Land Settlement and Labour Association, a sort of peasants' union formed in 1938, completed the picture just in time, as the cane cutters of eastern Jamaica went on strike. Suppression here failed to quell uprisings elsewhere, including a sugar company strike and associated riot in the opposite end of the island with dozens wounded and four killed by gunfire. Then the waterfront workers in Kingston launched something approaching a general strike in the city, spreading to the bulk of the island.[44]

It was as revolutionary a situation in the English-speaking islands of the region as had been seen since the days of slave uprisings. A generation after the birth rate had sharply increased (and the death rate mostly declined, save for the influenza epidemic of 1919–20), and for the first time the region faced no labor shortage, venerable estates closed suddenly or reduced production to a fraction of its former size. The money value of exports dropped nearly by half between 1928 and 1933, hitting bananas and sugar especially hard.[45] What had been endurable became unendurable. Racial arrogance long accepted was now increasingly rejected in innumerable small ways.

In Belize, as early as 1934, a self-described "Unemployed Brigade" seized the day, marching through the capital to meet the governor and plead for help for the starving unemployed. Unwilling to accept a pittance and a promise, a radical movement developed under the guidance of a well-known barber and orator, Antonio Soberanis Gomez. More disturbances prompted laws written specifically to justify his arrest on "conspiracy" charges—with a public mood so threatening that he escaped with a fine. Guyana plantation workers, St. Kitts cane cutters and sugar factory laborers, coal loaders in St. Lucia, and sugar workers in St. Vincent all but exploded. In St. Vincent, rioters actually struck the governor, cuffed the repressive attorney general, ransacked one of the richest estates, and broke into the prison, freeing the inmates before British warships arrived and the moment passed. (The locals leading them were known as "Selassie" and "Mother Selassie.") A British gunboat turned its bright lights upon the city of Castries, successfully intimidating St. Lucians. Clement Payne, born to Barbadian parents living in Trinidad, returned to lead the labor struggle in Barbados and was represented after his arrest by future prime minister Grantley Adams. Only in Jamaica and Trinidad did events leave an institutional imprint as well as personalities destined to last until the accelerating stages of independence.

Histories of modern Trinidad and Tobago often date to 1935 the return of the native son Eric Williams, educated personally by C.L.R. James, gone abroad to Oxford, and then come home. It would be just as true to say that 1935 marked a decisive disillusionment with Captain Cipriani, who signed on to a Wages Board report in that impoverished year concluding that few Trinidadian workers were underpaid. East Indian workers had already lost confidence in the captain, who urged patience in the political process despite the desperateness of the situation.

Violent strikes in the Sugar Belt prompted Indian lawyer Adrian Cola Rienzi—born Krishna Neonararine, more than a decade earlier the president of the San Fernando branch of the TWA and a source of anxiety to colonial officials because of his well-known sympathy for bolshevism—to break with Cipriani and form the Trinidad Citizens League. The following year, oil-field worker turned evangelical minister Tubul Uriah "Buzz" Butler also broke with an increasingly conservative (or at least cautious) Cipriani, demanded nationalization of oil, and launched the British Empire Workers and Citizens Home Rule Party. This was, as Kafra Kabon suggests, a "new kind of politics," for the region at any rate.[46]

Behind this wave lay less-understood developments, dating back at least to a Garveyite "back to the land" movement of the Trinidadian 1920s, to the National Unemployed Movement (NUM) based in landless laborers forced into cities without resources, and urban hunger marches (led in part by Ferdinand Smith). The Negro Welfare Social and Cultural Association (NWA), emerging in 1934, formed groups for discussions, worked with the unemployed, and stressed the connections of Afro-Caribbean with Africans in the condition of colonialism. NWA leaders, in touch with George Padmore in London, also urged internationalism and added a new note by promoting their own female leaders, a Caribbean first.[47] Added to the broil, calypsonians daringly sang about conditions and against popularly hated personalities, even when the commissioner of police called for censorship of popular music lyrics. The mass demonstrations held against this threat, and the withdrawal of the threat, as much as anything, gave NWA activists a growing sense of confidence: ordinary people had been won to their side. Cipriani, still mayor of Port of Spain, dug his political grave by turning upon the crowds that he had encouraged to demand their collective right to own the transit system (milked for profits by international interests) that they so badly needed. His day was finished, and with him an era.[48]

Butler had meanwhile placed himself as a sympathetic figure in the NWA and assorted movements, without committing himself to them. In 1935, he saw his chance to act when a desperate strike of oil-field workers in depression conditions faced the prospect of unemployment. As Cipriani dithered, Butler attacked him verbally and was thrown out of a public meeting. The strike was soon as good as lost—or worse, a smaller body of workers were given a slight increase, encouraged to form conservative unions, and made to feel themselves aristocrats of labor. Out of work, Butler traveled the oil region, an ex-soldier with all the talents of an agitator, to growing crowds.[49]

Bukka Rennie has argued that the subsequent strike wave, with all its vitality, has obscured in popular memory the importance of the factory and community organization of the NWA, its emphasis upon education and upon women's leadership through Trinidad's north, while oil-field agitation continued in the South.[50] The point is an important one, and not only because the NWA was forcefully internationalist and anticolonialist, while Butler frequently described himself as a "Black Britisher" loyal to the Crown despite anything and everything. Occupied with urban questions, attacked as "Communist," and undermined by the opening of a new harbor in 1936 with a supply of jobs, the NWA gave way to Butler and to working-class populism. It was a fateful development amid the unprecedented burst of labor activity, the most intense that the Caribbean had ever known.[51]

Butler did not precipitate the strike wave but placed himself in front of it in the fateful month of June 1937. He famously proclaimed: "The hour has come to show your might and power to get things for yourselves. Our brutal Taskmasters have proudly and cruelly turned down our prayers. . . . These men and bosses have challenged us to prove our right to life and happiness."[52] As police attempted to arrest a militant, a police corporal known for his sadism was soaked in paraffin and burned to death by an enraged crowd. By the end, fourteen people had died, fifty-nine were injured, and hundreds had been arrested. Soon after, the short-lived Trinidad Citizens League linked itself with the All-Trinidad Sugar Estates and Factory Workers Union, the Oilfield Workers Trade Union (OWTU) and others under a Committee of Industrial Organization (inspired, no doubt by the left-leaning U.S. industrial union body with the same initials), of which Adrian Rienzi was chair.[53] This was unionism of a new kind as well.

The colonial rulers answered the general strike with the predictable warships, and in time, Butler, given to wonderful flights of rhetoric against the authorities, was arrested and sentence to two years imprisonment for sedition.[54] Even the governor and his secretary admitted wages were too low; they were retired and transferred to another island for showing their sympathies. Conditions remained unchanged, and the union that struggled to improve them bordered on a personality cult for Butler. The London-based Forster Commission urged a paternalistic approach drawing union leaders into collaboration, converting "Red" leaders rather than suppressing them, and encouraging the formation of unions on a moderate basis.[55] This was successful, Rennie argues, because the emerging leaders of the OWTU, Rienzi and John Rojas, were themselves eager to institutionalize their movement by pacifying the most restless sections of workers. Like a number of Communists or near-Communists in the United States and the United Kingdom, they no doubt also judged that they had carried the struggle as far as it could go at the moment, in the global context of a Popular Front against fascism. At any rate, NWA activists found themselves walled off from agitation in the South. The revolutionary moment had passed.[56]

Butler seemed at different times either the more acceptable deviation from colonial rule or the less acceptable. Things could never be quite the same now that "Massa" had been challenged with Buzz's call, "Let those who labour hold the reins." If it certainly wasn't a threat of social-ism, it was definitely a species of anti-imperialism sufficient to get him jailed and exiled for the duration of the war. That he was called "Black" Butler underlined the racial implications of the shift, never much con-cealed. "Responsible unionism" of the British type could never restrain him, and the appeals of left-wingers for patience with the colonial process impressed him not at all. Attacked as a fanatic, mentally unbalanced, unsuited for parliament, he retained his popularity among a large section of ordinary islanders.[57]

We have more precise information about Jamaica's labor-radical personalities principally because one of its key participants has become its historian. Richard Hart, a light-skinned Creole and son of a promi-nent island lawyer, returned from a legal education in Britain in 1937 a convinced Marxist of Popular Front stripe. W. A. Domingo, W. Adolph Roberts, Rev. Elthred Brown, and Jaime O'Meally, all living in New York, had founded the Jamaican Progressive League in 1936 to promote independence. Roberts and Domingo returned to the island to discover others already hard at work toward the same goal. Formation of the news magazine *Public Opinion* the following year accelerated a wide-ranging debate over means and ends, with young Hart joining in and accept-ing the conclusion that national self-determination had to come before socialism.

The People's National Party was formed with Norman Manley at its head, a vacationing Sir Stafford Cripps (Left Labourite) on hand, and a crowd of five thousand in the streets of Kingston for the monumental event of the region. Cripps himself denounced imperialism, but Manley was characteristically cautious, suggesting that Jamaica was not yet ready for independence. Pressed by critics on the "Communist threat" (much feared though nowhere in evidence in the English-speaking islands), Manley batted away questions and later insisted that no member of the People's National Party (PNP) was a Communist—not quite true if the word had been improved as "Marxist" and not at all true if "socialist." (Sixty years later, Richard Hart quipped, "Frank Hill and I and others thought we were 'communists' until, in 1948, Norman Manley convinced us that we were not" and most amazingly that Hart and his Moscow-minded circle had supposedly never been more than Marxists in the general sense.)[58]

Against the foreground of these political events central to the political evolution of the region was a background of labor struggles that gave the politicos and intellectuals the force of influence and a degree of public authority. These struggles were also marked by a further peculiar cult of personality. The Jamaica Workers and Tradesmens Union (1936) and the *Jamaica Labour Weekly* had opened the way to agitation in which hundreds of sugar workers had stopped work in 1937–38 and Alexander Bustamante made into a hero. An agitator par excellence, he had served as a mediator (even while denying that he represented workers) and found himself as the symbolic head of still unorganized island labor. From the first—and this was also typical for large aspects of Caribbean development—the unions he created belonged to him. Not elsewhere would a labor organization actually bear the name of the champion, as did the Bustamante Industrial Trade Union (BITU), bringing together assorted workers, with Bustamante himself as the overpowering personality.

Bustamante's clash in early 1939, with what amounted to a smaller but now vastly more democratic Jamaica Workers and Tradesmens Union, prompted an unexpected call by the mercurial leader for a nationwide general strike. Workers themselves responded half-heartedly, and Manley intervened, bringing about a temporary labor unity, followed by a second split and a rapid decline. A second wave of strikes prompted by the outbreak of war in Europe and tightening labor markets fell under the grip of censorship. The little group of Marxists weighed their opportunities and took a disproportionate role in education, legal assistance to labor, and constitution writing. Bustamante attacked them, and Manley disowned them.

These patient comrades were the first organized Caribbean Communists. They remained determinedly loyal to the PNP and were actually taken aback when Manley expressed the aspiration for an ultimate vision of socialism for Jamaica. True to Popular Front logic, they believed the achievement of self-government was all that might be expected (or advocated) in the short haul. Doubly loyal, they supported Manley in his vague but definitely Christian vision of a socialistic, egalitarian society. As Hart teased out the meaning more than half a century later, the Labour Party had done so in Britain; this should be seen as the Jamaican seconding of the motion.[59]

But it proved, in other respects, a phantom. The war transformed everything, as world wars will do. It was still more true for the Caribbean, marking off past from future. The unions and political parties had been as much as created—in most cases, actually created—by the upsurge of struggle in the late 1930s. Independence, however long in coming, had been forecast and made inevitable. Not so inevitable was the sinking back of the postcolonial into the neocolonial and the exchange of British Empire for U.S. economic rule.

In the years shortly following the war, farsighted Caribbean leaders set out an agenda never accomplished. A Caribbean Civil Service Federation (CCSF), organized in 1944, committed to creating a single body in the region, free of colonial-era racism and thereby freed in a meritocratic sense to do its own useful public work. Meanwhile, the Caribbean Labour Congress (CLC), bringing together the leaders of the region—T. A. Marryshow, Norman Manley, Grantley Adams, Vere Bird, and others—advanced an aggressive program of socialistic reforms aimed at regional unity. On a regional basis, land reform joined the break-up of the plantation economy, with central planning to bring together the most and least developed island sectors. Not only blue-collar workers but teachers, lawyers, and even small businesspeople lined up behind the CCSF and its child, the CLC—until the cold war and the monied invasion of U.S. policy arms (in this case the deliberately misnamed American Institute for Free Labor Development) dictated otherwise.

It was thus a moment that failed doubly, because the compulsory alliance immediately corrupted society by pouring money toward those who supported the Americans and shunning or actually firing those who did not (at least they were not murdered, as in parts of Latin America). Civil service jobs and all else would be decided by favoritism after all, a particularly damaging blow in a region where good jobs were hard to find and desperation to live in a middle-class way meant the possibility of educating the next generation, along with the niceties of home or decent flat rather than lifelong economic uncertainty and likely squalor.

But the moment did not fall of its own weight, and that is a crucial point. The CLC had for a moment represented, in and through the trades unions, the regional socialist dream. The CLC has not found its scholar, but we know that it called for decisive land reform (no individual or corporation to own greater than five hundred acres), a unicameral legislature with full adult suffrage, central planning within a dominion status, and practical independence. With the British Labour Party promising a kind of socialism at home, the idea had even a sort of rationale in Fabian paternalism, as strange as that now seems. The Communists had deserted a Caribbean-led black nationalism a decade earlier; now was the socialist opportunity to do better.[60]

The cold war followed so swiftly upon the Labour Party election victory in Britain that the party's global impact was undermined and even reversed. Over the next few years, the point of paternalism was to keep the islands from going their own way or public sentiment from turning against the zeal of the cold war.

A division of labor confederations marked the sorry path ahead: the World Federation of Trade Unions (WFTU), representing the East along with many powerful Communist-led unions in parts of Europe, Asia, Africa, and Latin America; and the International Confederation of Free Trade Unions (ICFTU), breaking away to oppose Communist authoritarianism (and the top-down unions of the Eastern Bloc) but openly supporting U.S. foreign policy, organized and led by men in the pay of the Central Intelligence Agency (CIA). Grantley Adams and Norman Manley, true to the British Labour Party's obedient support of U.S. foreign policy, determined to move the Caribbean unions out of the WFTU and into the ICFTU by expelling all WFTU member unions from the CLC. Failing to gain a majority for expulsion, Adams resolved that the CLC had to be dissolved, a destruction that took a decade to complete. The new federation, meanwhile, was a mere branch of the CIA-operated Pan-American umbrella federation, ORIT (Inter-American Regional Labor Organization), dubbed CADORIT (Caribbean Inter-American Regional Labor Organization), formally based in sedate Barbados. As former CIA agent Philip Agee later remarked, drawing conclusions from his own fieldwork, there was never any doubt about CADORIT or its successor (which set up the Caribbean Congress of Labour in 1960) that the orders came straight from Washington, D.C.; Silver Spring, Maryland (AFL-CIO headquarters); and Arlington, Virginia (CIA)—on these matters practically the same thing.[61]

It remains an open question of what the radical, essentially syndicalist elements in Europe and elsewhere might have done in a ruined Europe without directives from Moscow, and what ripple effect takeovers of industry and commerce might have had upon working people outside the metropolis. Followers of Trotsky, including C.L.R. James, remained insistent, over a long period of activity and retrospect, that the moment had arrived and Communists had held the workers back from it.[62] Now we may be forgiven a little skepticism about the prospect of sudden transformation. It looks a good deal more like a great potential moment of transition, empowerment from below spreading out from unions and other grassroots organizations, restrained by circumstances (the residual strength of capitalism) from logical completion of the process. Within the metropolis, the prospect was to move the public interest of the New Deal or Popular Front up another notch; outside the metropolis, to wrest development from colonialists and corporations in the name of an enlarged community by actual uprisings or other means.

The events from 1946 onward ruined hopes so thoroughly that a sense of inevitability hangs over our retrospective. Western Europe, the crucial partner of non-Soviet socialism, was won back by the Marshall Plan. Meanwhile, the opponents of the cold war were practically neutralized by a combination of rising economy and ruinous state despotism in the East, which was faced with an impossible task of early recovery in any case but weighted down decisively by the faceless bureaucratic leadership installed from Moscow and kept in control by Russian tanks.

One increasingly gains the impression that, as in Ceylon, where organized Trotskyists successfully substituted themselves for the Communists, the results were not likely to be very different. Other Marxists, given the opportunity, could represent the radicalized petite-bourgeoisie just as effectively. Provided through an improved Marxism an explanation for national misery, they also gave a sense of identity for the intellectual, a feeling of populist zeal for the shopkeeper or the rising professional as the local or national leaders of the party and, through them, the voice of the masses. Given the successful continuation of global capitalism, the final results would not likely have been much different—until much later when the "new social movements" of ecology, feminism, and indigenism had made vandguardist Marxism-Leninism a thing of the past.

For the officials and members of the CCL, it was either play (play along with the American unionists under CIA influence, that is) or pay (with subsequent loss of office and influence). Housebroken, despite the retention of a few socialistic phrases, the CCL became for all practical purposes an American pet.[63]

Culture

C.L.R. James was fond of saying, during his "rediscovery" in late middle age, that the Caribbean had inherited nothing from Africa and began in effect anew. It was a metaphorical point at best, a matter of printed language and formal customs rather than the spoken word and folkways, in the light of the religious and cultural syncretism abounding all behavior.

Remarkably enough, however, the same James had foreshadowed the appreciation of disaporic gifts, and he had helped speed their tardy interest by his writings on music as far back as the 1920s. He and his friends listened to Louis Armstrong and other jazz musicians on the gramophone, and that may well have triggered a first critical appreciation of the calypso music exploding around them. The earliest calypso records stamped in

Trinidad—following the fashion of "race records" for black populations in the United States—found their way into his hands, because he was writing about calypsonians in Cipriani's weekly *Labour Leader*. For James, earlier than anyone else on the island, these island musicians were artists to be taken seriously and even in the light of classical music, not merely of popular or commercial culture.

We now know far more than James did, thanks principally to calypso singer-historian Hollis Liverpool. This Port of Spain schoolteacher (stage name: Chalkdust, familiarly, "Chalky"), has traced musical traditions and the role of the singer/griot back to specific African origins, and through parallel developments to calypso (sometimes directly influenced by it) in modern African musical traditions.[64]

Trinidad was central to calypso, for good reasons. Its phase of slavery had been shorter and release earlier, notwithstanding a decimation of ex-slave population (for whites and free coloreds rushing to the island in hopes of quick profits). Carnival day opened a cultural free space from the early decades of the nineteenth century. Masquerade (colloquially, "mas"), carried over from Africa with influences from medieval Europe, had offered a way of interpreting and dramatizing the role of natural and supernatural forces, the relation of human beings with animals and the environment. Most remarkably, the banning of the masquerade in postrevolutionary France (until the Restoration) encouraged exiles to practice, alongside transported Africans, what they could not practice at home. Likewise, Spaniards brought their own carnival traditions. Modern researches have uncovered multitudinous instruments, actually brought from Africa or made from objects at hand; dances accompanied the music, often satirical as well as celebrational, a reenactment of the spirits' role along with a commentary on the masters, rolled up into a seasonal ceremony, sometimes Christmas, sometimes Easter, sometimes fall harvest, or "cropover." Through these means, an extraordinary recuperation of preslavery tradition was maintained and updated, even when some rituals were permitted only under white supervision, if at all.[65]

In the postemancipation period, acculturation accelerated. "Freedom Day" occupied a central role, marked in Trinidad by stickfighters' contests; "mas"-imitated warriors, including red Indians (skin color rearranged with the help of plant dyes); and African champions. Calypso made its notable appearance with the (temporary) banning of masking. The Jamette—from the French "diameter"—designated a class beneath respectability but full of romantic interest. Bands of stickfighters, self-organized much as the later calypso and pan bands, had already designated themselves heroically and set out for a night's battle, after gathering with the call of conch shells and cattle horns. Violence, police suppression, and the renewed participation of the Creole and white upper classes in holiday events turned attention toward music and masking, widely accepted at the 1897 centenary of British rule over Trinidad. By this time, calypso lyrics—in English rather than patois—actually appeared in the newspapers.[66]

Fancy costumes and music replaced violence as competition, and dancers might be dressed as cowboys, ostriches, Scottish highlanders, or anything else in contemporary Anglo-American life and culture. But it would be a mistake to assume Europeanization could ever be comprehensive. West African spirits were vivid in the *Jour Ouvert* parades, and barely disguised curses at the white rulers could be heard easily. East Indians, Portuguese, Syrians, and others took part only in some "mas" events; Afro-Caribbeans dominated the streets on carnival day, another central factor in African retention.

In Trinidad, the carnival had been practically confined to the ruling classes, white and Creole, until emancipation. Slaves had been forbidden for centuries to drum, out of the reasonable fear that the "bush telegraph" would instigate and spread outright rebellion. No doubt they had found other means, well-studied for the U.S. slave population, to make sense of their own lives between sundown and sunup. But with emancipation, carnival immediately became central to the lives of the former slaves. Official efforts from the late 1850s onward sought to suppress the carnival fever, but these could only dilute the exhilarated expression. The Cambouley riots of 1881, indeed, seemed to demonstrate that the assortment of drummers, dancers, singers, prostitutes, and other revelers had made the carnival their own once and for all, the celebrative definition of their own ways of life. Riots a few years later caused the colonial legislature to bar the sugar plantation revelers—blacks and Indians alike—from entering the cities; the governor of the island in 1898 actually suspended the Port of Spain city council for refusing to enforce a ban. And the calyp-sonian Norman Le Blanc sang, "Jerningham the governor/It's a rudeness into you/It's a fastness into you/To break up the laws of the Borough Council."[67]

If Le Blanc was not and could not possibly be the political leader of the masses, he encompassed their sentiment. The Tambu-Bambu had already spread among Indians and blacks in Trinidad, a substitute for the forbidden drums, combined with dance, using the materials read-ily at hand. From Tambu-Bambu and without it (in some islands, like Antigua, that had no bamboo) came the iron bands of men (and also smaller groups of women) knocking pieces of iron together in rhythm. From iron, steel: the reworking of metal petroleum drums ubiquitous in the oil district of San Fernando, Trinidad, and passed through other parts of the island and elsewhere, in the rest of the English-speaking Caribbean with no petroleum reserves to tap. By the 1940s, steel bands made them-selves messengers of political demands and race sentiment (including versions of Islam). But the calypso tents had long since seen the most intense political dialogues of the region. Here, in true carnival fashion abandoned across the seas in Europe, the social order could be turned upside down, at least in imagination, and the foibles and corruption of white and brown revealed and ridiculed in rhyme, the highest prize often going to the sharpest tongue.

In the wartime economy and afterward, a handful of steel band and calypsonian musicians and singers could make a marginal living, and enough of the part-time musicians gathered to form (in Antigua) the Steelband Association in 1948, headed by outspoken socialist Ivan "Jones" Edwards. The planters naturally despised them, and the tiny black mid-dle class set dogs upon their parading bands. No use: the politics of cul-ture was here to stay and was destined to larger roles as independence approached.[68]

Formal claims on culture arrived with greater effort. Novels, short stories, and poetry written in the European fashion, but with some Native character, had begun to appear early in the twentieth century. St. John Perse of the French Antilles had actually won a prize for poetry in 1911. A.R.F. Webber's *Those That Be in Bondage* appeared in 1919, an idiosyncratic volume that included rural oppression among Guyanese blacks and Indians, interracial romance and sex (in Barbados), and "bondage" of different qualities, with moments of exaltation at the natural beauty of the surroundings. Webber lived long enough to have joined Captain Cipriani's movement in Trinidad and addressed mass meetings that James almost certainly attended. In Martinique, the poetry of Aime Cesaire had gained world notice by the 1940s, with one of the great literary works of the era, or perhaps any era, "Return to My Native Land."

In between the literary events of the 1910s and 1930s had been the most important influence on English language: the Harlem Renaissance. Unlike the Communist Party's approach to "the Negro question," this approach was far more African-American, far less Caribbean, in origin. But by no means entirely. Claude McKay, for a time both the most political and the most popular of Harlem litterateurs, served as the personal bridge. Author of two published books of verse before he left Jamaica for the United States in 1912, he joined the staff of the *Liberator*, succeeding the suppressed *Masses*, and became one of its most prized contributors. "If We Must Die," a poem hailing armed resistance in the face of Negrophobic rioting, was adopted by Jewish groups as their own sentiment, read in countless churches and some synagogues, and reprinted widely as a testament in courage and determination.

McKay toured Europe for years after 1919, was celebrated at the Comintern, and saw his poetry volume *Literary Shadows* praised extravagantly as the discovery of a new voice in American culture. His famed novels to follow—*Home to Harlem*, *Banjo*, and *Banana Bottom*—all stemmed from his exile years, perhaps doubly exiled because return to the West Indies seemed as impossible as return to the United States. He died spiritually with his return in 1934, broken and broke.

But the echoes had definitely been heard in the Caribbean. One might say that the appearance of short-lived literary magazines in Trinidad back in the 1870s, guided by John Jacob Thomas (who also wrote *The Theory and Practice of Creole Grammar*), foreshadowed the small literary explosion of the later 1920s. At any rate, C.L.R. James was to hail Thomas in the midst of that explosion at its epicenter: *Trinidad* (1929–30) and the *Beacon* (1931–33).

James was *the* black intellectual, his little circle of litterateurs the Creoles, most of them like James himself probably "graduates" of the Maverick Club formed in 1919 for local literary events. The most prominent was Alfred Mendes, soon to be author of *Black Fauns*. Mendes chose the same subject as James for his most poignant work: the community of impoverished black women, single, sometimes with children, "kept" by men's pay packets, living together with other such women in the slum barracks in Port of Spain. The eagerness for such a subject, the very opposite of Victorian propriety even when treated (as Mendes did) with basically picaresque traits, no doubt reflected the sentiment and style of the Harlem Renaissance, especially McKay's *Home to Harlem*. But the reality of them in the Caribbean, near the throbbing heart of mass culture, was shocking—just as James and Mendez intended.

Trinidad managed only two issues, Christmas 1929 and Easter 1930, but it kicked up a storm before collapsing into financial insolvency. James had announced that he intended to go abroad—as black intellectuals unlike their mulatto cousins were practically forced to do—and the literary baton fell to other hands. Alfred Gomes, another financier-publisher, took up the various cultural matters with more determination and success. For the first time, a Trinidadian (perhaps, for the first time, a Caribbean) literary magazine took up the issues of the East Indians. It also organized short-story contests; it embraced labor activists along with literary types in dialogue; it reviewed musical events and art exhibitions; it published enraged and quizzical letters from readers; and it printed stories with as much sexual frankness as contemporary British colonial standards would permit.

The arrival of the West Indian novel, as a genre, would have to await the advent of a new generation, educated in the (relatively) prosperous war years and able to travel abroad, mainly to the United Kingdom, during the 1950s for achievement and for recognition. But it may be fairly said that *Trinidad* and the *Beacon* had forecasted the mixture of realism and imaginative invention, the variety of styles, political engagement, and apparent political indifference, that would characterize the republic of letters in Caribbean cultural development. To borrow a notion from the discussions of Jewish and especially Yiddish literature, Caribbean

English in particular was in a sense a sort of "minor language" where all the issues would be condensed and appear somehow in nearly every text. It carried the burden of the political, economic, and social struggle for independence even when it did not wish to do so.[69] As Hector, decades later, would pay homage to all the region's literary heroes and heroines, Cesaire and James to Lamming, Jamaica Kincaid, and so many others, he placed them in relation to cricket, calypso, reggae, and other treasures of the everyday citizen, accumulating evidence that "all ah we is one."

The Depression fell hard upon the small world of Caribbean letters. It might almost be said that fiction and poetry shut down in favor of politics in the broadest sense, unemployed demonstrations and outright riots to strikes, and unions and political organization. But the cultural elements had never been entirely missing in all this. Small cultural publications like *Picong, Progress, Forum*, and *Callaloo* sprouted on various islands, although they took root only with great difficulty and often (as in the case of the *Beacon*) among Creoles still determined to separate themselves from a prosaic black culture. As a historian of Barbadian literature observes, the "social unrest" and "stimulation of the minds of the masses" prepared another day. Further outburst awaited the return of opportunity with the shocks of wartime occupation and wartime prosperity.[70] Next time, the literary class would be closer to the self-conscious radicalism of another political generation.

CHAPTER TWO

What Makes Antigua Different?

Ow is it possible, participant in long-vanished movements Richard Hart asks himself, that in Antigua, along with Dominica and Grenada, the great regional rebellions of the 1930s did *not* occur? Dominica and Grenada had proportionally more peasant farmers than elsewhere in the region, and that may account for the ability to struggle on with subsistence farms. But Antigua? It remains a bit of a mystery—at least to Hart, the outsider to Antigua and Barbuda who has been an insider in so many Caribbean political controversies.[1] Hector's effort to formulate answers made him journalist-as-historian, the writer who offered up lessons in the late twentieth century (and first years of the twenty-first) about events that seemed to concern scarcely anyone else. For him, those beginnings were not ancient history at all, but a saga with deep continuities into the present and solutions that, more than ever, needed to be puzzled out.

Hector had looked over his shoulder, always, to more than mere suffering. In the mid-seventeenth century, when blacks considerably outnumbered whites on the tobacco plantations and showed signs of restlessness, the return of a runaway was to be rewarded with six hundred pounds of sugar or tobacco, payable on execution of the Maroon. And why? Because, Hector insisted, these first freedom fighters of a 1680s escape and rebellion "were not content merely to establish a liberated area nor did they want to return to Africa. They wanted this: total freedom."[2]

Some seven generations later, as Hector liked to remind his read-ers at carnival time, the slaves gathered so numerously and joyously at Sunday market that their cultural behavior frightened the whites, who pushed through a legislative bill abolishing Market Sunday, the only day that blacks had for themselves. Their response spoke volumes: in March 1831, according to Colonial Office records, thousands gathered, this time in defiance, showing what the colonial governor described as "frequently violent and menacing [behavior] and accompanied by furious gesticula-tions and cudgels." When soldiers confronted them on horseback, the slaves responded first with a hail of stones, then with arson, but also with defiant carnival, "mas." It was the first carnival, marching "behind those with horns of oxen on their heads." They carried with them not only drums and masks but also the inspirational hope that abolition would come soon. Hector believed that this rebellion led directly to "Benna," the merger of African polyrhythms with Caribbean satire.[3] As past, as future.

Not So Long Ago

The concentration of wealth and power in Antigua was hardly unique but definitely intense. Unlike other islands (notably Trinidad) subject to a variety of colonial rule and accessible to different populations and markets, Antigua was almost from the first settled European moment a monoculture, owned by some sixty-five families producing for and buying necessities exclusively from Britain—after a seventeenth-century interim of French rule. Following an early spell of tobacco plantations and a diverse crop strategy (or mixture of commerce and subsistence) never replicated, Antigua was entirely sugar, even if sugar was by no means entirely Antigua. A paucity of whites commanded the quasi-military nature of the state, first against the efforts by Carib survivors to retake it, then for centuries against the transported Africans and their descendents. Creolized brown classes, as we shall see, played precious little role in the process.

Hector's student and his later friend Paget Henry has told the fuller story best. Sugar plantations actually came, during the last third of the seventeenth century, because of disappointment with other crops and due to the completion of British monopoly upon the slave trade. The British also took over from the Dutch the techniques of sugar production, but the new economy flowered only with the passage of several generations. The class society created in place of small planters (and, of course, in place of the exterminated Caribs) had the sharpest divisions between the owner or the owner's representatives, the little crew of managers, and the slaves, who naturally did all the work. The colonial seat of the Leeward Islands—within the arbitrary values of empire, it was much later to be designated a Windward Island—Antigua actually had a higher level of residentiary planter presence than similar islands. For this reason, among others, it also gained the vigorous presence of the Moravian missionaries from Germany, forming stable Christian institutions several generations earlier than on surrounding islands and encouraging at least a small degree of black literacy.

It took a century for the large plantations to accomplish near-total control, around the time of the American Revolution. Meanwhile, the white population of Antigua had actually declined from a high of five thousand or so to barely twenty-five hundred, as the slave population multiplied to nearly forty thousand. The large estates of the five-dozen planter families were permanently established and highly profitable, the export economy dependent upon a new kind of triangular trade that brought cheap food from North America—scarcely less convenient from the newly independent nation than the previous colony. With business first, imperial patriotism naturally came after.[4]

The compulsory task of all white males was to serve in the militia with a range of free coloreds, further protection provided thanks to the military presence of empire. The British kept a dockyard and naval station, likewise a garrison of troops, very much as the United States would in a later Antigua. Locals had to depend almost entirely upon the direct representatives of empire for their legal system (planter families hardly bothered to ponder the technicalities of official justice) and their parliamentary government. They were willing if not always happy to compromise with the powers above to ensure stability and, under favorable conditions, high profits.

Not that internal rebellion or marronage posed any standing threat after the early period. Unlike Jamaica, Antigua had no mountain fastness, and unlike Trinidad, no distances to make Maroons' lives possible. Maroon camps in the hilliest area of the island were wiped out during the 1680s. The last of the escapees were captured in 1723 and, like their predecessors, dismembered or burned alive. Slaves had actually murdered one of their plantation owners, in 1701, because he refused to give them the Christmas holiday. Soon after, striking or wounding a white became a capital offense, as the court chose. Three other slave conspiracies failed, the most significant involving some two thousand people, with a king crowned secretly and a plan developed to massacre the whites. Martial law was declared after slaves rioted. The next insurrection was postponed a century, arson reported as Afro-Caribbeans awaited word of emancipation.

The many difficulties of imposing a bipolar or tripolar system grew more evident with time. In particular, the question of transported Africans as mere property or inferior beings bedeviled both Anglican religion and property laws. Black culture, on the other hand, was bound to play an important role alike in production and civil society. The mostly West Africans who survived the Middle Passage or grew up as descendents of survivors shared beliefs and practices (notwithstanding wide variations) in what may be termed "nature religion" and associated rituals and knowledge, from dance to herbalism, that would be re-created under extreme conditions of learning a common language and understanding while under permanent military guard. Pidgin English, with all that it implies, and what Paget Henry analyzes as "magic" (that is, a system of ritual beliefs and practices), became common means of slaves relating to the whites and to each other, from workday until dusk and dusk to workday, respectively.[5]

The system, as a system, could produce large profits, but at the cost of stunting anything like the social dynamism required to move society from peripheral status into diversification, self-sustaining production or a coherent and cohesive culture of its own. The planters would not have understood or cared what it meant for slaves to lose West African traditions of painting, sculpture, or distinctly native music that had flourished at home for centuries. Worse, they would have considered those losses good because syncretic forms available through Christianity did not pose so much of a threat to the new order. One might say that by the early nineteenth century, the planters, for all their self-created distance from African populations, also hankered quietly after tradition, or if not, then a new synthesis that would allow them to continue as little changed as possible. The caste-system rulers thus never seemed to grasp the implication of blacks doing invaluable skilled work—except to the degree that, if necessary for production, it was also a source of potential future threats.

The fate of free coloreds was further indicative of the prison of caste. They, for their part, repeatedly petitioned whites, from the early nineteenth century, for more privileges, and with good reason: thanks to natural increase, they had come to equal the colonists in numbers. Relative to most islands, especially others of the Leewards, Antigua seemed to have the makings of a vigorous colored petite-bourgeoisie of merchants and artisans. Successfully petitioning the Crown, they were allowed to vote after 1817, and they repeatedly sought to advance themselves legally for the right to become overseers, gain commissions in the militia (that is, defending society against the slaves), join juries, and receive church assistance when necessary.[6]

If accepted to some small extent, free coloreds were never situated to become an entrepreneurial class except on the smallest scale. They had no niche in the highly structured rulers' society that attended Shakespeare performances, expended capital on luxury goods for choreographed social events, and constantly dreamed of return "home." Thanks to the profits and the stability achieved, colonial authorities nevertheless considered Antigua unusually "civilized" and pushed the island toward full emancipation, by contrast to the transitional "apprenticeship" visited across the rest of the region.

The British never practiced benevolence (let alone sentimentalism) without profit, real or anticipated, and the imperial shift away from mercantilism would prove catastrophic. The free traders had overthrown the Royal African Company's monopoly on slaves in 1698, but that was only the beginning. Overcoming support for protection took more than a century—and never succeeded entirely—but demonstrably gained strength with British manufacturers' search for new markets in places like Brazil, Cuba, and India, bearing their own sugar or cotton to sell. Free trade was the tool of the future ruling class, and the abolition of first the slave trade (in 1804) and then slavery itself marked one of the free traders' chief victories—however much it may also have been urged by humanitarians. Still other sugar producers now undercut the English Caribbean, and newer-created peripheries in Asia and the Middle East brought accelerated competition as well as prompting the British merchant class toward abandonment of the mercantilist framework entirely.[7]

Antiguan planters, foolishly confident that they did not need to compete with, say, the production of Cuban sugar, badly miscalculated. High prices rather than efficient output had always been the standard for profit, hence a collapse in credit prompted a collapse in confidence and a steady downward spiral. Emerging global sugar producers raced ahead, in beet sugar as well as cane, around the world and even in the U.S. West. Meanwhile, Antiguan sugar production output actually fell, and many planters sought personal protection in bankruptcy. The American Civil War opened an important new market, but it was hardly salvation. By the early 1880s, Americans bought half of Antiguan sugar, an early sign of what controlling influence lay generations ahead. Slowly but surely the transfer of island control was passing, under the sign of free trade. Planter families were steadily displaced by the merchant class, itself inherently unstable. The old social system increasingly shattered—with nothing as certain destined ever to take its place.

During the era when sugar lost its primacy, the ruling families might have drawn on the diverse personal and cultural resources of the inhabitants, modernized production, changed crops, and otherwise sought to capture a regional market. They neither directed nor permitted any of these developments, attempting instead to hold on to what they knew, through minor adjustments. Hector would often say that because expatriates had determined to stay only as long as necessary, they had practically no interest in agricultural or any other innovation; if labor was cheap, why should they invest in machines? The changes that interested them were in fashion and furnishings across the ocean, craved especially by wives and daughters with little else but provincial gossip to occupy their time. Only the difficulty and length of the journey to England created and maintained the conditions for any distinct colonial white culture.

Modernization in a full and successful sense, of course, would have demanded some kind of decisive adjustment in the postslavery relations of upper and lower classes. Elsewhere in the Caribbean, some ruling groups made attempts—far less than they might or should for their own interest, given the resources they had at hand—to "reculturize," to make the black and brown poor feel part of a coherent society. State-sponsored projects of Christianization and education scored some real successes, albeit mainly confined to the Creole classes.

After slavery's abolition, paltry additional attempts were actually made in Antigua—mostly after demands from below, resisted by planters but judiciously accepted by the Crown's representatives—to give former bondsmen a stake in the society. Some unused land was opened for purchase, and nearly thirty villages grew up. But the Contract law, applying to most laborers, amounted to slavery by another name. Former slaves received the use of small cottages—the same old slave huts—with gardens in return for long days of labor at pitifully small wages. They usually could not leave "their" plantations and, as in the post–Civil War southern United States, overwhelmingly did not choose to do so because of their many ties with extended families. The small proportion of former slaves living in their own villages simply continued the essence of the old ways, slavery routines now adjusted by contract labor, binding the worker and family to the particular plantation year to year on penalty of arrest. If a compromise, it was one heavily weighted toward the plantocracy. A parallel replacement of the old militia with a police force had a similar effect, except that Creoles and some blacks enforced their own collective misery.

The changes had an unforeseen impact upon the island's civil society: the emerging state was de-democratized so as to ensure that planters' power could be maintained in the face of a nonwhite citizenry. But as elective features were stripped off, power inevitably returned to colonial authorities. The elite removed more and more of the requirements for them to continue permanently as anything like a functioning class of rulers.[8]

The sense of crisis in identity or utter lack of identity propelling the comfortable classes toward a sort of re-Anglicization in the last half of the nineteenth century brought with it the conscious reintroduction of all manner of costume, architecture, and manners, as much as disowning any previous accommodation or deviance. Faster ships carried more goods and people; now, newly arrived colonists gained the deference of those whose families had been in Antigua for generations or centuries.

Appreciation of European classical music, for instance, symbolized holding the line against non-European culture, quite as much as it may have indicated an effort at cultural uplift for its own sake. Theater, another key marker, was both enormously popular and strictly imported: not a single play written in colonial Antigua survives, and perhaps none were written. Traces of poetry reflect strictly English themes and approach. Not even Creole culture has a place this colony, a most telling detail. Antigua's single nineteenth-century novel, published in 1890, describes the horror of race-mixing with its catastrophic results for a young woman who discovers her "tainted" blood.[9] Racist themes burgeoned in popular novels imported from the United States, where a small but growing number of Antiguans had already begun to flee with their possessions. The usual plot in a counterpart to the race-tainted novel would have involved the taint of hereditary insanity; in a way, these plot devices were usually the same, a hopeless downward trend for the unlucky and the unwise from the purity that civilization demanded.

Needless to say, purity did not describe precisely the relation of white men with nonwhite women on the island or, more important, the consequences. This gap between racist ideality and racist reality worked a double disadvantage: the plantation system desperately needed and on some other islands successfully trained Creoles, as well as a small number of Afro-Caribbeans, for the tasks inevitable for advancing mechanical and clerical operations, ranging from accounting to the creation of water systems, and so on. But in Antigua, all valued knowledge came from abroad; as in generations earlier or later, higher professional advance and/or escape was to be had mainly by way of education in the United Kingdom. The modest advancement of secondary education in Antigua did not change that circumstance greatly. Instead, by a perverse logic, better ocean travel actually advanced the possibility for further "authentic" cultured Europeanization. Use of local patois, it almost goes without saying, would never be encouraged, even when it served as an effective second language to Creoles working with full-blooded Afro-Caribbeans.

Perhaps the greatest of the changes could be found in the educational offshoots of religious practices. Most of the funds of the empire that did not go to compensate slave owners for their loss were devoted to subsidizing Christian missionaries, whether Anglican, Moravian, or Methodist. Missions set up primary schools, with the colonial offices providing continuing funds and also guidelines for keeping the students close in gratitude and sympathies for the homeland. At that, those allowed to attend school were almost exclusively whites, along with the children of a few well-off Creoles. During the 1890s, the average annual attendance for boys was under fifty pupils, for girls barely over thirty. A society soaked in ignorance and parochialism reinforced its own limitations.

Did Afro-Caribbeans find formal means to express themselves, their understanding and way of life, at all? Yes, in the sense described by U.S. slave scholar George Rawick as "Sun Down to Sun Up," at home without the peeping eyes of whites. Not only there. "Cropover," an Afro-Caribbean moment forged from a mixture of carnival, plantation cycles, and cultural retention, grew up at this moment into the "mas" first seen in 1831 but now formalized, street theater and music touched with comic irony, masking, and extraordinary symbolism (like the John Bull drama reenacted to show resistance against whites). Arguably, the very totality of repression in Antiguan life made the "mas" more necessary and perhaps at times more expressive than in the more complex societies in places like Trinidad and Jamaica.

Potential adjustment of the existing system was dubious, in any case, thanks to the decline of its economic base. The moment of change, signaled by a financial crisis, brought only reinforcement in economics as it had in culture—because the planter families and their successors considered any real change impossible no less than undesirable. As Antiguan property continued to fall to merchants, by way of unredeemed debts over the last decades of the nineteenth century, the family basis of the plantation system finally collapsed. The paucity of untended land effectively excluded black escape from the system that planters elsewhere met with infusions of Indian laborers. In Antigua, African descendents had virtually nowhere to go. Thousands settled in rural villages whose land might barely support self-sustaining communities but whose constrained atmosphere afforded no real opportunity.

The poverty of those Victorian years is legendary. Wattle-and-daub houses, dirt floors alive with chiggers, hollowed gourds for household utensils, light from rags set afire in bottles, water from ponds where sewage of humans and animals flowed—all these made epidemics common. Rioting intermittently broke out, with petitions hopelessly presented to colonial authorities for better wages and more educational opportunities.

The birth of a new century saw dramatic changes in large parts of the world, none less dramatic than in North America. The acceleration of industrial development, the emergence of sophisticated chemical production, the replacement of iron with steel, the beginnings of the electromagnetic revolution, and the emerging consumer economy (with "automobilization" at its apex) all appeared nearly to pass Antigua by. Like Rhodesia of the 1970s where nostalgia-stricken whites still danced the fox-trot, Antigua's elite enjoyed a handful of automobiles and read about the latest fashions in British and American magazines. But they lived in the shadow of Victorian empire, devoted to its values and always fearing that its decline would lead inexorably to black over white.

Antigua suffered one further and, in Hector's mind, virtually unique perversity. The "coloreds," whose numbers accelerated from interracial contact and who by the early decades of the twentieth century actually outnumbered whites by approximately four thousand to two thousand, were destined never to become the "brown people of the cities," as rural blacks have characterized the Creole middle classes who were replacing white colonial bureaucrats in so many societies across the world. Antiguan Creoles instead commenced a virtual disappearing act: the successful ones had been fleeing since the middle of the previous century, more and more finding in Canada their promised land, leaving poorer relatives behind. Those latter remained, by Antiguan lore based in community memory, extraordinarily barren, opting for childlessness rather than the dreadful demographic alternative of mating with Afro-Caribbeans. "Not even the venal mulattoes of Haiti," known for their violent hatred of their black relatives, "were so self-destructive in their race hatred," Hector insisted, choosing extinction rather than alliance.[10]

How unsurprising then: the patriotic binding of colonials to the homeland in crisis, the rousing of white and Creole sentiment, and a few dozen actual volunteers in 1914 to fight on the European mainland (or in other colonies, far away) in any available war but especially a world war. This response to distant trumpets amounted to one more manifestation of Antigua's shadowland existence. In the United States, contemporary Harlem grew into the black metropolis, and elsewhere in the United States race riots (actually, pogroms of slaughter and burning) punctuated the attack on black communities by nervous and enraged whites, furiously determined to keep blacks underfoot. Harlemites accurately saw in the rise of Garveyism the desperation of their people everywhere but also the promise of something better. Some Antiguans must have known that their countryman, Bert Williams, was already a giant on Broadway.[11]

Prices meanwhile shot up in Antigua as well as in North America during World War I. In the war's final years, St. Johns saw one of the worst of the Caribbean riots driven by desperation in the face of inflation and lower wages, with several plantations set afire, overseers attacked, and a few rioters shot to death by police.[12] Rumors of Garveyism if not many copies of the *Negro World* itself managed to reach the island and circulate widely. No record of black organization, formal or informal, seems to have survived except for the records of the many small and semiformal sickness-and-death benefit societies established as "lodges," rather more on the American than the British model. It was precious little to build from, but it was something.

Beneath the ferment and violence, a Pan-Africanism of sorts took root in the same lodges, and Hector's fascination with these developments mirrored C.L.R. James's urgency to find the truth in mass movements behind the appearances of passivity or mere thrashing about. The Ulotrichian Universal Lodge was held up with special scorn by the authorities ("To the speeches of some of its members can be traced the awakening of the resentment of the Negro against the white, which is the most dangerous feature of the recent history of St. Kitts and Antigua," reported the governor in 1915.)[13] The Antigua Progressive Union, the most political of the

lodges, conducted forums with the distinguished and remarkable participation of some of the island's elite. Should the Contract law (essentially
making trade unionism illegal) be abolished? The distinguished panel-
ists resolved, "No." Workers in the capital of St. Johns answered with an
uprising, and what became known as the "Weston Riot" quickly spread
to rural areas.

Local leader George Weston himself fled to Harlem, where he joined
Garvey's Universal Negro Improvement Association (UNIA), ultimately
becoming one of many vice presidents. Weston's own visits to Antigua,
in the following years, stirred interest in Pan-Africanism and mark one
of the few visible points of rising political consciousness in the decade or
so to follow.

The black and colored middle classes of the cities, deeply frustrated
at their own circumstance but also (especially in their own minds) far
removed from the circumstances of the black peasantry, knew only that
they needed to organize. The colonial office sent the first of its distinguished bodies, the Wood Commission, out in 1921. No doubt the commission was responding to unrest on many of the islands, but especially
in Grenada, where T. A. Marryshow led a formal protest movement. The
commission recommended, in any case, a serious consideration of constitutional reform, although mainly for a few freely elected seats in the
island legislatures. Its presence and work mainly constituted a sop to the
middle classes. If Grenada, St. Vincent, and Trinidad actually adopted
these very modest changes, Antiguan legislators ruled such changes out
for the time being, thanks to the planters' influence. But things were
about to change.

Papa Bird Spreads His Wings

The birth of Vere Cornwall Bird in 1909 must be recorded as a major
moment of Antiguan history. Raised in a poor family in St. Johns's worst
slums, the illegitimate son of a father who later committed suicide, Vere
was raised by a single mother known popularly as "Aunt Baba." Her
own father had been a white planter, altogether indifferent to his brown

daughter's fate. During the first years of Vere's life (and that of his one younger and two elder brothers), things had gone relatively well for sugar, consolidated into ever fewer hands. Therefore, things also went well for trade and even for petty tradespeople like Bird's father, a wheelwright and cooper who lived some streets away from the family. As times went bad, he emigrated to Bermuda, no longer supplying even a minimum of support for his family. Bird's mother took other boys in for care within her small but reputedly spotless house.

One scholar reports that the young Bird had not been able to attend the Anglican secondary school because it did not recognize illegitimate children, but this is inaccurate. In the near-starvation conditions and with no health care, he fell ill and missed almost a year at Boys School. Falling a grade behind, he nevertheless made himself a leader of games and, later, formal church youth activities. In the Boys School, training was strict, and young Vere took severe punishment without a whimper. Intellectually, he was average or just above, neither budding scholar nor dropout. Then, in the middle of his adolescent years, Vere found himself.

The well-off Antiguan in black as well as white society—in different congregations, of course—attended Anglican services of the island. The poorer classes of blacks found Methodist or Moravian churches, or the one other interdenominational alternative: the Salvation Army. At fifteen, standing under the tamarind tree on New Street where the "Army" held both church and Sunday school, the boy became a ferocious disciple.

Some say he created his own version of the Sunday school and developed his own rituals, perhaps because the Army had so little youth following on the island. At any rate, he was as fanatical as any socialist convert, speaking and thinking of almost nothing else but the salvation of souls and the social transformation that the Army sought. At eighteen a lieutenant, he was shifted to Trinidad, his first step out of the little world of Antigua. There, taught the crucial art of bookkeeping, he further trained for leadership and reputedly gained admiration for developing his own methods of recruitment. He performed administrative work in the Sailors' Home on that island as well, made captain, and transferred to Grenada.

He returned home suddenly at the end of 1929 and resigned from the Army, for reasons never disclosed. Here can be found a first note in the murkiness of Bird's background, suggesting a life of petty and grand theft within the framework that slaves had long since taught themselves for survival and sometimes advancement. He later insisted that he had learned leadership in the Salvation Army, but also that he had suffered from its racism, compelled to sleep away from the superior quarters of the white soldiers and otherwise poorly treated. This seems likely enough, although political foes pestered him in later decades with alternative stories of fraud and disappearing funds.

Bird later on added new layers to the mystery. He claimed that the riot of 1918 had been the burning memory of his childhood and that he had been drawn into the Garvey sentiment as he came of age. These stories are not necessarily contradictory in the life of an islander at the time: Garveyism had an appeal, but the Army offered a way up and out. Like many an early labor leader (including that staunch champion of conservative craft unionism, the American Samuel Gompers), Bird gained his organizational bearings and personal contacts through a society far removed from labor or radicalism. Having learned what he needed and having gone as far, perhaps, as a black man could go, Bird needed the Salvation Army no more. Experience with it left an inclination, some said, toward a certain mysticism, useful in a future charismatic figure.

Back at home, Bird did not seem to know at first just what he wanted to do, spending time with a brother who worked as an overseer on one of the sugar estates. He spent many hours on horseback observing the work process but also avoiding an estate supervisory job that would find him trapped between white rulers and black ruled. He took a job as a clerk for a Portuguese baking firm, in the tiny sector neither black nor Creole but nevertheless cut out of the white hierarchy of business and social life. Then he became, in succession, the manager of the bakery and the enterprising owner of two V-8 taxis and a house of his own (mysteriously destroyed in a fire and the object of a subsequent insurance battle). Some say that he did extraordinarily well at the bakery until the owner asked to see the books; according to legend, he immediately tossed them into the stove. No fire, not even the prospect of hellfire, contained this enterprising entrepreneur.

We know at least that he quit the bakery and ran a small import-export business, moving into the front ranks of those dark-skinned but ambitious merchants perpetually enraged at the benefits bestowed on their white expatriate competitors by the colonial administration. The Small Trades Association was a class and race movement in itself, of a distinctly petite-bourgeois variety. Several of its members would play important roles in the Antigua Workingmen's Association, albeit apparently not Bird himself. They provided the financial backing, through advertising patronage, for the seminationalist weekly, the *Magnet*, that put the nerves of colonial administrators on edge. And they led the lodges where a kind of politics or at least political discussion could emerge.

Here was a basis for a political machine. Bird's personal life remains, by contrast, somewhat of a mystery. We know that he fathered a daughter without benefit of marriage in the early 1930s, that he married a second woman a few years later and fathered four sons by her.[14] He separated from his wife, and in 1939 he became a founding member of the Antigua Trades and Labour Union (AT&LU), successor to the Antigua Workingmen's Association.

Bird later bragged, no doubt to distance himself from any notions of socialism, that he had never read a book and was free from presumably foreign influences as he shaped himself. Antigua is so small a society and so intimate a part of an international movement that Hector learned personally from Pan-African giant George Padmore that Padmore had energetically stoked the young political leader's interest in the 1930s and 1940s with books, articles, and ideas offered during Bird's occasional trips to London. More definitive: Hector came into possession of the very copies of the British *Marxist Quarterly* whose pages contained the underlining of Bird and his political savant, McChesney George. Bird's only written document—probably put to pen by George, but reflecting the thinking of both men—explained basic purposes in Fabian terms, as the official 1948 minority report of the Soulbury Commission of Lord Earl Baldwin, governor to the Leewards. Bird and his colleague mainly urged, with entirely good logic, the rapid diversification of crops as a step away from the chronic importation of foodstuffs—and the takeover of plantation lands for that purpose. Milk-and-water socialism surely, but socialism of a sort it claimed to be.

Bird was said to have been warned by those around him that he was likely to get a different reward from the one that he expected: the "educated sons of the peasants will cut your own political throat." But for that moment, Bird personally summed up the basic wisdom of fellow islanders.[15]

Big Crisis Reaches a Little Island

Between the colonial days of the 1920s and the nationalist struggle of the 1940s had, of course, come the global economic crisis and the intimately related crisis of confidence in the future of capitalism. The Hungry Thirties also precipitated, as we've seen, the uprisings of West Indians on other islands and the founding of labor organizations and a labor press. Antigua was behind, if not entirely far behind, the others. The Antigua Sugar Factory reputedly continued to pay the highest dividends in any sugar colony to its absentee owners and shareholders. But not without challenge for long.

Documents dating to 1932, tucked away in the Colonial Office archives until some sympathetic archivist passed them on to Hector, revealed the governor of the colony deeply worried in these years about the return of unrest seemingly quashed a decade earlier. "Newspaper articles and speeches which might seem trivial if written or uttered in England," he warned, might well "assume a really serious nature in these islands among an easily stirred-up people." The *Magnet*, the new tabloid in question, had actually raised only modest questions about royal authority. But even this was too much, and the governor looked to "underground influences at work, probably from Russia," as the real source of trouble, fingering the editor of the *Magnet* for arrest and possible prosecution. The manager of the Antigua Sugar Factory, another senior member of the regime's Executive Council, had written the Colonial Office a few months earlier that in such nervous times, disloyalty simply could not be tolerated.[16]

The powerful still held all the power. But for the first time, assiduous colonial officials made changes in the conditions of government, mainly opening it to the middle classes. A colonial commission had prompted the allotment of five seats in the Antiguan legislature for direct election in 1935. Whites and Creoles naturally took these seats, and the one reformer who appealed for changes in treatment of the poor was ousted after a single term, on the basis of insufficient property qualification. Registered voters, as Paget Henry records, amounted to only 7 percent of the island's population, and yet they were feared. A letter from three top members of the executive committee to the Colonial Office in 1937 claimed "to voice the views and fears not only of the white minority but also of responsible opinion of all colour" in regard to the dangerously rising tide of race resentment.[17]

More telling, perhaps, was the long-delayed eradication, in 1937, of the Contract Act legally binding workers to their plantations. This had long been more symbol than substance: the great majority of laborers and their families had already removed themselves into villages. But the legal shift at least marked the end of the premodern rules by which blood counted more than money. The abolition had been forcefully demanded by a white lawyer and the personal owner of little Guiana Island, Major Hugh Hole, one of the first and last of the great white reformers in modern Antiguan history. It had also been demanded, so to speak, by the unrest sweeping the region.

The Moyne Commission, the most important of colonial ventures in generations, meanwhile casually added Antigua to its list of islands surveyed, and predictably recommended further modernization. The Moyne Commission no doubt prompted the Antigua Recovery Program, urging settlement on unused acreage, increases in public works of various kinds, increases in local food production, expanded state intervention at various other levels, and, as expected, continued Crown support for sugar.

Little result could be seen from these initiatives, apart from public works. Probably the rising expectations contributed to the explosion to follow. A strike at the Antigua Sugar Factory in March 1939 set off the Antiguan version of the near–General Strike sweeping the other islands. Workers from the sugar factories and the estates, waterfront workers, and government sanitation workers created what American unionists called roving picket lines, traveling to make sure that others did not work. Within two days, virtually all wage labor had ceased, and in a few cases, estates had been set afire. On the third day, the defense force joined the police in making arrests. Protests now practically ceased without any further major confrontation.

Little had been gained in practical fact. Promises of slight improvements, land resettlement, and committees to examine working conditions altogether heralded next to nothing. But the moment had been prepared for Vere Bird to step into the spotlight.

In 1933, an Antigua Workingmen's Association had been founded, very much on the model of the Trinidad Working Men's Association (TWMA), itself a shadow of the British Labourist model. As we've seen, the TWMA of the 1920s succeeded in raising Captain Arthur Cipriani to the mayor of Port of Spain, a figurehead of working-class demands if not much more than that. The Antigua Workingmen's Association, concerned mainly with waterfront workers, had no such importance and had rapidly faded away. But the model of labor leader as political leader survived.

More than the real-life model, it was the presence of Lord Citrine that proved decisive here. A most thoroughgoing Fabian of the Moyne Commission, the visiting Citrine delivered a talk on trade unionism in January 1939, prompting one of those otherwise forgotten local Afro-Caribbeans who had spent time in the United States to propose an organizational meeting. Vere Bird sat on the resulting executive committee.

The formation of the AT&LU could not have come at a better moment or, just as important, under better auspices. Class consciousness had reached new highs. British Labourism, a huge disappointment at home (where Labourites worked cheek by jowl with Tories on economic policies, yielding far more ground than they took), nevertheless had the effect of damping down potential planter reactions in the colonies. Likewise, the stamp of British approval consolidated the growing resentment of the middle classes, black and Creole, toward the planters and their willingness to look to "respectable" labor movements as their own representative or, at the least, their ally. As the AT&LU pressed for recognition, its potential membership once more took to the streets for protest and quickly learned to advance or retreat in orderly fashion. They buoyed the confidence of their would-be leaders.

Bird was not alone, of course. George Weston, the leader in 1918 who had traveled to Harlem and become an ardent Garveyite, was back by this time, agitating among sugar workers. Norris Allen, a petty merchant and like Bird an activist in the Small Trades and Workingmen's Association, had spent almost a decade in the United States, active in the left wing of the great industrial union movement. He personally put forward the proposal for AT&LU's formation, with an independent jeweler as president, joined by a black lawyer and several others on the executive committee. Bird, an executive committee member, had at first followed his friends into labor organizing. Thanks to dedication and ability, he soon would surpass them.

Organizing themselves as the leadership of the masses, AT&LU activists secured an astonishing 50 percent increase in wages for their members in 1940, as the Depression eased. A new moment had come to Antigua, not least of all in the state itself. War had already come to the Continent, and British leaders, settling in for a long siege, had in effect nationalized large sectors of the domestic economy and services in the name of coordinated national defense. They were also quietly negotiating a new contract with their newly appreciated diaspora, the historic empire that they rightly feared they might soon lose. It was a contract that included ambitious state programs of economic development.

The expansion of tasks and even purposes of the colonial state, as Paget Henry as argued, had at least two sharp edges. In the past, the state had been cotangent with the planters and saw as its main purpose the protection of whites' property and safety; now it had assumed the role of overseeing the relation of whites, blacks, and Creoles among each other, and intervening directly to shape development. But development to what end? Up to this point, it had mainly responded to the threat of independence with strategies of containment. The emerging pattern was suspiciously familiar. The Antiguan government in 1940 thus borrowed an unprecedented ten thousand pounds for construction of a hotel, previewing the era of tourism and non-British investment, the creation of a new kind of overlordship after the long-postponed demise of the planta-tion economy.

In the British colonial context, the aim of the Labourist-shaped AT&LU was no less statist. As surely as Welsh miners believed for genera-tions that the nationalization of the pits would bring a form of socialism, AT&LU members and followers believed in the gospel of state develop-ment, with working-class needs and aspirations at the center of the state program. By a great historical irony, if the slave economy had rested upon imperial funding, navy, and soldiers, then the modern economy rested upon versions of imperial democratization in a tiny corner of the empire, with a potential postcolonial state assuming the reins. Even more ironic, the latter project took the phraseology and the credibility of "socialism" by which, in Karl Marx's own vision, workers would precisely free them-selves from their assorted masters. The "emancipation of the working class will be made by the working class itself," the *Communist Manifesto* had said, setting off modern socialism from the condescending programs of utopian reforms designed from above. But not here.

One could also add that the infrastructure of black middle-class life, so evident on some of the larger islands, especially Trinidad, was miss-ing here. The kind of organization that founded a women's self-help movement, creating islandwide conferences of women professionals, and after the war a Federation of Women's Institutes, could not be created under Antiguan conditions. The growing differentiation in educational opportunities for men and women—adolescent males directed toward skilled trades, women toward unskilled work and housewifery—from the early twentieth century therefore struck Antiguan women all the harder, with fewer assists from better-off islanders. The wartime labor shortages, resulting in greater opportunities for women, did not, of course, last. A new service economy brought at least some of them into the palaces of the rich, but under conditions that could hardly be considered favorable, and many struggled on with small businesses of their own, or the tradi-tional recourse of washing, sewing, and assorted homework. Still sharing agricultural labor in many cases, in countryside or city they joined the national struggle—as Hector would say frequently—double-burdened but undaunted.[18]

The third irony and deepest of all was the chief source of rapid Antiguan modernization: the creation of a U.S. military base in 1941. The product of a complex deal by which the struggling British Empire received fifty destroyer ships and the United States got in return ninety-nine-year leases for military bases in Trinidad, Guyana, Antigua, St. Lucia, Jamaica, the Bahamas, Newfoundland, and Bermuda, it amounted to a take-over of practically the whole region on the installment plan. In other words, the vision of the Monroe Doctrine was now to be completed, the Caribbean an "American Lake" forever.

Americans, their racial practices no less rigid than the British and often more bluntly expressed (nevertheless, according to the calypsonian Lord Invader's famous "Rum and Coca-Cola," with considerably more money to spend on native women), occupied the northern third of Antigua. They efficiently trained Natives for the necessary work. Under wartime pressures for speed and efficiency, they also responded to the insistence of AT&LU leader George Walter—a future prime minister and the only successful rival of Bird—that the wages suit the work. Bird himself, a timekeeper on the base, was reputed to have broken an incipient strike because he could not accept the strategy of further demands. He was rising, wanted to risk no trouble, and had already acquired a reputation for organizing brute force.

A section of the American ruling class came with the fleet, the Mellons and Harrimans ordering megamansions to be constructed at Mill Reef, a most picturesque spot on the southeast coast. Here, with the burgeoning of the Smart Set, grew the idea of Antigua at the "up-market" end of some future tourist trade. With it, the vision was confirmed of Americans instead of the British as the bringers of wealth and comforts, even selected services like emergency health care, thanks to the first modern hospital on the island. After the war, across the Caribbean, the Americans eventually returned nearly all the bases to Britain or turned them over to the new governments after protracted negotiations (in some cases, struggle). Not in Antigua.

And so the irony became paradox. The economic shift behind the demand to break free from Britain politically, and thus to replace the plantocracy, came from the American millionaires and military, neither of these forces known for noblesse oblige, let alone any intention of empowering the Antiguans themselves. The presence of an American leisure class no doubt prompted Bird to move Antigua toward a resort and casino economy, eventually a global economy (with less-than-legal connections around the world), earlier and more vigorously than almost anywhere else in the English-speaking Caribbean.

The planters, for their part, did not take the ongoing changes lightly. The Antigua Sugar Planters Association (ASPA), formed to combat the AT&LU, had no desire to give up its members' prerogatives. The ASPA thus insisted upon the right to settle sugar prices among themselves, for the 1943 season. The colonial government refused to accept this position, quietly encouraging the AT&LU to press for a series of wider demands, including better wages, an end to the twelve-hour workday, and changes in the work process—much as many other unions still outside the fascist grip or military conflict demanded around the world. As so often in contemporary wartime America, wages and hours concessions were then made, while the union for its part accepted the existing structure of authority, fully prepared to discipline its own members. Thus things changed somewhat, but nothing was resolved.

By 1946, amid postwar strikes breaking out across the hemisphere—merchants and landowners determined to return wages and hours to prewar standards, and workers determined to hold on to their gains—the AT&LU led a widespread, ten-week strike. Dock workers and sugar cutters won important changes in working conditions. Three years later, Bird himself led workers against the Johnson Construction Company, a U.S. company building luxury homes in Mill Reef. Lacking any means of transportation, some of the laborers had walked ten to fifteen miles in blazing heat, had to wait hours for their wages on payday, were refused a raise for four years, and were replaced with strikebreakers at the walkout. The police sided with the American company, and the strike seemed truly broken.

But then a truck transporting strikebreakers, slowing down to round a bend amid cane fields, was felled by a dynamite explosion (mercifully, too late to kill but just adequate to scare the scabs into hiding). Bird, summoned to Government House for discussions or negotiations, left empty-handed, gazing at the fires that already burned in some fields, echoing images of Resistance fighters behind fascist lines in Europe willfully burning their own villages rather than leaving food and materials for the advancing enemy. Several strikers were ordered to jail, but now Bird refused to give in. Almost spontaneously, unionists from St. Kitts and Monserrat to Nevis ordered a halt to goods being reloaded to Antigua. Other island labor leaders prepared their followers to take up the fight. For the first time in Caribbean history, the Colonial Office ordered a regional leader actually brought to London, so as to settle a dangerous strike at all costs.

Hector called this coordinated action of Afro-Caribbeans a "living, literal Federation in struggle," and he is surely correct. Bird made nothing of it openly. But he showed colonial officials careful records of the Johnson Company, with most of its employees as productive and loyal union members. Under the circumstances, the evidence convinced. The strike was victorious in one of the most dramatic peaceful showdowns of the incipient regional independence movement.[19] If the strikes of the later 1930s had made independence ultimately inevitable, these events brought it closer and brought regional workers closer to each other as well.

Much of it was personalist, of course. In Monserrat, for instance, Robert W. (Bob) Griffith, son of an estate manager, won a seat in the legislature. He had already won a public, as a Methodist minister and owner of a popular hall in the capital. He personally organized the Monserrat Trades and Labor Union (MTLU) in 1946. Accoutered in red cape and accompanied by a steel band, he gave public scriptural lessons about colonialism, sharecropping, and tenant eviction. Leading and sometimes winning strikes, Griffith made himself a near-martyr by barely evading a prison sentence; soon after, he began a slow fade out from significance.[20]

More dramatic action, and some of the best fighting rhetoric of the region, fell to Vere Bird, by this time popularly seen as "Papa" to the incipient nation. Alexander Moody-Stuart, arguably the most powerful figure in Antigua in 1951 as director of the Antigua Sugar Estates, Ltd., could not believe that field laborers would now suddenly refuse to work for the traditional shilling per day. Through exquisitely personal confrontation, Moody-Stuart promised to crush Bird and everything that the workers' champion represented. But in the most famous political speech in the island's history (also the most famous Antiguan prose until the writings of Hector and Jamaica Kincaid), Bird answered that his people would "eat cockles and the widdy widdy bush" and likewise "drink pond water" rather than yield. The tamarind tree in a remote village on the southeast side of the island became instantly famous for the site of this declaration.

A few months earlier, Bird had warned Moody-Stuart that the year's crop would not be planted without a pay scale announced in advance. The strike was already under way, and the governor had agreed with Moody-Stuart's demand to have martial law declared. It was to no purpose, or rather to great purpose of the opposition: Bird, in his triumphant moment as labor and incipient strike leader, exhorted the nearly starving workers to continue. They saw in him more than he was; but they accurately saw in him the counterpart to the labor and nationalist leaders gathering strength and confidence across the region, many of them destined to guide the movements for independence and the first postindependence governments. Bird would have the dubious distinction of being the last of the giants to bring the Anglophone Caribbean toward independence through a labor movement and labor government. But distinction it was.

More in accordance with changes in neighboring colonies and less from pressure in Antigua, constitutional change did finally come. Adult suffrage sans income qualification was mandated in 1951, with a modernization of legislative set-up, from the number of districts to the seats in the legislature. In 1956 came the ministerial system of government, the increase in the number of seats from eight to ten in 1961, and the chief minister and prime minister (inevitably, Bird himself) established. In 1967 the British granted a status known as associated statehood, with the British still controlling all defense and external matters as the prime minister became premier and a bicameral legislature was formalized. Ultimate decolonization was, by now, not too far away.[21]

But Bird himself seemed, to many observers, increasingly unequal to the tasks at hand. Not every emerging regional leader, by any means, was an intellectual like Norman Manley or Eric Williams. As Hector later noted, Bird as a personality was singularly narrow. He had no apparent cultural pursuits whatsoever, as he had no interest in regional history or even hobbies. Apart from womanizing, Bird was "all politics." He could deliver, in that narrow but all-important sense. He had chaired the island's Labour Settlement Board since 1946, raising peasant farm holdings from 270 acres (and six hundred peasants) in eight years to 8,000 acres (and more than four thousand participating peasants), including more than 70 percent of the population. It was, Eric Williams once declared, on paper the greatest land reform carried out in the Caribbean until Castro. But economically speaking, the transfer came with too little infrastructure and came too late.

The sugar industry, long dying on the veritable vine, had practically been abandoned, by this time, to the government for the relief of plantation debts. The Bird regime, perhaps arranging matters through quiet consent in advance to give the emerging government an illusion of greatness, took control of the plantations but at vastly inflated values. The "fair price" exacted a huge, irrational investment of national funds and, adding insult to injury, retained the same old division of labor. "The exploiting planter," in the phrase of a later ACLM manifesto drafted by Hector, had been at once both "saved and knighted." What quickly became known as "realienation" followed when ten thousand acres of the best lands were actually leased to an American corporation at an absurdly low rent for fifteen years (renewable for another fifteen). It was a decision made almost understandable for a country without a ruling class of its own, the planter-merchants gone and no one, not even a Creole elite, to replace them.

The last misadventure ended when the American company, turning from sugar to corn production on the unchanged monocultural model, went out of business. Other sugar lands were turned into a state farm, also without noticeable shifts in social relations. Only a small portion was turned over to farmers who sought, with a logic that escaped the government, to plant vegetables and root crops most suited to diversifying the island's agriculture after centuries of single-minded production for export. At this crucial moment, the peasant sector was deprived of access to resources, land, and water to experiment in a fashion that might have changed the economic and social structure of island life profoundly.[22]

What happened instead can be summed up in a single word: tourism. Or better, in two words for Antigua: casino tourism, the high-rolling, nightlife, sin-tainted style of tourism unsuited for sedate Barbados but just right (many investors and tourists themselves thought) for a kind of little Las Vegas or pre-Castro Havana, the Antigua of the Birds where anything goes. The high-end nature of the island's tourism had been forecast, not only by its unique pink beaches but by the further development of Mill Reef as a mansion colony with fabulous views of the ocean and loads of low-priced house servants who served (in so many capacities, gardener to cook, nanny and mistress) much as the house slaves of old.

The short-term visitors in their fancy hotels also made possible a certain prosperity, if never as much as expected. Executive jobs, even most of the skilled trades work, went to whites who took their salaries and eventually went home. Drawers of water and hewers of wood continued at their tasks, although less rural and more urban, raising themselves up a notch with some access to consumer items, nevertheless continuing within the scope of a familiar poverty, with limited opportunity to school their children into generational mobility. And yet Bird, in a perverse way, had charted a future. As Hector put it in a public eulogy, "Bird had changed Antigua and Barbuda from a plantation society, underwhelmed by disease and poverty, to a modern consumer society, overwhelmed by alien production and alien accumulation, with a huge foreign debt."[23] It was a kind of progress, perhaps the curse of modern interpretations of progress, to abandon the production of goods for a service-and-consumer society, however fragile and mediocre.

Tourism on a mass scale waited for the middle 1960s, when irredeemably revolutionary Cuba shunted development dollars in all sorts of new directions. Within the eastern Caribbean, Antigua had the second-highest standard of living, but at a cost. As other islands developed a mixture of relatively modest (never modest by the standards of ordinary islanders themselves) cottage colonies, Antigua and the Birds became known for jumbo-sized combination hotel-and-gambling complexes noted for characteristically faulty sewage systems, imploding when not simply flushing the wastes into the Caribbean a short distance beyond most swimmers.

Few came to swim, anyway. No wonder the offshore betting scandals of the 1990s found Antigua an epicenter of U.S. sports wagering.

The almost unbelievable Bull Project drove this point home most lamentably. Gerald Bull believed himself the greatest artillery engineer in history (a television biopic, scripted, ironically enough, by a victim of the anti-Communist blacklist, was titled *The Biggest Gun in the World*) and swore that he could build his own gun that launched a shell into outer space.[24] It interested weather scientists. But the real customer was the U.S. military, which put up half the funds for its own research base in an obscure corner of Barbados, then was forced to move in 1976 after criticism from an incoming government. Meanwhile, artillery bound for apartheid South Africa, eluding a United Nations ban, was discovered when a crane loading containers in Antigua revealed a skullduggery the Bird government and Central Intelligence Agency (CIA) officials alike denied. Secret research and perhaps also illegal weapons deals would nevertheless continue in the northeast corner of Antigua, secure from inquiring eyes and from restless workers, thanks to a private military force commanded by a retired U.S. Army officer. Exempted from customs and other regulations, military officials from across the world could come and check on the hardware's progress. A muckraking Tim Hector blew the whistle and got himself arrested for his trouble.

But I am getting ahead of my story.

Enter Tim Hector

Into this impoverished and confused but highly agitated world plunged Tim Hector. He had been prepared for it since childhood. Born in 1942 on Lower Newgate Street, neither the best nor the worst of St. Johns, he had a father not only out of sight but also unknown (at least to him), and no siblings. To his mother, Mable, mainly fell the real task of parenting. Commenting on her death in 1978, Tim called her "quite an ordinary Caribbean woman," at various times seamstress, small shopkeeper, and teacher. Hector later recalled that "money was always the scarcest commodity" in the household. "Manufactured toys were few. For presents, I got books about poetry, comics, literature, cricket, history, science fiction, westerns, and later jazz and art."[25]

Issues of race were never absent. He recalled his white next-door neighbor, obviously poor as well, but managing a marvelous rose garden. She taught him, from age seven, how to play serious pieces on the piano, including Bach, Beethoven, and Brahms along with moderns like Casals. She was, he later reflected, civilizing the backward nonwhites, as God had called upon the colonizers to do. But there was no closeness. Only upon the occasion of her husband's death, when Tim's extended family's emotional support was happily accepted, did the boy perceive anything like warmth. "The white man in his castle. The poor man at the gate. God made them high and low, and ordered their estate—eternally." A less sensitive child might not have gauged the contradictions or, in a different light, the perceived absence of them.[26]

A yet deeper pathos occasionally emerged into Hector's prose, as he described his female-dominated childhood home life. Reflecting on how, at a regional conference, Angela Davis and Alice Walker had turned their wrath on him (in their eyes a representative Caribbean male), he recalled a childhood where

> back then I was the boy who looked from the window, like a good girl. Sternly forbidden, as a "nash" [tender], "sickly" child, to venture out among what I suppose were the more robust and active girls and boys. All but my last Aunt, the youngest, Aunt Gwen, devoted to the letter, this caged child's order: Church and school, and straight back home.Five minutes late and the wrath of God would descend, on my small back and bottom, which, apparently, were no longer "nash."[27]

So much like C.L.R. James looking out the window at the cricketers almost half a century earlier, Hector, kept at home, turned bookish. He also had from earliest age an intellectual mentor: his grandfather, an autodidact former policeman, left-leaning, and intensely race-conscious, a man also determined to engage his only grandson. "Tim" was extended playfully by the old man into "Timoshenko," the name of a then-famed general of the Red Army saving the world from Nazi domination. Young Tim was soon given the sober task of reading to the increasingly blind grandfather and relating to him firsthand the story of the sports matches, cricket to boxing, that the boy had been given the money from the hard-pressed family to attend. After his grandfather's retirement, more so after his grandfather's stroke, the police pension kept the family afloat, and with increasing weakness came less authoritarianism, more family counsel, with the occasional moment of studied rage when the boy failed to understand the depth of race issues and past unheralded attempts to struggle against racism.

Here the memory of the old man's wife, Hector's grandmother, comes squarely into view. "Read what you like, but measure what you read against life," a pronouncement that was to take ever more meaning as he grew up. Writing to him a decade later in Canada, she advised sagely, "Don't worry with the high and mighty, it's the little people who have much untold to tell." A black woman from a little island, as he called her, she had a view large enough to anticipate what E. P. Thompson had seen within the history of the British working class.

Because the men in his family (other than his grandfather) were largely absent, settling arguments by force was eschewed. Less political-minded than her husband, but a dedicated public health campaigner against the mosquito-born diseases all around them, Tim's grandmother had a definite materialism. Passions were poured out in her card games with his mother and two aunts, no quarter given to the lad's amateur play. He was being treated, in some key respects, as a grown-up, and with lasting effect: "Thanks to my grandmother I have always shunned abstractions, for [concrete] ideas, which allowed penetration into the opaque and the concrete."[28] One of his first self-assertions was to break with Catholicism—and the dim notion that he might actually become a priest—and to embrace Islam, at age eleven. He shrugged off the latter in a few years; it had performed its service in helping further to free him from blind beliefs.

The presence of scattered whites in the society around him also had a liberating effect. Those whites next door were actually victims of the heavy-drinking husband, and Tim's piano teacher also taught him almost unintentionally the cultivation of roses, knowledge considered by whites of the region to be a mark of civilization and therefore theirs alone.[29] To this, he attributed his indifference to the foolishness of blacks being intimidated by whites, uncomfortable in their presence and unwilling to speak up (except, perhaps, to shout). The rest of his musical appreciation could be measured in black notes, because he rebelled quickly. Another of his nearby neighbors was the first organizer of Antiguan calypso and of the island's first calypso tents. Soon, then, "a steelband could not issue a note and I would not be there," as a nonplaying participant in the scene. "I was on the ground floor. It was my first home-coming. A major re-making of self, so to speak"[30] Many of the Antiguan calypsonians and steel band players actually held court at his home, and one of the best musicians, Ivan "Jones" Edwards, was a close family friend.[31]

At the time of Hector receiving the first "People's Award" on the island, in late 1996—with seven thousand signatures in his favor—an old friend recalled Tim's stirring address, as Head Boy of Antigua Grammar School, on "cricket, dominoes, the common man's cause," topics suggesting the time he spent in adult company, including that of his family. He struck his fellow students as the brightest contemporary they had ever met, not only because of his sharp focus but also because of his omnivorous curiosity.[32]

Hector liked to call the 1950s the "Antiguan Enlightenment," and if the island had no outstanding intellectuals, it had a preindependence vigor of discussion matched only in Hector's own newspapers afterward. The *Workers Voice*, the organ of the AT&LU, had indeed provided the material for his first regular reading aloud—to his grandfather, almost on a daily basis. The *Voice* was a family endeavor in another way. Two of his mother's sisters worked on the paper as compositors, and its reports of struggles in the sugar fields and elsewhere were naturally the conversation of the dinner table. Its editor, Rolston "Checkie" Williams, was regarded as an intellectual hero for his tireless efforts to provide reportage and interpretation of the worldwide anticolonial struggle. Williams occupied one of the few roles available as intellectual/political leader on a small island, and it is difficult to imagine him not being a role model, in some measure, to the future editor.

Moving into his teen years, as Hector told Trinidadian oil field workers' leader David Abdullah decades later, he broadened himself with the daily newspapers of Trinidad (no dailies were yet published in

Antigua) and with radio broadcasts of Legislative Council debates in that island bubbling with independence fever, orators like Eric Williams and Winston Mahabir offering him models of oratory as well as political points to ponder.[33] Williams, in particular, as the "second brightest man in the world," offered a beacon by declaring that the era of colonialism was finished. "Dr. Williams opened an entirely new world" to Hector's teenaged mind. His further historical awakening, race and region, owed much to this beginning.[34]

Locals spoke to Hector or those around him, and he listened. Not only were the admired musicians visiting his family frank about their socialistic politics, but peasants bringing their cotton to the gin next door explained their work and their plight to other adults, with the boy listening carefully. One of his very best childhood friends, later politician Robin Bascus, urged on Hector both the theory and practice of understanding the agrarian economy of the island. The same Robin Bascus gave Hector a printed version of *Massa Day Done*, the pamphlet version of Eric Williams's famous address that (Hector claimed) meant as much to him as James's *Facing Reality* was to mean later.[35] Friendship with a local jazz aficionado meanwhile inspired him to admire and closely follow jazz, black high art in music, for the rest of his life.

But it would be too much to emphasize only the contemporary, informal side of Hector's intellectual education. His grandfather loved a religious debate and demanded assistance in preparing for discussions with an instructor visiting weekly, none other than Tim's first head teacher. Tim thus read both the St. James and Catholic versions of the Bible, page by page and verse by verse, clearly influencing his prose in decades to come. Father Brown, who came to the home to discuss biblical issues, invited him to use his private library—and there, with theological literature like Pierre Teilhard de Chardin, C. S. Lewis, and G. K. Chesterton, was also Richard Wright and James Baldwin, even Henry Miller's *Tropic of Cancer*.

Most of a lifetime later, in 2001, Hector paid a visit to St. Michaels School and recalled both the poverty of children a mere decade before his own grammar school days. Parents worked in the fields for twenty-four cents per day, and schools with but rare exceptions set upon instilling the colonial mentality, the quest to "pass through" or drop out entirely rather than excelling. Not much had changed since the time Hector had attended. He marveled at how students had been taught, from the class-room to the sports field to the music room, mere subordination. "We did not really belong," one of the cruelest of all possible realizations, mirrored what Antiguan whites had always thought of Afro-Caribbeans: only hands for work, brought in as slaves centuries earlier for economic purposes, deprived of culture, therefore lacking culture, and therefore (in the eyes of the colonial authorities and those lesser figures whom they appointed to run things) lacking everything that counted.[36]

And yet: the "we" who did not belong were not entirely "he," because he was being picked out as special. Before age sixteen, he was lent Freud's *Interpretation of Dreams* and *Civilization and Its Discontents* by a good friend, while with another good friend he tried reading the first volume of Marx's *Kapital* in the public library (remarkably enough, it was on the shelf there). During his last year of school he was taught by Gregson Davis, who had set off a small storm at Harvard as a graduate student before returning home; with Davis (aided by another Harvard graduate), he carried on discussions about Erich Fromm, David Riesman, Oswald Spengler's *Decline of the West*, and various Caribbean writers. The occa-sional school controversy provided him an insight into the larger politics of the island and his own responses.[37]

Meanwhile, sports had provided him the best path as a real leader of the popular culture of the island. As a boy, he had been all but forbid-den to play soccer (in realistic fear of an injury that the family could not cover financially), and no doubt partly for that reason he became a fanatical follower of the Atomic team that swept the league from the middle 1950s onward. The middle-class team (named Maple, as the "brown" team of C.L.R. James in Trinidad) was, significantly, fading away with the landed aristocracy and the democratization of the most physical of local sports after boxing. Cricket gave him another and more lasting pleasure and object of examination. Poor with the bat, he was fine in the field and undoubtedly appreciated more for his mind than his play. He had intimate discussions of the game, from philosophy to the fine points of practice, with some of the island greats.[38] One day he would be an outstanding administrator, and if he had stayed away from politics, he would likely have become the finest booster of amateur sports Antigua and Barbuda had ever known.

But he and Antigua were waking up politically, mostly in response to events in the world outside. Into Mable Hector's little shop, owned with her brother (Tim had, from early on, the tedious job of weighing out sugar or cornmeal or flour before he could go off to play, and if slipping away instead of doing his tasks, he could count on getting spanked, "licks like peas"), came several determined left-wingers, regaling the youngster with arguments and details about the cold war, colonialism, racism, and socialism. One of them, Ivor "Jones" Edwards, had also led the movement of local steel bands, sweeping culture smack into the center of politics. Just outside the shop, on the street, a nearby spot gained the cognomen of "University of Chelsea" at the corner of Thames and Newgate streets, its cognomen a clear imitation of the "University of Woodford" that served a larger but similar purpose for Eric Williams in Port of Spain, Trinidad.[39] Here, in St. John's, amid endless games of dominoes, debates of the later 1950s and early 1960s ranged over every topic imaginable, especially embracing anticolonial revolts and the Cuban revolution. Encouraged by his grandfather, mother, and aunts into the logic and love of serious debating, Hector relished the conversation. At first taking a firm adolescent stand against socialism on the usual lines of "human nature"—he had been an avid reader of *Time* magazine and needed to unlearn what he had learned—but then carefully weighing the arguments, he found himself convinced in the other direction. And so he grew.

It was said later that a lengthy letter of Hector's published in the *Workers Voice*, describing in detail a riotous soccer match—with many asides to history and culture—stamped the fifteen-year-old Hector as a journalist with a difference. It may be remembered that a young C.L.R. James had begun his extraordinary writing career by reporting cricket matches in his native Trinidad thirty-some years earlier. At any rate, numerous readers wrote in their own agitated responses to the remarks of the young man who, in such a small island, everyone knew by reputation; others, the vast majority who did not bother to write in, doubtless also wondered about him. Hector was one of those promising young people (in his era almost exclusively boys; Jamaica Kincaid was only a few years behind, shipped off to school abroad) who inevitably seem to represent the whole island, but almost invariably leave the island behind them so as to succeed in the wide world.

Young Hector clearly had literary talent and classical tastes, including an early turn toward Shakespeare. It is valuable for that reason among others to contrast him to another figure destined for a very different path: the region's first Nobel Prize–winner in literature, Derek Walcott.

Born and reared in St. Lucia about a decade earlier than Hector, Walcott stemmed from a near-aristocratic Creole family whose white ancestors had lived as plantation lords and ladies in Barbados. His father was an illegitimate child but a proper Creole, a minor government functionary and a founder of a literary club that could be seen as the counterpart to James's circle in Trinidad (baby Derek was pushed around with his twin in one of the first double-prams seen on the island). This could not be described as anything like real prosperity, but it was respectability with the possibility of a middle-class bohemianism unimaginable to Hector. It was also a cultural life in the cold war years that led Walcott into the extended tentacles of the Congress for Cultural Freedom, quietly funded by the CIA, eager to take on promising youngsters with no known left-wing tendencies.

The playwright-poet's biographer insists that Walcott's St. Lucia was not a likely place for nationalism and black power, even if labor uprisings in the 1930s mirrored those of other islands in the region.[40] The more that the young man studied the peasantry (still very much present around him) in particular, the more distant he felt himself from them.[41] If the New World was truly "new," as he often and eloquently wrote, then Walcott wished to leave the cultural traditions of Africa further behind him than he had left those of known civilization, that is, Europe. Not that he scorned the Caribbean, as Naipaul would. The soaring heights of Walcott's verses lifted up the drama of the region, flora, fauna, and natural forces, with stunning brilliance. But the contrast with Hector is nevertheless dramatic in Pan-African terms, among so many other Caribbean radicals of Hector's own generation, especially but not only jet-black skinned, precociously literary-minded men and women whose turn to politics often surprised themselves.

Other precocious youngsters Hector's age, on the larger islands—including most of those who would become outstanding academics—were frequently offered the opportunity to continue their secondary education immediately. More like C.L.R. James in Trinidad forty years earlier, Hector graduated from secondary school and immediately began teaching, one of the youngest instructors in the history of the Antigua Grammar School. Paget Henry, Hector's Fifth Form student, recalls most vividly the young instructor lecturing on black American poet James Weldon Johnson and Nietzsche on the transformation of values. Thereby, as Henry says, Hector signaled the transformation of colonial to postcolonial life facing all Antiguans.

Hector meanwhile set himself on reading "every major critic on the major English writers," Hemingway to Whitman, Langston Hughes to Paul Lawrence Dunbar, then the West Indian novelists (including the early fiction of C.L.R. James). George Lamming's novels especially shook his world. He and an older fellow teacher, Venetta Ross, indeed prepared the first of the Antigua Broadcasting Service programs on Caribbean literature, in 1961–63. Then, after two years and amid much political agitation on the island, he made a difficult choice to try for a scholarship.

Several of those whom he admired had opted to join the local political fight straightaway. He recalled with keen regret not providing political and personal support in particular for Milton Benjamin, editor of the *Workers Voice* and a high-ranking official in the AT&LU. Hector and a youthful friend actually taunted Benjamin for a failure to teach workers about the history of revolution, especially the Glorious Revolution of the British (in whose history literary islanders had been so miseducated, but for which a new Marxist scholarship was being set solidly into place), failure to use his columns to educate readers about the Chartists and the mass strikes of the 1930s, and so on. Worse, Benjamin had fought shy with the corrupting drift of Papa Bird—until he broke, wrote a stirring editorial, and lost his livelihood. Like Hector, Benjamin went abroad, but as an employee, not a college boy. He had nevertheless been mostly if not entirely wrong to twit Hector's small circle for being the overeducated, pink tea-party socialists living in a mental world outside the daily realities of Antiguan working-class life. The educated classes on this small island were too small for that kind of clear division, even for those who dreamed of vistas afar.[42]

For that reason, perhaps—but mainly at the insistence of his grandmother than he undertake something other than "hoity toity" office work—Hector looked to blue-collar jobs when he joined the student body at Acadia, in Nova Scotia, on his scholarship to Canada. In some ways, it was extraordinarily bracing, for Canada was more than going to university. It was a modern industrial society, huge beyond Caribbean imagination, "one twentieth of the world's surface. I reveled in its wide open spaces. Its prairies." And in the news of struggles farther from Nova Scotia, in a political sense, than the contemporary bubbling Caribbean, that is, "in the Civil Rights and Student movement then sweeping the U.S."[43]

It was not an entirely happy resettlement, by any means. He repressed his classical music knowledge (as "white," no doubt), and recalled later that his professors were sure he was faking his knowledge of the classics— the petulant black boy who could not face up to his own limitations. He needed to support himself, beyond his scholarship, and he worked first as a busboy, then as an industrial worker in a garden house factory, finally as an assembly line autoworker. Of this experience, he was retrospectively gratified: "The little boy from Antigua [now] had firsthand experience of modern industrial work and life. My reading became clearer set against the work I was doing."[44] Although he might be accused to reading back his later political training into this experience, he also no doubt accurately recalled the eagerness of even the most racist workers to describe to him, a good listener to anyone, how they could easily manage production themselves, without the supervision of the bosses.[45] Of the real-life, grinding alternative, a degree of alienation as severe if entirely different from the ordinary alienation in Antigua: "I had [now] seen and been in Blake's 'dark satanic mills,' where humanity is reduced to a mere fragment of a person, in dull, repetitive tasks. Where violence is firmly entrenched in the passions on the assembly line seeking release in mindless TV chock a brim with violence as catharsis for the dread immiseration of modern industrial work. Philosophy was becoming real."[46]

Finishing his bachelor's degree in haste, he was, without knowing it, getting himself ready. He was en route to Montreal and Marxism, for a definitely unique Pan-Africanism and for the most formidable personality in his life and that of his closest contemporaries: C.L.R. James.

What awaited Hector on his return home to Antigua in 1966 was nothing so grand as a victorious election—after all, he had come of the most modest background, not the political royalty of Michael Manley's lineage—or as violent as guerrillas with guns. But his circumstances contained all the elements of corruption and idealism, black nationalism under Rasta influences, uprisings of sorts, despair, and renewed hope. In the troubled Caribbean, it could not be otherwise. Circumstance, however, contained more than mere marginality; it was marginality with promise.

CHAPTER THREE

Independence and Neocolonialism

The heartbreak of independence struggle leading toward neocolonialism and enforced economic (also cultural) dependence
within political independence is the great tragic story of the
modern Caribbean. Not that the region is so different, in this respect, from
most of the rest of the "underdeveloped" world. But each region and each
society has its own story to tell, its own high hopes of the early independence era dashed by the power of the multinational giants (enforced, if need
be, at the point of a gun), reinforced by local elites who frequently talked
about national dignity but wanted, most of all, a share of the spoils.

The English-speaking Caribbean is unique, among other ways, as a
laboratory for labor-oriented political movements steeped in British parliamentary traditions. It is a laboratory marked with generalized indifference to anything resembling Marxism-Leninism even when (sufficiently
influential for fraudulent claims in Guyana and ambiguously developed in
Grenada) linked sympathetically with the Soviet Bloc. Inflected by Black
Power and the Caribbean's own unique contribution of Rastafarianism,
by varieties of calypso, reggae, and other forms bearing severe criticisms
of society and an apocalyptic egalitarian lyric, Marxist parliamentarism
and assorted movements or groups took on peculiar Reddish hues rarely
seen elsewhere.[1] To say that Tim Hector was a participant-observer in
all this is an extreme understatement. To make an analogy: Rather than
musician in personal life, he was a sportsman, but his ear for the music

of rebellion, African American jazz to local steel band, was extraordinary. He heard the strains of symphonic possibility as well as aural utopia.

Being who he was, Hector's interpretation of Caribbean literature's explosion during the 1940s–50s and after would necessarily be decisive. George Lamming, one of the several regional writers whom Hector admired most, proclaimed (in *The Pleasures of Exile* [1960]) that the West Indian novel had "restored the West Indian peasant to his true and original status of personality." These peasants and low-class city-dwellers were the ones most invisible to Caribbean intellectuals who lived off colonial imports, the same ones (as Sylvia Winter said) whose lives had to be recaptured for West Indian literature to come into its own.[2]

The literary surge forward can be said to have taken shape with Vic Reid's *New Day* (1949) about the Jamaican popular resistance to colonialism. It picked up speed with fellow islander Roger Mais's novels *The Hills Were Joyful Together* (1953) and *Brother Man* (1954), because Mais (himself a political prisoner for a time in the 1940s for his protests) explored the life of urban slums and the Rastafari, that is, the circumstances and consciousness of the displaced peasant. The decisive step in the global recognition of the region's emerging literature had to be the Caribbean readings of the British Broadcasting Company (BBC). These broadcasts established the network of publishers and reviewers that made writing—albeit mostly from abroad, in Britain—almost a viable occupation for those who could live poor, teach on the side, or otherwise manage.

It might have been no surprise to the farsighted (although a great and painful surprise to James) that the most successful of the new writers, V. S. Naipaul, would turn from the folkish and socially sympathetic if also critical themes of *Miguel Street, A House for Mister Biswas,* and *The Mystic Masseur* to the unforgiving and mean-spirited attacks upon the lives and cultures of ordinary West Indians. James was less surprised to see the attacks applauded loudly by metropolitan intellectuals like Irving Howe—decades earlier, James's own socialist comrade—increasingly inclined to romanticize colonial days and enraged at attacks upon the West's empires, most especially the American empire.

But no one could fail to be amazed at Wilson Harris, the so-called James Joyce of the Caribbean, whose *Palace of the Peacock* (1960) sent the former Guyanese surveyor and British factory worker into a career that should reasonably climax in a Nobel Prize. With Reid, Mais, Naipaul, Harris, but also Earl Lovelace (among the next generation, a particular favorite of James's), Samuel Selvon, Jean Rhys, and a host of younger writers, including Jamaica Kincaid, the regional Anglophone novel truly came of age. So did the poetry, with Derek Walcott at its head. Hector's favorite and friend Martin Carter, Linton Kwesi Johnson, Jean Binta Breeze (personally very close to James in his final years in London), and others were not far back, whether writing from the islands or the United Kingdom. And so did criticism, increasingly the practice of Caribbean academic intellectuals likely to be ensconced in Britain, the United States, or Canada.

Lamming, head and shoulders above the rest in political engagement of social and cultural issues, had long since shown the way with *Of Age and Innocence*, *In the Castle of My Skin*, *Season of Adventure*, and *Water with Berries*. Treating the colonial past, Caliban was freed to discover himself and the possibilities before him.[3]

But there was a tragic side to all this, not especially well hidden even at moments of enthusiastic expectation. The collective self-contempt that was unchanged through exchanging British for American popular culture and the psychological self-division of the writer in exile found their way into the works of an ever-sensitive Lamming. He told Tim that the appeal to him, living in isolation in London years after his writing *The Emigrants*, one of the most terrifyingly disillusioned novels of ordinary West Indians emigrating to find their fortune and losing themselves in the process, had saved his life or at least his hopes. Lamming was called back to the colors by a new generation, and it was what he needed. Naipaul and even Walcott, who returned to become a Caribbean theatrical savant, thrived on other kinds of affirmation.

Culture could not be separated from politics any more than politics from culture. And it was not at all surprising that Hector, drawing from his engagement with C.L.R. James, should filter the local lessons through James's own recent experiences in Trinidad. Jamaica, the most politically developed English-speaking island, had the earliest New Left, thanks in part to the patronage of the Manleys, father and son; Guyana had the only large-scale political movement avowedly anticapitalist. But Trinidad was, despite its large Indian population, in some ways closer to the experience of the other islands, modulating one-man (or one-family) rule with extreme outbursts of militancy. It happened also to be the only island whose political leader had learned his childhood lessons in literature, his scholarly methods and his first political training from James himself. For these reasons, as well as boyhood hours spent listening to "wireless" broadcasts from Trinidad and Tobago, the developments of that society would be central to Tim Hector's understanding.

Trinidad and Tobago, Eric Williams and C.L.R. James

What came to be called "Doctor Politics," the world of Eric Williams's following, was not only an expression of the individual leadership common in the Caribbean but also of the intellectual giant rare in party politics anywhere. Magnificent scholar, Williams was a far better (if less prolific) historian of his society and region than, say, Winston Churchill of Britain and its empire, because unbound by the race-romance of conquest and the unending justification of colonialism. No wonder that Williams, whose addresses to crowds on a corner of Port of Spain made him legendary, came to be regarded by common folk as the greatest genius of the planet after Einstein. That he not only failed in the end but turned the society seemingly in his hands into an interracial conflict for power over the spoils of office is far from exceptional. But Williams's *Capitalism and Slavery*, based upon in part on a thesis set forward by James, had nevertheless, in vital and lasting ways, given West Indians what Patricia Mohammed calls a "new way of seeing themselves."[4] In a limited sense, for his own twinned islands, he had done the same politically.

There was a large, tragic dimension to Williams's accomplishments. A quarter century after the publication of *Capitalism and Slavery*, and just as James himself emerged as the eminence grise of Pan-Africanism, touring campuses with messages of emancipatory possibility, Williams had withdrawn into personal isolation combined with continued political authority. His personal style had always led him to overwhelm his supporters as well as his opponents, not only by his towering brilliance but also by playing one individual or institution against another. Stunned by a Black Power revolt against his government, he was unable either to abandon power or to make sense of his own role as he continued on until the approach of his death, a decade later.[5]

The student had outdone the teacher, then had fallen back, himself undone by events, the subject of history's irony but in some degree of self-betrayal. *Outlet* carried most eloquent testimony. George Lamming poetically attributed the failure to Williams's "flying in the face of God," attempting what could not be done there or elsewhere, seeking to overcome the weight of colonialism and its gloomy heritage with rational, secular humanism, evidently discounting the tragic dimensions of civilization.[6] Others were not nearly so generous. James observed sorrowfully, as the teacher pronouncing on the former student, that Williams had left "nobody nothing," neither Trinidad nor the region, whose hopes for federation Williams had helped to smash. This was too negative a judgment, because Williams had contributed mightily to national identity through Afro-Caribbean leadership and to regional identity by his force of example, the great intellect. But it was scarcely a realization of the early promise either of interracial democracy or democratic socialism, the two amounting finally to the same goal unattainable in the historic period.[7]

Growing out of a modest, lower-middle-class background in Port of Spain, Eric Williams was recognized as an exceptionally bright boy—even before James took him ("still in kneepants," as the former teacher liked to say) in hand—and by his teen years, set about straightforwardly for a college education and a profession. Making his way to Oxford despite his father's stern advice to become a lawyer or physician, he steadily made a name for himself as a veritable Caribbean DuBois, if such a lopsided comparison can be made without losing all meaning. Williams could not have combined the qualities of that novelist, magazine editor, political mastermind, and scholar as the intellectual giant did, because no one else of any color or nationality has done that. Nevertheless, Williams was absolutely brilliant in exploring and explaining regional history, the crimes of colonialism, and the right of the Caribbean man (most especially the black man) to seize destiny, as in the title of his famous 1960 address, "Massa Day Done."

Reading at Oxford in the 1930s, Williams went heavily against the grain of the British scholars of West Indian history, firmly fixed on the familiar white man's burden. Resolving to take up the slave system, he buried himself in available records at the British Museum (where Marx's *Das Kapital* had been researched) and elsewhere, producing "The Economic Aspect of the West Indian Slave Trade and Slavery," which earned him a Ph.D. in December 1938—only a year after the publication of James's monumental *The Black Jacobins*. Thenceforth, he took a position at what was known as the "Negro Oxford," that is, Howard University in Washington, D.C., teaching there until 1948 but from 1944 also spending time at a research position at the Anglo-American Caribbean Commission. He published his first major articles in Carter Woodson's *Journal of Negro History* and a survey volume, *The Negro in the Caribbean*, in 1942—notably put in print by the Pan-African Congress— establishing him as a scholar of political bent. *Capitalism and Slavery* (1944) was his monumental achievement. Offered a position at prestigious Fisk University in 1947, he declined, and when a first history professor was to be appointed to the University College of the West Indies in the early 1950s, he was most conspicuously *not* named to the post. His destiny, probably to his disappointment, lay elsewhere.[8]

That Williams taught himself to reach crowds in oratory and written polemic, far enough above the masses that he seemed like a god but also close enough to be well understood, speaks volumes. That he applied himself to politics day by day and night by night, during the fight for independence, was a matter of personal temperament but also regional proof that the supposed innate inconstancy of the African diaspora could only be a myth. His love for empirical detail, convincing his audience with evidential effort, was greater than even in C.L.R. James, the studied Marxist who wrote history with the pen of a novelist. Lamming like to say later that Williams set himself on the task of seeing and understanding the region as a whole, learning the languages, mixing with people from different islands, establishing a precedent that his academic successors, retreating into insularity, would not or could not maintain.

But at least for one generation (including Lamming's), he was teaching Caribbean intellectuals something vital, something that they had never grasped before.[9]

Not that the prospect of personal reward had ever been entirely absent from Williams's mind. The British were evidently preparing themselves to shed considerable sections of their empire when Williams purposefully returned to Trinidad in 1948, a man apart from as well as with the masses, a politician who enjoyed the house and car appropriate to the successful section of the black commercial class. Serving on the Anglo-American Caribbean Commission offered him both dignity and a springboard for organizing a political movement. As his critics often later observed, the way had been prepared for him (or someone else) to do it.

The populists and radicals of the previous generation were by this time, if not played out, at least unable to command the kind of attention that Williams could. It was old Buzz Butler, elected to parliament in 1950, who introduced the practice of holding mass meetings in Port of Spain on Friday and in San Fernando (home of the oil workers) on Monday each week after parliament closed, and Butler's protégé, oil-field worker George Weekes, destined to be C.L.R. James's closest follower in the labor movement of Trinidad and Tobago, who proved more typical of the new generation of red hot platform speakers.[10] But as Weekes's biographer freely admits, it was nonetheless Williams who successfully "captured the hearts and the imagination of the mass of Africans in the society," Port of Spain especially—although definitely not of the East Indians in the countryside.[11]

It is illuminating to observe that at a moment when James became the veritable man without a country (actually, he appealed to Sir Anthony Eden to protest his expulsion from the United States to the United Kingdom in 1953, and Eden wittily responded that repatriation to England could not be viewed as punishment), Williams was the man who stood *for* a country. Colonialism became more unworkable by the year, and Williams brilliantly walked the narrow line between anticolonialism and the loyalty to the West that always signified loyalty against communism. Butler, for his part doggedly faithful to the empire, had called for "Home Rule" and something vaguely like socialism; Williams called for a more radical independence, but without the threat implicit in Butler's rhetoric to nationalize the booming oil industry paying vast dividends to the stockholders of Texaco (United States) and Shell (United Kingdom).

Breaking with the Anglo-American Caribbean Commission in time for the 1956 elections, Williams personified as well as led the new People's National Movement (PNM), stepchild of previous nationalist parties and labor radicalism. As Selwyn Cudjoe was to summarize the PNM's achievements and failings, it set out a policy of honesty and nondiscrimination in the office and workplace, likewise of better education, health, and schooling. But if firmly against British rule, the PNM rarely elucidated what it stood for in any wider sense, how the postcolonial state would be fundamentally different in structure and purpose, and what the ideas or ideology the new emerging state would bring forth. PNM voters could be forgiven for concluding that the old masters would essentially be replaced by better (as well as darker-skinned) ones, led by Williams himself.[12] As James later observed, "The Doctor" seemed to be led onward by the people, rather than vice versa, denouncing colonialism and racism, calling for such drastic near-time change in society that James actually feared the consequences.[13]

No wonder the excitement of the moment understandably swept away a young Tim Hector in the middle and late 1950s, his ear fixed to the broadcasts of parliamentary debates from Trinidad. The crowds and the agitation were Williams's meat and milk, and recent scholars take special note of his careful attention to youth and to women, people whom he wooed brilliantly. He obviously had a unique appeal, especially among women, for that little-understood third category of Trinidadian demographic life, the Chinese and other Asians who occupied the ranks of shopkeepers and lower professionals for generations before East Indians attained that level outside the insular rural areas. Understandably never really attracted to Black Power, the island's Asians could easily share the sense that Williams conveyed an egalitarianism guided by an idealistic minority, a section of themselves included.[14] The Doctor-led "March in the Rain" on the U.S. Naval base in Chauguaramas in 1957, demanding an end to occupation, was a symbol of extraordinary self-yearnings, because everyone knew that the sailors' presence meant money, compared to which dignity might easily grow empty. Calypso hits "Rum and Coca-Cola" followed by "Jean and Dinah" verified the sense of exploitation, rage, and triumph, albeit expressed strictly and somewhat perversely in terms of gender relations.

Williams must have sensed the inner contradictions (or lackings) in his work more than he ever admitted, because the personal invitation to C.L.R. James to return to Trinidad, as editor of the PNM newspaper the *Nation*, implied the sort of partnership that the headstrong Williams would not have granted anyone else. At a minimum, his former teacher and world-famed Caribbean litterateur would help consolidate the nation-building project. But no one who knew James could seriously expect him to stop at that goal.

Williams, as James explained the figure, had never shaken off the old view of the great leader and his party being handed by the masses the mandate for absolute leadership. Williams looked to the most brilliant man he had ever known (and notably, the most brilliant black man) to assist him in that leadership in the Caribbean, non-Leninist, British-like equivalent to a Vanguard Party, but without any real participation of the party's rank and file, let alone the wider population.[15] The paradox was that he would of necessity defend James, still in the eyes of many a dangerous Communist or at least a revolutionary—while coming to power without the familiar face of colonialism to attack and to blame for all the ills of the society. Williams would have known that the great thinker had a track record of starting near the top of political organizations, building his own base of support downward. He miscalculated in anticipating that James, satisfied with the editorship of the party paper, would not want to make the party into the thriving, bottom-up democracy that it was not, inevitably undermining the rule-by-personality that was Williams's character.[16]

Most West Indians, including educated ones, knew little or nothing of James beyond the rumors. *The Black Jacobins*, out of print for decades, would return to print and its first extensive Caribbean distribution after 1963; a decade or so later it would become a veritable textbook for the advanced student, much as E. P. Thompson's *Making of the English Working Class* would enter the curriculum of the United Kingdom. And yet James was being "discovered" as a great historic figure of the region awaking to itself, and arguably the greatest visionary of federation. In June 1958, months after being called back by Williams, James had delivered an important lecture in British Guiana (the next year it was issued as a pamphlet, with an introduction by none other than Forbes Burnham), "On Federation." He recalled that only twenty years earlier, talk of independence was treason (he might have added on a personal note that authorities in Trinidad of the late 1930s were convinced that James, across the sea in Britain, had somehow infected strikers with his Bolshevist doctrines). Now he had been asked to attend the celebrations of the Federal Parliament's inauguration in Trinidad. He argued forcefully that only through federation could the region leave behind underdevelopment and join the modern world. But behind this conclusion was also a larger historical vision:

> The times we live in are a time of transition, the world we live in, the world in which we have lived for three centuries as colonial possessions of imperialist powers, is falling apart. The chief imperialist powers, Britain, France, Italy, Spain, Holland the Belgium, are all states of Western Europe. The important thing, the thing that is new about them, the thing that concerns us is that they are no longer world powers. The world in which they ruled and shaped our destinies according to their will, imposed upon us their ideas of the economics and the politics that they thought suitable for us, that world is gone. We shall enter as a free people into a world that we never knew and which our masters never knew until recently. If they were merely losing their colonies and continuing as before that would be one thing, not only for them but for us. What is happening is something entirely different and, I believe that most of the shortcomings in our thinking of our future spring from an inadequate grasp of this central fact.[17]

It was a very large thought, and unlike the "masculine" Black Power politics so often implied by the rhetoric of Williams and others, not only a matter of sloughing off the masters but of seeing the whole world as a different place. Perhaps to his own surprise, James around this time displaced his previous Marxist-style vision of global proletarian revolution (including African, Asian, and Latin American worker-peasant participation) with a vision of a postcolonial world of mainly nonwhite peoples reordering itself. Mere nationalization on the British or any other model held no charm for him, and this was to become more and more crucial to his late-life politics. Rather than salvation from above, the "mobilization, the education of the population as to what is being proposed . . . in the interest of consolidation and establishing a sound and stable basis for the future development of our economy and our social life" was paramount.[18] The masses, with some degree of leadership and other assistance, would free themselves, and he could declare as he did introducing *Party Politics in the West Indies,*

People of the West Indies, you do not know your own power. No one dares tell you. You are a strange, a unique combination of the greatest driving force in the world today, the underdeveloped formerly colonial coloured peoples, and more than any of them, by education, way of life and language, you are completely a part of Western Civilization. Alone of all people in the world you began your historical existence in a highly developed modern industry—the sugar plantation. All those who say or imply that you are in any way backward and therefore cannot in a few years become a modern advance people are your enemies. . . . Be of good cheer. Know that at this stage of world history and your own history there can never been any progress in the West Indies unless it begins with you and grows as you grow. . . . You have to know who you are, and what you can do. And this nobody can teach you except yourselves, by your own activities and the lessons that you draw from them.[19]

This vision evidently lay beyond Williams's expectation and likewise his task as editor of the *Nation* to promote and organize. Perhaps the prime minister, en route to a stumble from which he never recovered his true footing, did not really know himself. James believed that Williams, responding to the enthusiasm of the masses, broke with the subservient stance of other independence leaders, realized that he would have to take on his own party apparatus as well as the Americans (and British) to go all the way to a new society—and then returned, making James a sort of personal operative along the way.[20] Selwyn Ryan suggests, in a similar spirit, that Williams was feeling his way.[21] James had no intent of posing such radical demands as the expropriation of foreign-owned industries, regarded by many Marxists (and not only Communists) as the only way forward. He definitely had no intent of challenging Williams personally in any way. But his aim to build the PNM internally, gaining the trust and support of an East Indian community that Williams had sometimes ignored and at other times thoughtlessly alienated was a fundamental if largely unintended challenge to "The Doctor" and to the exclusionary politics that he represented.

On the surface, the task that James undertook seemed to go well, in no small part because he brought his own one-woman support group. Selma James, his third wife, gave her own extraordinary energy to the managing end of weekly publication. The Jameses together created a remarkable paper that refused to make itself the organ of the party's official views, seeing itself instead as opening its pages to the "problems of the people in particular as stated by the people themselves." Forcefully anti-imperialist but not polemical, the *Nation* (as James himself had renamed it from the *PNM Weekly*) gave as much attention to the crusade for a West Indian cricket captain (that is, Frank Worrell) as to political particulars. It also gave much space to the importance of calypso, to national and international figures of history such as Captain Arthur Cipriani and Abraham Lincoln, to the budding regional literature, and so on. Williams's own column in the paper was doubtless the most definitive for the PNM, but James titled his own column "Without Malice," and there is every reason to think that he meant it.[22]

Such a journalism and, for that matter, such a political relationship of coactive husband and wife was nearly unknown in the region, outside of Cheddi and Janet Jagan, and arguably created a model for Tim and Arah Hector, among others. In short, it was an intervention with enormous potential going out in various directions into the Caribbean present and future.

Swedish scholar and close observer Ivar Oxaal, a leftish liberal, was to suggest later that he'd heard the Central Intelligence Agency (CIA) demanded James's ouster as the price for continued good relations of the State Department with a Williams-led regime.[23] If true, this would have been a necessary but not sufficient condition for the organized ouster of James by the PNM's inner circle of functionaries, evidently not only resentful but terrified that James as "No. 2" was in danger of becoming "No. 1." Somehow, as Williams's trusted adviser and *Nation* editor, his presence seemed to threaten their positions of responsibility and salary—and, in the large sense, it probably did. James struck back, in literary form rare for him, with a pamphlet pointing crucially to the sheer mediocrity of the local middle classes unable (as well as unwilling) to transform themselves from the colonial mentality, eager to continue colonial-style bureaucratic rule with themselves in charge.[24]

The oil-field workers, the most powerful and radical of organized labor, dramatized the problem with a bold strike in 1960 under their rising dynamo, George Weekes. Popularly regarded as the "son of Butler," Weekes increasingly took the place of the mostly absent Buzz Butler by the later 1950s. In the last days of June 1960, some seven thousand oil-field workers left their jobs and marched to the tune of a current Mighty Sparrow hit, "4% is murder," that is, the miserable offer given workers amid inflation. A one-hour national work stoppage (not universally successful, but met with sympathy among stevedores and others) drove home the point that nation-building was not easily to take the path wanted by the petite-bourgeoisie in the PNM. For the moment, Williams postponed any forceful attempt to put the oil workers on a leash. But the stirrings clearly shook him, and the day of union challenge to his power would not be distant.[25]

Williams, at any rate, soon believed he had to choose between his entourage and his mentor. He quietly supported the party functionaries' ongoing conspiracy to make the Jameses' continuation on the *Nation* impossible.[26] And he did so at what must now be considered a crucial phase of the nation-building process. Williams's own past gestures toward the East Indians had received a cool reception but not an entirely hostile one. Now, rallying his faithful with clearly coded racial phrases, he began increasingly to speak of the East Indians as an "alien" force in the land, giving the opposing political machine all the room that it needed to exploit its own nationalist position ruthlessly.[27] In the same political moment, the PNM followed Jamaica's move to quit any positive movement toward federation, prompting the British government to terminate all prospects of West Indian unity, granting independence hereafter on an island-by-island basis.

Tim Hector would bemoan, throughout his journalistic and political career, the succession of events that had found regional leaders unwilling or unable to educate their constituencies to the importance of federalism. At least Norman Manley had tried, although his failure to reach the rural population had long since backed him in a corner. According to some observers, neither did he try quite hard enough. Williams acted worse, threatening to resign if Trinidadians voted to join a federation whose leader would inevitably be Jamaica. The smaller eastern islands' leaders, rather passive, had hoped more modestly to be federated with Trinidad. Further efforts failed and worse, led to the interisland squabbling of small men with large ambitions to hold on to their positions. Apart from Manley and Barbados' Grantley Adams—the two figures James singled out for praise in his *Party Politics in the West Indies*—no one in leadership had really made the effort to achieve anything like a West Indian nation.[28] James put it himself more simply: "We have failed miserably." Failure, however it might be dressed up as independence, added up inevitably to accepting conditions of neocolonialism intimately close, in fundamental respects, to the same old conditions of colonialism, including ethnic divide-and-rule.[29] Further, more modest efforts at economic integration, Caribbean Free Trade Association (CARIFTA) and the Caribbean Community and Common Market (CARICOM), could never approach the original vision and, within an invasive world economy, could hardly do so in any case, short of a major political decision unwanted by the usual island leaders.[30]

Williams's compatriots would hereafter rule their two islands with the single aim of retaining power and its perquisites, holding off those political rivals whose aim differed only (apart from race) in the desire to get the power and perquisites for themselves. James left under conditions so strained that hundreds of copies of *Modern Politics*, a series of lectures that he delivered in 1960 at the Port of Spain public library, barely touching on Trinidadian life, were seized by the government upon publication and held for years in a warehouse. After a near-fatal automobile accident the following year, a much-wearied James took to London to recuperate. He appealed, a few years later, to be asked to return and to contest Williams in the prime minister's own home district. He returned, in a meaningful way, only as a cricket reporter and eminence grise. The day for a more important role in Trinidad for James, and also the best moment for what might be called Jamesean politics, had passed.

The formation of a Workers and Farmers Party (WFP), founded in 1964 by James's followers (and James himself as candidate) to challenge

Williams, failed miserably in elections, despite the ardent support of George Weekes as oil-field workers' leader. A youth wing, New Beginnings, would successfully train the likes of New Left intellectual (and Hector's comrade in Canada) Bukka Rennie, future editor of the oil-field workers' paper the *Vanguard*, among James's faithful Trinidadian followers of future decades. But the WFP and New Beginnings went up against obstacles too great to be moved aside or beaten down without massive support from the populace that was not forthcoming.[31]

Looked at differently, however, James, who under other conditions might have been tied down in Trinidad-Tobago politics, by the middle 1960s found himself in Canada. There, for a third time in his life in a willed exile, he once again trained young radicals, this time including Tim Hector. Unconvinced by the continuing call for nationalization of business and industry across the Third World, he was nevertheless also growingly influenced by Black Power sentiments, ready by the middle 1960s to draw new and more openly revolutionary conclusions.

Crisis Waits for No One

It would be impossible to overemphasize what the U.S. civil rights movement (better understood in its own popular phraseology, the "Freedom Movement") meant to young West Indians from the later 1950s onward. When Sparrow made his 1961 hit, "Martin Luther King for President," the chorus phrase ("After Kennedy Go") recalled how glorious the promise was and how soon to be punctuated by horror, with much more of the horror to come. As Garveyites and Marxists had returned home during the 1930s–40s bringing race pride and radicalism along, so progressive entertainment giant Harry Belafonte (from Jamaica) and younger black militants like Stokely Carmichael (born in Trinidad) spoke with their considerable American status to peoples of their homelands and would have done so powerfully if they had never visited, entertained with talk or music, or taken public stands on Caribbean issues.[32]

Before Hector's departure to Canada, the impact of Martin Luther King Jr.'s crusade was already fully felt. King had been personally cautious as the 1960s dawned, partly to distance himself from the rhetoric of black nationalism bubbling up through the Nation of Islam, partly to stave off (liberal or conservative) cold warriors' charges that demands for rapid change were feeding the fires of global communism. But as Hector later recalled, the effects of the "I Have a Dream" speech in 1963 were monumental, because West Indians could easily hear in it a call for something more than meritocracy. Hector wrote later, "Not to see [King's call for equality] as a socialist's demand for the re-distribution of wealth, as a pre-requisite to equality, is to be purblind."[33] Malcolm X (and his assassination), the first articulation of Black Power by Stokely Carmichael (destined to be one of Hector's most prestigious political friends in global meetings of Pan-Africans) and others, the anti-apartheid campaign, but above all the mass movement showed the potential of popular mobilization for radical change and government. It was an earth-shaking development better interpreted by James than by anyone else.

The ongoing Caribbean transition from Old Left—such as it was, very different from cultures where outright Communist parties had deep roots—to New Left could perhaps be seen earliest in Jamaica. There, the conservative wing of the People's National Party (PNP) had anticipated victory over Bustamante's Jamaica Labour Party (JLP) in the next elections but feared the "communistic" label; thus the PNP purged four leading, albeit leftward, organizers of the party at its trade union base. Norman Manley himself, their former ally and patron, insisted upon the expulsion, telling critics that he would otherwise resign from leadership and adding for the public record that he simply wanted the victims "to go their way and let us go ours." They were, he suggested, "free to form a Communist Party if they wish to do so," although this obviously would have been Sisyphean and downright foolish.[34]

Like the expulsion of the eleven left-wing unions from the American Congress of Industrial Organizations (CIO) in 1949, the expulsion had the effect of cutting off younger members of the next generation from the radicals of the past generation. A backstairs struggle by Left-connected labor organizations, especially the Sugar and Agricultural Workers Union, were battered as their parent organization, the Jamaica Federation of Trade Unions, was decimated after reaching a high point of influence in the early 1950s. The PNP that won the 1955 general election was not the same organization that it had been.[35]

A half-generation passed after this political debacle disguised in electoral triumph. The time-servers moved in forcefully, grabbing the goodies, but predictably failed even in their own terms to keep the masses' political loyalty. A Young Socialist League (YSL) was therefore founded in 1962 as an offshoot of the PNP, at the initiative of the brain trust Policy Planning Committee and with the blessing of Norman Manley, following the election defeats of 1961 and 1962. Young Michael Manley, back from his English education, had vigorously sought from the mid-1950s to build a National Workers Union, more moderate than the Communists had been but still a real union and not an expression of personality, like Bustamante's federation. It might be said that the process of self-education in meeting Jamaican working people would have given young Manley the common touch and a substance to his socialistic beliefs. Yet something more was needed to bring new life to the PNP and to begin to rethink the place of egalitarian labor politics in the light of global developments. More Fabian by design than either Marxist or black nationalist, the YSL nevertheless offered that something more.

The new body quickly outstripped its origins, drawing sons of old Garveyites, labor activists, militants of the unemployed movement, and others actually trained by Old Left lawyer-organizer Richard Hart during the 1950s in the short-lived People's Freedom Movement organized by expellee Richard Hart before his departure to Guyana.[36] YSLer Norman Girvin, in Jamaica of the early 1960s and a short time later in London, brought into the conversation a very young Robert Hill, who early on began to give public speeches and write papers for its conventions. The YSL, altogether too independent-minded for the PNP, was itself doomed. But its offshoots, including a fresh injection of popular culture into politics, continued in outward ripples, proposing a rather different route from New Beginnings, that is, James's Trinidadian disciples proper—but definitely moving in the same direction.

The pace of developments in Jamaica had been stirred by a level of violent unrest as yet unseen elsewhere in the region outside Cuba or mainland Central America. It had been long prepared, as Horace Campbell explains, not only by the continuing attraction of Garveyism and the personage Haile Salassie—who made an unheralded visit to Jamaica in 1966—but also by a massive displacement of rural and semiurban Jamaicans during the 1950s. Expansive bauxite mining (owned almost wholly by outsiders) swallowed large quantities of property; up to half a million former subsistence farmers were thrown off the land, along with skilled and semiskilled tradesmen of the villages. Hundreds of thousands of Jamaican natives left, in the same decades, for the United States, Canada, or the United Kingdom. Those who stayed found themselves largely driven to the outskirts of Kingston and Montego Bay, creating the notorious "shanty town" ambience of reggae lore.

Norman Manley, who had founded the PNP around himself and led Jamaica step by step through the paces toward independence, had envisioned a freer if not postcapitalist society of the future. But as his son observed late in life, after the family's dreams had been dashed, the political leaders of the region had never possessed the power to control the international movements of capital. That was the crucial limitation. Rather than moving toward national development in a future independent state, Jamaicans actually lost a considerable amount of agricultural production, enforcing a further dependency toward the status of an Antigua, unable to survive a month without U.S. food and other imports.

The dependency and the growing sense of calamity fed renascent Rastafarianism better than any cultural or political current or cult alone could have done.[37] Following the publicity around the Mau Mau in Kenya (sporting, in widely circulated photos, the dreadlocks that Jamaicans would adopt) as a visible identification with all things African, hundreds rallied in Kingston repeatedly in 1958. They chanted to drums the songs of African Repatriation ("By the Rivers of Babylon, where we sat down/ And there we wept, when we remembered Zion/But the wicked carried us away in captivity/Required from us a song/How can we sing King Alpha song/In a strange land," as Jimmy Cliff would later sing so memorably in *The Harder They Come*, one of the region's two or three most memorable films.)[38]

On the anniversary of Emancipation Day, August 1, 1959, the Reverend Claudius Henry announced to his flocks that two months and four days hence would see the "Miraculous Repatriation Back Home to Africa." Reportedly, Rev. Henry had actually visited Haile Selassie during the previous year, clearly an apotheosis of the self-made preacher's life story. Born in 1903 in Jamaica, he had emigrated to the United States in 1944, coming home in 1957 after a vision that God wanted him to return Africa's children to the promised land. As the day neared in 1959, crowds gathered in increasing numbers, whether curious or dedicated. For some, at least, Henry was a real prophet.

Come October 5, police charged the church headquarters in the Kingston slums, seizing thousands of detonators, a few guns, several sticks of dynamite, and a goodly quantity of machetes reportedly sharpened on both sides. The millenarian movement seemed to end in a scandal suitable for the always lively tabloids.

But not quite. A few months later, Henry's son Ronald returned to Jamaica with a group of street toughs from the Bronx and Harlem that he called the "First Africa Corps." These young men, choosing new names such as "Kenyatta," had been active in various U.S.-based black nationalist movements and armed themselves in preparation to returning home. Anticipating unrealistically the help of the Castro government (never offered or even suggested), they planned to infiltrate Jamaica in small numbers, apparently to move from the countryside to the city, Cuban Revolution–style. But there was another twist, characteristic of the English-speaking Caribbean. Nearly all of the Americans assumed the task was seizing Jamaica, whereas their island sympathizers thought the task was to prepare a return to Mother Africa. Skirmishing with British soldiers in the bush, the poorly armed cadre scattered and attempted to flee, the last of them captured in a small shop. The aftermath to this strange millenarian revolt known as the Henry Rebellion was deeply old-fashioned colonialism: young Ronald Henry was hanged.[39]

Most observers inside Jamaica and commentators outside shook their heads. The neo-Nazi survivalism of rural American whites during the 1980s or David Koresh's followers of Ruby Ridge in Texas later on could not have appeared further from anything resembling the kind of social democratic politics preached by an aging but powerful Norman Manley, ultrarationalist father of Jamaican independence.

But to see it this way is incomplete at best. The alternative to the elder Manley's policies and his PNP had been, for nearly two generations, Alexander Bustamante and the Bustamante Industrial Trade Union (BITU), with its rural base established for the future (and highly misnamed) JLP. At once rhetorically populist and deeply conservative, the JLP obviously prepared itself to represent the "loyal" side in the cold war—at a moment when the CIA and State Department were preparing the overthrow of an elected Guatemalan government and arming the right wing to drown that nation's restive Indian populations in an ocean of blood. No doubt fearing a similar CIA-style overthrow, Manley had understandably acted cautiously.

The expulsion of the party's Marxist left wing, seen in this light, had made perverse sense of meeting the British, under the heavy pressure from the Americans, halfway and, with this compromise, moving toward the independence reached in 1957.[40] If this move had deprived the nation of potential leaders like Ferdinand Smith, left-wing leaders back from the United States under expulsion and still full of energy and skill, it actually impelled the younger Manley to out-organize Bustamante. The most generous of the father's abused and disenfranchised critics, putting aside the ill effects upon their own lives and upon the party itself, could take the point.[41]

Moving in counterstrokes that longtime Caribbean observers appreciate best, Manley soon invited back from Britain his son Michael, who threw himself into building a new union federation more militant, more effective, and more democratic than the BITU, meeting and working with ordinary Jamaicans across the island. The same younger Manley, taking over the PNP from his retiring father in 1969, won the 1972 election with a "Rod of Correction" rhetoric lent to him by another father, Claudius Henry, and with the slogan "Change Must Come," a whiff of the very Rastafarianism considered the dialogue of madmen and women only thirteen years earlier. It was a stunning turnaround, appreciated to the full by few outside the region.[42] It was also, in very complicated ways, one important part of the Caribbean New Left come of age. That it came of age as the Caribbean moved toward federation, and faltered, offered up possibilities of both its promised destiny and its tragic fate.

Guyana and Jagan

C.L.R. James placed great weight upon the actions of the mass movement in British Guiana, soon to be Guyana, in his 1958 address in Georgetown. Although bitterly opposed to the Moscow orientation of Cheddi Jagan, the elder statesman of the Caribbean Left indicated his respect and even admiration for a political leader in the region who had built a real party around himself through decades of concentrated effort and selfless devotion. If the Guyanese could overcome (or at least abate) their racial divisions and move toward federation, he insisted, great things could be done. Compared to the timid Fabians of the political movements in other islands, these were the real revolutionaries—or at least taken to be so by critics and devotees alike.

The Cheddi Jagan story, once told as a major regional cautionary tale against "communism" (or even sympathy for the Soviet Union), now reappears after Jagan's death and Janet Jagan's final loss of the Guyanese prime ministership in 2000 as a massive tragedy of anti-imperial challenge and defeat.[43] Two competing political parties, each claiming to be more revolutionary than the other—but held together, respectively, by clan loyalties of Afro-Caribbeans versus Afro-Indians—have now both practically faded into the neocolonial picture, even if Guyana is still marked by extreme political violence. The pro-Soviet authoritarianism of sometime prime minister Forbes Burnham that landed him a Russian state funeral turns out to have been only another form of state-managed capitalism, although his followers may well have believed something very different.

Cheddi Jagan's aggressive social democracy through three victorious elections and two periods of national leadership surely would, in other circumstances, have become the basis for the region's most egalitarian society. In the existing circumstances, it provided the political infrastructure for a largely petite-bourgeois Indian culture to claim the middle-class dignity denied for generations—except, of course, that violence and repression drove the luckiest and most enterprising of them into exile. Walter Rodney offered a distinctly different path, steeped in the bottom-up politics of C.L.R. James, and Walter Rodney was murdered. But we need to go back to the origins to see it more clearly, and first to the pregnant question, why Cheddi Jagan?

It's a good question, in some measure answerable only in the familiar Caribbean terms of the great individual representing masses of poor, barely educated but fanatically devoted followers. In this case, the individual was as selfless as the region has ever produced, and in that way not at all unlike Rodney, James, and Hector. He was, however, and despite the absence of even a drop of racism, very much the East Indian from start to finish. His parents were sugar-estate laborers, part of the first generation from the homeland. In a touching tribute to a figure whose global views he had so often opposed, Hector recalled learning with amazement that Jagan's father was only ten at the time of the arranged marriage, his mother still younger, the two living apart six years and then joined with her in-laws in a house of two rooms, mud floor, a couple of windows, and grass growing on the roof, with plaited ropes across boards serving as beds. They worked from dawn to dusk for sixty cents per week.[44]

What miracle, then: Born in rural Port Mourant in 1918, Cheddi was the brightest student than anyone thereabouts had ever seen. Only a year before his birth, migration from India had been ended by British fiat, opening a new era of sorts for assimilation of sorts. The young man's entry into Queens College seemed to promise something almost unimaginable to the humble East Indian community.[45]

Jagan initially had in mind the usual path of becoming a lawyer, for which study in the United Kingdom would have been both proper and inevitable. But much as his parents had sacrificed to send him to secondary school, they could not afford this step. Instead, he headed for a scholarship at Howard University in segregated Washington, D.C., amid the upheaval of the New Deal and the American Communist Party's peak influence in the Popular Front. He spent seven transformative years in Washington and Chicago, coming back a nationalist and a revolutionary, but of a sort that the Caribbean had never seen.

It is not entirely coincidental that in seeking a practicable career, Cheddi Jagan turned to dentistry. Trotsky had once sneered at the pre-1920 socialist movement of the United States as a "party of dentists," and in the Communist milieu of the 1930s, Jewish dentists were remarkably common, African American dentists far from absent. Nearly all had been denied entrance to medical school or had simply abandoned hopes for a profession with its distinct racial quotas against non-Aryans. They were, by and large, humanitarians with expectations of a low-paying but badly needed practice. They were also, along with small businesspeople, the heart of the respectable lower middle class of left-wing American Jews, within which a youthful Jagan would feel altogether comfortable.

Embedded within the leftward edge of the New Deal (until the death of Franklin D. Roosevelt), this American Popular Front Left actually conducted itself in a social democratic manner, apart from abject loyalty to all Russian Communist decisions and bitter criticism toward those on its left flank. Along with its wide labor support and its wealth of talent in every avenue of culture, Hollywood to Broadway and mural to easel and not forgetting the sports arena, it had one leading trait: its antiracism. In an era when other aggressive opposition to racism was rare in the United States, this carried considerable weight among the African American elite of artists and intellectuals. The Popular Front also carried the stamp of anticolonialism, even when antifascism and support of European democracies muted the earlier militant rhetoric. Jagan notably "married in," that is, into the Jewish American Left, a common practice of non-Jewish intellectuals and activists seeking deep ties in a country where the Left remained, especially west of the Hudson River, thinly scattered, often concentrated at leadership levels of unions and civic organizations. Janet Rosenberg was to be his life's companion, chronicler (she always referred to him in print as "Dr. Jagan"), and, for a few years after his death, as much as ruler in his name.

Cheddi Jagan returned to British Guyana in 1943, dental degree in hand, and set up a practice in Georgetown. Within a few years he was treasurer of the Man-Power Citizens Association, the earliest union for sugar-estate laborers, and in 1946, the Political Affairs Committee. Running as an independent, he won a seat on the Legislative Council in 1947. Three years later he and a handful of friends founded the People's Progressive Party (PPP), often described as the first real mass party in the history of the colony. A British scholar, Richard Drayton, has described in detail the consequences of the PPP's electoral victory, the first under adult suffrage, in 1953, as the early point in an extended Anglo-American conspiracy to keep Jagan out of office.[46] For the following three years, British Guiana remained under a Foreign Office "State of Emergency." It was not that Jagan had proposed anything like a Communist revolution or organized anything like a Vanguard Party. Rather, he had linked nationalist politics to a peasant base and anti-imperialist ideology to support for the anti-imperialist rhetoric of the Soviet Union.

His PPP never lacked a business and professional wing of East Indians eager for an independent country in which they would occupy the upper stratum. Likewise, Jagan's perspective was no more threatening than the (very) long-run social transformation through social democratic, welfare-state measures badly needed for health, education, and economic development—in short, what the British Labour Party would presumably have promised in a Third World situation. It is impossible to say what a British (Labour or Conservative) government, left to itself, would have done about Jagan. As diplomatic documents now reveal, they set out to smash the alliance between the Indian rural workers and the mostly urban Afro-Caribbeans (and those working in the all-important bauxite mines). Their unlikely cat's-paw was the rising black orator of the PPP, lawyer Forbes Burnham. Identifying him as the coming figure of politics, and as much as urging him to split from Jagan, they succeeded in 1955 when he formed a rival organization. Despite gerrymandering of election boundaries and CIA funds delivered quietly to Burnham, the popular Jagan nevertheless won again in the 1957 elections after constitutional government had been restored by the British. Burnham put forward the same demand for independence as Jagan but under the leadership of his own group, the Progressive National Congress.

The internal government conceded by the British in 1961 raised the stakes still further, and with the approach of the election, the CIA put its extremely heavy foot down. The PPP won once more, but Americans delivered multimillion-dollar bribes to the officials of anti-Jagan unions of Afro-Caribbeans, a measure purposefully and effectively increasing racial tensions. By the time Tim Hector reached Canada in 1965, Jagan's government had been overturned by months of calculated strikes and riots, with heavy doses of arson and explosions, while Burnham's party flooded the countryside with rumors of "coolie" takeover, prompting pogroms of a type then unique in the Americas (except, of course, for the familiar kind directed against indigenous peoples). If the United States had lost out in Cuba for the time being, they intended to win in Guyana.

Historian and Kennedy White House adviser Arthur Schlesinger Jr. apparently helped formulate the new mix of terrorism and extreme proportional representation, providing Burnham a comfortable power base while making life under Jagan impossible. It was, for the region, a classic move of American cold war liberalism. In the 1964 elections, Jagan once more got the most votes, but Burnham ruled the narrow parliamentary majority, this time thanks more to State Department manipulations than to the decisions of the compliant colonial authorities.[47]

Burnham was altogether predictably a monster in office, destroying the economy through nationalizations followed by political appointments of incompetent and corrupt figures to run the operations, meanwhile rigging votes and arranging arrests, beatings, and the occasional assassination of opponents. The country became hopelessly split along ethnic lines, and independent Guyana gained a new dubious distinction as the greatest proportional exporter of citizens in the world.[48]

To get ahead of our story: by the time Jagan was allowed by the United States to come to power in 1992, it was too late to do anything but accept the International Monetary Fund's (IMF) bidding. Schlesinger Jr. had won at great cost to the region. And yet, writing at the prime minister's death, Hector would recall Jagan's perfect absence of bitterness, his courage and steadfastness, his bearing among young radicals who sometimes treated him with contempt, and his high standing until the end.[49] He was one of the great dignified figures of modern politics, exemplar of the empire's victims unbowed by repeated trickery and defeat, martyr of and for the Caribbean, and "foundation pillar for the beginning of a truly Caribbean era."[50]

Hector added one serious criticism to these kudos. Jagan had failed to find the way to unite his party with Walter Rodney's Working People's Alliance (WPA), and the moment of promise quickly passed. There lies another story near the heart of Hector's vision of a renewed Caribbean and his generation's potential role in it.

Walter Rodney

Walter Rodney, Hector declared, was "far and away the most significant intellectual and political personage of the post-independence history of the English-speaking Caribbean."[51] High praise touched by deep sorrow decades after: no event hit Hector so hard as Rodney's 1980 assassination, save the murder of his wife, Arah, a decade later. Perhaps no other political event hit him so hard as the destruction of the Grenadian Revolution, the murder of Maurice Bishop, and the invasion of the U.S. Marines.

Jagan represented the preindependence generation in its high nobility of character, and Rodney represented the new generation. About the slain activist's political moment, mentor C.L.R. James had spoken most eloquently to a college audience:

> To be born in 1942 was to have behind you a whole body of work dealing in the best way with the emerging situation in the Caribbean and the colonial world. That was Walter Rodney. He grew up in the world of the wars and also in a world where Nkrumah succeeded in securing independence in the Gold Coast and establishing Ghana; then a little later Julius Nyerere did so for Tanganyika, which united with Zanzibar to become Tanzania. Walter had an upbringing and development that many of you cannot appreciate, because to you it is natural. To him, it was not; it was something new. That is why when he completed his studies, he was able to build on these foundations. The work that had been necessary to motivate him to study Africa and the Caribbean had been done already. That is an aspect of the importance of the personality and particular politics of Walter Rodney.[52]

James was, of course, referring to himself in more than passing. But it was not a lack of modesty that caused him to do so. Rodney was an intellectual child of James almost as much as he was a political child of Guyana.

Born into a lower-middle-class (or better, a skilled working-class) family in Georgetown, son of a hard-working tailor and a seamstress, Rodney grew up knowing his parents as Afro-Caribbeans involved in Jagan's PPP. As a teen, Walter would distribute party manifestos and sell fund-raising trinkets in neighborhoods thought to be friendly, hoping for success and fearing angry responses or dogs set upon the youthful tractarian.

If young Cheddi Jagan had been a perceived genius, young Walter was hard working and bright, as studious as "those Indian students" who provided a (however resented) model for ambitious Afro-Caribbeans to emulate. His classmate, later literary scholar and critic Gordon Rohlehr, recalled that the new generation of the 1950s saw a significant widening of the colony's elite. Not one shone as brightly as Walter Rodney, president of the Historical Society, vice president of the Debating Society, editor of the school magazine, and winner of several prizes, including, most important, the Open Arts Scholarship to enter University of West Indies (UWI) in 1960. He had already joined a political study group and begun, in his school paper, to explore the constraints of colonial life. Not that he was particularly clear-minded yet in politics: he returned briefly in 1961 to campaign for Forbes Burnham, who he then regarded as the nationalist black leader supreme.[53]

Jamaica's UWI Mona campus of 1960 was ruled over by Arthur Lewis, an ardent regionalist who stressed strong academic preparation for lives of public service. Around the campus ranged the first full generation of West Indian artists and writers: Rex Nettleford, Edna Manley, Derek Walcott, Orlando Patterson, and many others who came to visit and lecture, including George Lamming, Wilson Harris, and V. S. Naipaul. The history department that attracted Rodney's highest interest boasted of the young Elsa Goveia and Roy Augier. Rodney, president of the debating society in his first year, was part of a student delegation visiting Cuba in 1962 (which probably cost him the presidency of the student body: facing defeat, he was viciously Red-baited for the first of many times). Perhaps most characteristic and most like Tim Hector, Rodney argued in an early essay that Marxism-Leninism and Labour-style social democracy were both putting the cart before the horse because West Indians needed to look first within themselves.[54]

Rodney had also begun to pose the issue that would occupy him the rest of his life: the supposed backwardness of Africa's children at home and abroad. Encouraged by his teachers, he moved on as a graduate student at the School of Oriental and African Studies (SOAS) in London, then one of the very rare places in the world for concentrated African studies. He saw himself as a future professor and (following his marriage to a fellow

Guyanese student in London) as a provider for a growing family. But he was also becoming a Marxist, thanks largely to a study group congealed in James's flat. Orlando Patterson, Joan French, Margaret Carter Hope, Stanley French, Walton Look Lai, and Rodney represented altogether half a dozen islands—even Manhattan island and Brooklyn, in the person of Selma James. They commenced, under C.L.R. James's guidance, a serious and lengthy examination of past revolutions and revolutionary writings and lives, and a wide-ranging view of the present day, not excluding the work of Guyanese novelist Wilson Harris (who had himself shortly relocated from Guyana) and of Garvey. Uninterested in contemporary (overwhelmingly white) British Marxism, whose advocates always seemed rather condescending to the issues of small islands, Rodney tended naturally toward the Pan-Africanism dramatized by the struggles in Tanzania and southern Africa.

So Rodney turned to West Africa and its colonial history for a dissertation, more than six hundred pages of the kind that Tim Hector in a different lifetime might have done in the same spirit and with the same concentrated energy. Rodney's clear notion was to teach briefly in Africa and to take what he had learned back to the Caribbean. Dar-es-Salaam offered him a position in 1966, destined to provide not only the sole reliable institutional base for the rest of his life but also the least troubled site of his years ahead.[55]

The importance of *How Europe Underdeveloped Africa* for Tim Hector and others cannot be overemphasized. Published in 1972, it was not merely an indictment of capitalism's crimes. A careful yet highly popular exposition of a new perspective—that African societies had been at a sort of takeoff stage of development akin to Europe's at the moment of the slave trade's decisive expansion—had explosive political implications. The ravaging that lasted for three centuries, dragging off a decisive portion of the labor force among other major disruptions, had been succeeded by a nineteenth- and early-twentieth-century colonization that intensified exploitation many times over and robbed the continent's societies of practically everything worth expropriating. Nascent African capitalism had thus been blocked (at least) twice over, adding precious few internal improvements and those only for accelerated removal of valuables.

What Rodney's biographer calls a "tour de force of theorizing backed up by wide-ranging empirical knowledge and good writing . . . a classic of historical research and synthesis" was one of those rare documents accessible to ordinary readers as well as intellectuals, a living example of "what is to be done" in literary terms for the likes of Hector's ongoing journalism.[56] In lifetimes of copious and mostly fluent literary production, neither James nor Williams nor, for that matter, Jagan had done better.

But this was already the notorious Walter Rodney, driven from the Mona campus where he had studied and distinguished himself because of rampant fears of disorder. Robert Hill (destined to be James's literary executor and the director of the Marcus Garvey Papers at UCLA) and others young and active in the early 1960s have emphasized the unmistakable effect of the contemporary Rastafarian movement and its influence upon sections of the black working class. Rodney offered something for them, while intellectuals on the make turned in precisely the opposite directions. C.L.R. James, in chastising Orlando Patterson's ridicule of the Rastafari in *Children of Sisyphus*, argued in 1964 that "Mr. Patterson does not, cannot, convince the reader that the life he is describing is absurd. Horrible, horrible, most horrible it is. But it is not absurd." Rather, "as long as they express themselves, the form may be absurd, but the life itself is not absurd." Here James called down criticism on Patterson that could last for the rest of the future Harvard professor's career as public intellectual; seeking to define the "civilized" in terms of race relations, Patterson always seemed to be warning against impulses from below. As James observed at the onset of the notable career of a leading West Indian intellectual, the determination of the novelist (at the time ensconced in London and writing for a British audience) to separate himself from this misery was worse than failure. The "fate of Rastafari and Mr. Patterson himself are very closely linked," James pronounced, with a "common destiny" whose trumpets of battle needed to be sounded at home "in Kingston, in Port of Spain, in Bridgetown, in Georgetown [because] from London (and in London) they are horns from an elf-land, blowing only faintly."[57] Had he been able to see the future, James would have added: from the Harvard Yard as well.

This indirect condemnation bore heavily upon young radicals like Rodney who were precisely determined *not* to live abroad and write for the European audience. "Brother Wally" readily accepted the necessity for what he was to call "groundings with my brothers," the opposite of the emerging West Indian middle-class aspiration to act white and marry white (or light). Rastafarians had placed the issue of race and its relationship with Africa on the center of the political map. The issue could only be escaped personally, not evaded.

Hector Abroad and Back Home

Restless at the intellectual insularity of the Maritime Provinces, Hector had moved on, in 1966, to McGill University in cosmopolitan Montreal. First he studied philosophy, aiming toward a Ph.D. and the professorship that would have found him prominence and respect at home as the "big professor" who visited occasionally. His major professor at McGill was soon severely disappointed to learn that the young man was not, after all, training for a distinguished career as a literary critic and scholar. He was downright disgusted that Hector intended to ruin himself in a noncareer of socialist agitation.[58]

But there at McGill of the mid-1960s, what Paget Henry calls the "fateful encounter with the ideas of C.L.R. James" took place, putting a stamp on Hector until the end of his days.[59] In one of many tributes to his mentor, Hector was to say that James's genius "lay not so much in his definitely remarkable intellect, but the application of that intellect to the creative possibilities inherent in the working class in developed and underdeveloped countries." The sometime Pan-African magus also—and this is crucial—himself personified the Caribbean's great contributions to human progress.[60] No regular class, no discipline, no professor could offer that much to the young man.

The group of Caribbean intellectuals gathered in Montreal, most of them going to school at McGill, constituted an intellectual and political powerhouse in some ways fulfilled, in other ways destined to be denied the realization of its promise. Bukka Rennie, Rosie Douglas (later prime minister of Dominica before a premature death), Franklyn Harvey, future Canadian MP Anne Cools, Alvin Johnson, Hugh O'Neal, Robert Hill, and Alfie Roberts, among others, were all part of the Canada-wide West Indian movement that centered in Montreal and Toronto, with extended links to Vancouver and other distant parts. It is difficult now to appreciate how so much political-intellectual energy could be concentrated in the circle of a few dozen temporary (in some cases, permanent) exiles, and how widely their influence would be felt at the high tide of Pan-Caribbean, Pan-African left-wing nationalism.

But the deeper causes were clear enough. Not only had strict racial segregation and its power to demean been a lifelong Caribbean experience, formally (if by no means entirely) lifted in Canada. Its reverse served as magnum symbol during the last stages of old-style colonialism. "Black Is Beautiful" came of age as the United States faced defeat in Vietnam—an almost unthinkable defeat of the world's military juggernaut by a peasant people—and seemingly projected events at least as dramatic dead ahead. "The riots erupting in Watts and Detroit, I thought I was witnessing the dress rehearsal for the final showdown."[61] That the circle around Hector was young, alive to the rapidly changing music and art of the era, heightened the effects enormously. It was an era when the young, worldwide, seemed to be leading the grand changes, watching themselves on television, listening to cultural history being made.

Something like this, but more insular, had come together around James's apartment in 1950s London, and something like it around a stove (with James very much on hand) in London twenty years still earlier. But if, in those earlier times, independence overrode all other purposes—even the socialistic politics of C.L.R. James—then independence alone would not be nearly enough for this latest crowd. They had the same class origins as the rising middle class ascending to the highest posts of the soon-to-be-independent islands. But they were rebels from their status assignments as professionals likely to do well at home or abroad. The profession they sought was revolutionist, and it made at least as much sense, for that moment, as the cynical turn of Naipaul and so many others just a generation older.

James, uncorrupted and charismatic, was a natural attraction for these young people. If he had symbolized for a Malcolm X in the 1950s (according to Malcolm's attorney, Conrad Lynn) the black Marxist who was as learned as any white radical in the world, his status on that score had jumped upward in a decade. Unlike Malcolm X, these youngsters had the opportunity to read James's more difficult works. Some of them were even able to reproduce unavailable ones (as Robert Hill brought out a mimeographed edition of dense study of dialectics), the more precious because apart from *The Black Jacobins* and *Beyond a Boundary*, assorted obscure books and pamphlets of his that were practically passed around hand to hand.

Moreover, for them James was a Caribbean, former mentor to Prime Minister Williams in Trinidad—whose renowned histories of the region could be regarded as extended footnotes for James's works—and a respected commentator on regional sports and culture at large. He was a giant, and thanks to assorted developments, he was theirs.

In fact, James's own political group, never more than fifty or so members, would formally dissolve in 1970. If he had spent a political lifetime attracting young people, this would be the last milieu created more or less in his image. The publisher and distributor of pamphlets and longtime leader of the Detroit group, Martin Glaberman, was an intellectual mentor to those who traveled to see him, because he gave the Jamesean touch to Marxist study. But the Third World nationalism adopted by the Caribbean circle was too eclectic (and too accepting of the "Stalinist" leadership of the Vietnamese and Cuban revolutions, among others) for Glaberman and other old-timers of the group. On the lecture trail but also in his personal affinities, James had gone beyond his erstwhile disciples, inspired in no small part by the young enthusiasts who adopted him.

These ardent young intellectuals and activists met formally and informally, naturally more often at close range as friends, to discuss and argue over texts, to become the intimates that only fellow exile-revolutionaries are likely ever to be. They also hosted James in visits that would change their collective lives. First he came to see them before returning to Trinidad, where they raised money to support his efforts to build a political opposition, and on his return after an ignominious defeat. This time he remained fixed in Canada as an organizing base, until permitted reentry into the United States as college lecturer in 1970.

The young expatriates held unprecedented, major conferences of Caribbean intellectuals, calling back from relative obscurity (or at least despair at isolation) some senior Caribbean intellectuals but also the likes of cricket giant Garfield Sobers and the Mighty Sparrow, destined to be the first calypsonian awarded an honorary doctorate by the University of the West Indies. Along with the ongoing New World group's reanimation of Caribbean letters, the youngsters helped revive among themselves a Pan-Caribbeanism that had so lapsed among island leaders as to become practically a dead letter.

Robert Hill, who invited James to the second annual conference for West Indians in Canada in 1966 and thereby brought the senior revolutionary and the future disciple together, recalls a crucial part of it. Current graduate student and future UWI professor Norman Girvin had taken Hill to a North London lecture by James in 1963, and Girvin arranged a lunch with the eminence grise in his flat on Staverton Road. The visit had been impressive enough, a voice from the increasingly distant past of 1930s–40s Pan-Africanism. Returning home to Jamaica with some of James's books and pamphlets, Hill recalled that he felt the sky had opened: this nearly forgotten fellow Caribbean giant, like no one else anywhere, offered a road starkly different from the standard neocolonial (or Communist) alternatives of economic growth and the Vanguard Party.[62]

Hector himself recalled the events from a slightly different angle. When James went off to his home island, they anticipated the overwhelming odds and their champion's defeat, yet "we followed it as if our lives depended on it."[63] James's return to Canada found them reading all his available writings and engaging him as he engaged them in an extended nonacademic tutorial. They would present analyses; he would listen and then ask questions that prompted the speakers to see the error of their own thinking. He taught them Caribbean history as it had been written, and then offered Marx's analysis against the grain of the accepted historical account. For Hector, the key questions were also philosophical, complex issues of dialectics and their relationship to historical developments: Hegel and the modern class struggle.

And then there was Pan-Africanism, its history seen better or at least viewed differently through the rear-view mirror. Robin D. G. Kelley has

glimpsed most keenly of the decisive turn that James had made from orthodox Marxism during his London sojourn of the 1930s, and the influence
that this turn had on all his subsequent work.[64] At a moment when socialists and Communists alike thought of African freedom from colonialism
as generations if not centuries in the future, James and his little circle
had began planning something entirely different. The Italian invasion of
Ethiopia gave them a decisive issue, and the break of James's childhood
friend George Padmore from the Comintern gave them connections and
energy badly needed. James led the formation of the International African
Friends of Ethiopia (IAFE), with himself as chair, and a prominent group
of activists including Padmore, Jomo Kenyatta, Amy Ashwood Garvey
(the black prophet's first wife), T. Ras Makonnen, and Grenadian intellectual Albert Marryshow.

These young black men and women determinedly carried over energy
from the Pan-African Congress of 1921, in a real sense reviving the Marxist
version of Pan-Africanism whose banner had fallen with the close of the
Crusader and the African Blood Brotherhood in New York a decade earlier. Unlike the Communists, they would not subordinate the anticolonial
struggle to the needs of the Soviet Union, and that principle had been
decisive. Less decisive but important was the pursuit of radical allies, in this
case the Independent Labour Party (ILP) that gave James a hearing and a
platform in its publications. The International African Service Bureau,
succeeding the IAFE and publishing *International African Opinion* under
James's editorship, meanwhile set the agenda for Pan-Africanists of a certain kind for decades to come: those who believed that Africans had to free
themselves and that their own ruling groups would not contribute much if
any to that liberation. James might seem to leave these things behind—in
large part because his dubious legal status in the United States from 1939
until his expulsion in 1952 practically forbade such international trips and
activities. But they were there, making him a larger-than-life figure for
young black intellectuals of the 1960s.[65] It was natural that they should
form a Caribbean Service Bureau in expectation of future Pan-Africanist
activities.

And there was more. James's visit to Ghana in 1957 had prompted a
further projection that Africa and especially its peasants (as James was to

affirm about the peasantry during the Vietnam War) might be decisive in the anticapitalist offensive of the age. It was a crucial point, all the more so because the CIA, through the arms of the American AFL-CIO, could easily bribe sections of the small, urban labor force who lived apart from the rural masses, and because the nationalist regimes virtually without exception sought to squeeze the "interior" to create surpluses for economic growth, exactly the wrong plan to sustain a peasant-based democracy.[66] If the projection of Caribbean unity with James as an important figure had fallen down, due to the manipulations and island self-centeredness of certain leaders, the black revolution lived and was finding itself in the Black Power slogans in the United States.[67]

That would have been enough to make James a magnetic figure. But it was never a matter entirely of politics. James meant to educate in the broadest sense. To James and the intense conversations between the two, Hector credited his reading of Naipaul, Lovelace, and Walcott, not to mention Althusser, Heidigger, Sartre, Marcuse, and Merleau-Ponty and of course the magic trio Hegel, Marx, and Lenin; also his listening to Bach, Mozart, Beethoven, Stravinsky, Art Tatum, Dionne Warwick, Aretha Franklin, and Ray Charles; his appreciation of painters Picasso, Cézanne, Cuban surrealist Wilfredo Lam, and the forgotten geniuses of the Sistine Chapel.[68]

Only a few years later, as it turned out, Hill and others, including Lloyd Best, were hosting James for lectures and long sessions of conversation, including some stay-over weeks in Canada. Already in his middle sixties, the once-vigorous and athletic James was by this time badly weakened. He had become razor thin, and his hands shook so uncontrollably that eating with knife, fork, and spoon had become difficult. Lacking anything like a career and in the process of breaking up with Selma, his dynamic third wife, James nevertheless found the strength inside himself for a late-life political and personal renewal. Thoroughly defeated in Trinidad by Eric Williams and by this time best known as author of the magnum cricket history *Beyond a Boundary*, he finally found another generation of likely disciples-of-sort within the Canadian circle. Their 1966 conference sealed the relationship for decades to come. Hill, taking the train back and forth from Toronto to Montreal, effectively led a study circle in James's writings among mostly McGill students. Here in this milieu, whatever his earlier anticipations of certain views, Hector was certainly changed for a lifetime. Or better said: the process ongoing through his young life was finalized.

We know about this development in several ways, complicated almost from the outset because Hector was perfectly capable of taking James's core teachings beyond James's own immediate conclusions. Hector later recalled a three-hour phone conversation, in 1966, between Walter Rodney in London and himself in Montreal, with asides at James's strategic advice, taken both positive and negative. Both felt impulses of Pan-Africanism that needed no stirring from the elderly James, much as he had nurtured it around the potbellied stove in London. Nkrumah, though banished from power, and Julius Nyerere, discredited in power, had nevertheless made revolutions and articulated the need for a postcolonial African unity on the basis of a unique history and culture.[69] Hector all but demanded that Rodney return from London to Guyana instead of heading for Africa, because (in Hector's mind) the Arusha movement in Tanzania had been exhausted or worse, betrayed, while Guyana itself was the logical place for functioning cooperatives, the alternative to neocolonialism and state socialism.[70]

James, looking with hopes too great upon a former comrade of the anticolonial struggle, tenaciously held on to his confidence in Arusha and its architect for years further, seeking near the end of his life a positive substitute for the ruination of Nkrumah's and Ghana's dreams. In a small way, we are told, James never forgave Hector, unwilling to yield a crucial point even to his greatest teacher. Hector, James counseled, should have written out the point, not argued with Rodney so vividly, advice keeping with James's older and more formal way of thinking. And perhaps he was still right: even in a day of frequently contentious e-mail, it is still easier to bear a challenge in type than to hear it over the phone or in person.

But Hector did, as he recalled later, properly press the central issue of state socialism and its alternatives to Rodney. Forbes Burnham's scheme of nationalizing businesses in Guyana was no liberation, but instead an opportunity for political corruption. Only "factories and fields vested in public companies, with worker-shareholding, and national shareholding" could provide the kind of transition toward the self-managed society mobilizing its population.[71] Making these kinds of arguments, dispensing this kind of advice, Hector was definitely talking like a revolutionary rather than a future professor. Some of his fellow study class members made that transition; more of them either did not or postponed professorhood until their main political days were finished.

Whatever James's views on current particulars, he had in his past writings given Hector, among others, an utterly unique view of economics and politics—before and after formal independence. By contrast, as Paget Henry has seen so acutely, the mainstream Caribbean development models owed most heavily to Sir Arthur Lewis and what might be called the technocratic solution. A brilliant scholar of historic labor conditions, Lewis unforgettably analyzed the grotesque and dehumanizing experiences that had slowed meaningful development through poor health, poor housing, lack of education, and low wages for the workforce. When independence actually approached, Lewis seemed to throw all this overboard so as to boost, through the careful planning of experts, a nascent bourgeoisie rather than workers but especially rather than the peasant sector. Future economists who would modify Lewis's programs, notably George Beckford, sharpened the focus on the role of the economic technician as creating and maintaining the proper "mix" of industrial and agricultural development as the moving factor of the situation and potential success of the emerging nation.[72]

By the mid-1960s, it had become clear that the future of the region would not unfold as Lewis and other optimists had predicted. The bourgeoisie remained timid in respect to global enterprise. As increased communication brought the world of American consumerism closer to elites' daily life, the ruling strata actually operated more and more like an unproductive latifundia, attaching itself to neocolonial projects and goals in ways that only deepened dependence.

Toward this new and heightened challenge, James and his faithful disciples had less than certain answers, but offered devastating critiques based upon a different internal logic as well as straightforward democratic principles. As the master theorist scrutinized the plans of the planners, he observed that they did not even include working people and peasants as intelligent beings, only as "factors," those whose responsibility was to take orders, laboring dumbly to carry them out. Thus, the Caribbean was robbing itself of its greatest resource: human talent. He called for a public mobilization—with urgings and education from the governments—that would place in front of the masses the issues at hand and how these could be resolved for the common good. State socialism on the Russian model would simply not work. As Hector was to repeat in future years about the Burnham regime, replacing ordinary capitalists with state bureaucrats, however accompanied by socialist or anti-imperialist rhetoric, did not empower either the worker or the public but instead deepened cynicism.

A similar critique, applied to the sudden overthrow of a government, guerrilla-style, was hardly likely to apply to most of the Caribbean but was not quite unimaginable, either. James had traveled to Cuba and often praised Castro as the most significant figure in the region since Toussaint. Indeed, in his afterword to the 1963 edition of *The Black Jacobins*, James pointed to the Cuban Revolution as a new stage of the region. But it was not because of the Cuban Communists, the model Vanguard Party in Russian-version (or for that matter, Chinese version) Marxism-Leninism beginning to be embraced by some militants in Jamaica. Far from it.

Still less than a decade after the Hungarian uprising of 1956, James saw industrial societies leaping out of capitalism or state capitalism through workers' councils. Less-developed societies had a different and more complicated road to travel. But they would travel, in important ways, through the same basic venue of what the 1960s generation called "power to the people." To take the bureaucratic path—as argued by documents on Nkrumah and the degeneration of the Ghanaian experiment that James had not yet released publicly—only courted disaster.

Not many followed James's pronouncements with the credulity and vigor of Tim Hector. The ready adoption of the master's ideas coincided with certain anarcho-syndicalist tendencies of the New Left (the "student syndicalism" of the Students for a Democratic Society [SDS]) that turned from the campuses to labor, parallel to the hopes and dreams of youthful revolutionaries in so many other parts of the world. James's own writings appealed, in the United States, especially to the enthusiasts of the most proletarian sector of the Black Power movement, of Detroit and the

League of Revolutionary Black Workers. These, like a section of the New Left drawn to him, were the children of evanescent impulses, limited to temporary formations and, after a few years, scattered individuals.

The complexities of the Canadian situation were underlined not only by the overwhelmingly white character of the nation (French Canadians had been known for a century, from Rhode Island to Quebec, as the "niggers of the north," and they played the role of the largely missing blacks in other respects, figurative drawers of water and hewers of wood restricted to the lowest occupations) but because black nationalism moved forward in the most curious ways. Rosie Douglas, destined to be one of Hector's closest political companions in the last Pan-African adventures, was in the mid-1960s an outstanding youngster in Prime Minister John Diefenbaker's Progressive Conservative Party, royalist not Marxist or even liberal. Douglas, always one for maneuver—down to his last years as ally of Momar Khadaffi and Liberian dictator Charles Taylor—supplied most of the funds for the Canadian group, from what must be presumed to be politically conservative donors.

In 1968, it was Douglas himself who led the rebels at Sir George Williams University, seizing the computer center in a demand for Black Power on campus. It was the most dramatic campus event of the Canadian scene during the era, sparking sympathetic demonstrations as far away as Trinidad. When such a small group could bring such drama to a large "white" nation that had so long ignored or abused its other minorities (most obviously indigenous peoples, by the time themselves clamoring for land and compensation), a new day had arrived.

The Caribbean element in James had, of course, a more widespread and more lasting impact on "his own" people, the more so because of his personal relations with young radicals. But why did he have such an impact on Hector, apart from a certain regional pride and personal loyalty? A part of the answer is the role of culture in James's vision: neither the detached avant-garde of the Parisian (or London) intellectuals disdainful of working-class life nor the "socialist realism" of the Popular Front model could have a political appeal to young Caribbean intellectuals. His grasp of cricket (most especially but not only for cricket fanatic Hector) as evidence and secondary source of regional development, along

Tim Hector with other founding members of the Afro-Caribbean Movement, 1968.

Hector with his mentor
C.L.R. James (seated)
at a public forum in
Antigua, 1975.

Poster of Hector as the ACLM (Antigua Caribbean Liberation Movement) candidate in the 1980 general elections.

Leonard Tim Hector against corrupt officials
ACLM 1989

Editorial cartoon depicting Hector fighting corrupt government officials. In 1989, he ran as the ACLM's candidate in the St. John's City South constituency.

Arah Hector, Tim Hector's first wife and leader of ACLM's Sisters' Liberation Committee. She was murdered in 1989.

Poster of Tim Hector as the UPP (United Progressive Party) candidate in the 1994 general elections. Hector ran against the ALP (Antigua Labour Party) candidate Vere Bird, Jr., in the constituency of St. John's Rural South.

OECS (Organisation of Eastern Caribbean States) Mission to Libya, 24–29 August 2001. From left to right: 1. Tim Hector; 2. Dr. Ralph Gonsalves, Prime Minister of St. Vincent and the Grenadines; 3. Col. Mu'ammar Gaddafi, president of Libya; 4. Dr. Keith Mitchell, Prime Minister of Grenada; 5. Elvin Nimrod, Foreign Minister of Grenada; 6. Pierre Charles, Prime Minister of Dominica; 7. L. Leroq, Minister of Foreign Affairs and International Trade of Dominica; and 8. Dr. Earl Martin, Minister of Health and Environment of St. Kitts and Nevis.

Weston-Mandela House, c. 1988. The building served as ACLM's headquarters and as the home of Outlet Publishers.

Hector and his second wife Jennifer on their wedding day, 31 December 1993. To the right is Hector's lifelong friend George Odlum, who was the former Minister of St. Lucia.

Professor Selwyn Cudjoe presents Hector with the C.L.R. James Award, 2001. Paget Henry, Hector's friend and editor of the *C.L.R. James Journal*, is in the background.

Hector (right) and the Leeward Island Cricket Team, 1973.

Hector (second from left) demonstrating against the landing of the British "Red Devils" in Antigua in 1968.

Ella Hector (1888–1968), Tim Hector's grandmother. He credited her as being the greatest influence on his life.

Hector (right) with Kwame Ture (Stokely Carmichael) in Antigua, 1994.

Hector addressing a mass gathering in Guyana, at the funeral ceremony of the noted Guyanese scholar and political activist Dr. Walter Rodney, 1980.

African Liberation Day Rally, led by Hector and other ACLM leaders, May 1977.

Police and Defence Force personnel bear the flag-draped casket of Tim Hector,
19 November 2002.

Hector, Rosie Douglas, and Jerome Bleau in a jovial mood.

with his long-standing Pan-Africanism and Pan-Caribbeanism as a black contribution to global solutions (coinciding, as it did, with disillusionment in "white" Russian communism), made him, at least for handfuls of a certain kind of intellectual/activist, an ideal mentor. The notion, for a radicalized Antiguan, that the masses' self-learning in cricket, in "mas," and in steel band offered important evidence of political maturity was in some measure irresistible. And Hector did not resist.

Hector had come to Canada to gain a Ph.D. and to teach at the college level, very likely in the United States or Canada. He recalled later that he had been disgusted by local (white) Communists who sought to recruit him into a Third World Popular Front, intuiting already a different kind of Marxism of James with emphasis on power from below and a tilt toward a particular Caribbean contribution.[73] James for his part, basking in the first years of late-life celebrity, fixed his star upon Pan-Africanism as it had not been since the 1930s, dramatizing the distance from state communism and the Communist movements. In the light of recent events, he began proposing the reorganization of an overarching Pan-African body like the vanished African Service Bureau, with an agenda that James would later unsuccessfully attempt to affix to the Seventh Pan-African Congress of 1972.

A International Caribbean Service Bureau would serve as a strategic opener, young Tim Hector as functionary of the larger project, James the architect and ideologue. It had worked before, and brilliantly. James might even have imagined Hector a young Eric Williams or Kwame Nkrumah, trained by him personally for leadership. Hector, seizing the chance history offered him, dropped out of graduate school to travel widely for the ambitious effort, meeting old and new contacts, high office or no office, setting a pattern for the rest of his life.

Montreal-based activities around Caribbean concerns would continue and even flourish, but the dream of a revived international movement dissipated. Only the Communists and their allies really did have sufficient material backing (of the Soviet Union but also left-wing trade unionists and functionaries, or alternatively, of China and its own followers) to open up grand new efforts. The project failed also because nationalist leaders of new states in Africa and the Caribbean wanted to quell and not encourage radicalism, especially movements that questioned their own status as domestic rulers. It had, ironically, been easier or at least more straightforward for the militant Pan-Africans before the end of formal empire: they only had to overcome colonialism.

Perhaps there were also other reasons for Hector's withdrawal from school. His was a restless intellect, already at home more in the classroom or cricket field than in a cloistered study; the notion of being a professor had only thrilled him briefly. Instead of reentering school, he returned home. It was the most fateful decision of his life, because once reengaged, he never ceased engaging. One step led to another and another, as Hector came to epitomize the radical homeboy who had returned to challenge the mighty Bird family. David Hinds, radical academic and editor of the online *Rodneyite*, would later say that "my generation got in touch with James through Tim's theory and practice," and thus he carried the torch lit for himself in Montreal from the receding past of James's boyhood Trinidad into the future.[74]

Returning, as so many of his fellow Caribbean intellectuals who came of age during the 1960s did not (or only for visits), Hector met the crisis with vigor and confidence. It was to be understood that, as the outstanding intellectual of the Antigua Workers Union (AWU) shortly before it was established to contest the ALP, Hector would be the editor (and a principal writer) of the AWU's newspaper, the *Trumpet*. He now occupied the high ground of the radical, fearless journalist that he would cling to for more than thirty years—until the end, when he was writing editorials from his deathbed.

The *Trumpet* gave forth its earliest notes in December 1967. Within two months, during the second week of 1968, Antigua and Barbuda experienced its biggest demonstration in history, climaxing in a general strike, the first in thirty years. Bird met the crisis with a state of emergency, a showdown between the workers and the police, who could not successfully suppress the popular sentiment and pulled back. A badly shaken Bird pronounced Hector a "Communist," not for the last time.[75]

By-elections, called for the following August 7, saw dissident ALPer George Walter determined to unite all opposition around AWU officials, making himself the grand leader. Hector and the militants, seeking to clarify their position, formed the Progressive Labor Movement (PLM), with Hector its first chair. In an effort to stir public interest, he proposed election primaries, so as to encourage competition rather than an alternative one-man rule. This was also Hector's own first opportunity to run for office, and he characteristically turned down the appeals of friends and readers to do so. Some weeks later, he and Walter found themselves, respectively, the general manager (with a column) and editor of the *Antigua Star*, a weekly that had passed from the planter elite to the young radicals, a paper switching political (or class) positions while remaining in opposition to the Bird machine.

Hector was also exceptionally active in cricket circles, attending at the first opportunity of scholarship an advanced university program for sports administrators (sponsored by the International Olympics Committee) at Sussex University and throwing himself into the reorganization of regional cricket. As Conrad Luke observed, Hector soon "served at every level of cricket administration in the region, from executive member of the Antigua Cricket Association to the Leewards Board, to Manager of the Combined Islands," finally a member of the West Indies Cricket Board, and a familiar figure on regional television (as James was to be in later years in the United Kingdom) pronouncing upon cricket and its significance.[76]

But it was the political activist and politician who took on the weight of controversy. In 1966, it had been decided that Antigua and Barbuda would become one of the United Kingdom's "associated" states—the first in the Eastern Caribbean. It was far from complete independence, and the island's foreign policy and national defense were still to be governed by Britain. But internally, it was to be its own—or Bird's. In buying thirteen thousand acres of sugar lands with a British loan, Bird united the economic, political, and union authority into himself. Within that first year, he showed that his true colors were hardly Red. When the AWU demanded recognition as a contesting labor union, Bird turned the police on the populace: no more than two citizens could even walk down the street together. When these measures did not suffice, he ordered the police to use teargas. Hector was later said to be the artist-athlete who taught the crowd to catch or pick up the canisters and throw them back at the police. When police rushed the crowd, Hector meanwhile directed his friends to go to rooftops and hail down stones on the misguided authorities. A veritable platoon of civil servants quickly and perhaps shamefacedly defected to the opposition, and Bird had no choice: he recognized the AWU.[77]

The situation was complicated if not muddled by the reappearance of middle-class politics opposed to Bird rather than anything resembling socialism. The Antigua Progressive Movement (APM) and the Antigua and Barbuda Democratic Movement (led by one of the last prominent planters) represented the sort of elite coalition of professionals and businesspeople who, in other peripheral societies emerging from colonialism, sought solutions that would have worked better in Europe, the United States, or the rapidly industrializing societies of South Korea or Malaysia.[78] Alas for Antiguan elites, no manufacturing sector, no well-educated working class, and no prospect for a happy leap into development were in the cards. Bird continued to rule by virtue of old loyalties but also because his opponents lacked the social infrastructure and the collective will to go a different way.

Hector recalled later that he had pleaded with George Walter to seize the moment and build a real political party (echoing James's plea to Eric Williams in 1960: "Build your party, Bill, build your party"). The sugar workers, who had seen Bird as a savior for almost two generations, remained loyal to him. But the new generation working in oil companies, tourism, and assorted service industries felt differently, the more so because their employers were for the most part foreign. Hector urged Walter to "lay the base of a new working class party, based on shop stewards, advanced workers, and the progressive intellectuals." Walter chose instead those from the professional elite who had no particular loyalties and would not turn on him in disappointment.[79] The middle classes represented in the APM might have provided an organic substitute for union members and certainly wanted badly to detach two-party politics from labor affiliations. But the Antiguan middle class, as always, proved too small, too weak, and too lacking in self-confidence. Besides, without the AWU, Walter could not possibly succeed. The APM formed the Antigua Political Party, which, after a short life, rejoined the Bird machine: if they could not successfully create a bourgeois politics, they would settle for patronage.

Disillusionment with the AWU and George Walter (on his way to a brief premiership, between spells of Birdism) brought Hector and other mostly young radicals of the Political Action Committee (PAC) to urge a revised course. The main body of Walter's supporters demanded the dissolution of the PAC; the radicals essentially appended their section of the AWU to the Afro-Caribbean Movement (ACM) formed a year earlier, in 1968.[80]

It proved a fateful step for two reasons. First, the keynote of the ACM was the black revolution worldwide, the ways in which the fate of Antiguans was intimately bound up with that of their brothers and sisters from Mother Africa to the rest of the far-flung diaspora of which the Caribbean might well be a leading part. Second, it marked the definitive appearance of Hector as a political leader.

Hector wrote the defining document of the ACM, *The Caribbean: Yesterday Today and Tomorrow*. It was, as Paget Henry concludes, a masterful synthesis of Marxism (James style) and black nationalism. Hector drove home the historical lessons with a Jamesean look at slave uprisings in Antigua and the region. If Jamaican blacks sought to overthrow all property relations in 1841, it was in a quest to form a new society—the task that remained foremost a century and a half later.[81]

The movement had come just in time. The continuing collapse of the old colonial framework and the sudden expansion of power and influence by a tiny (but almost entirely black) elite raised problems of representative government heretofore inadequately understood on the island, and for which the government and the people were equally unprepared. The very development of parliamentarism found the parliamentarians unready, the division of parties based on little more than lining up favors, since Antigua had neither the noxious racialism of Trinidad and Guyana nor the carefully cultivated social democratic traditions of Jamaica, let alone the Communist/labor nexus of Cuban twentieth-century history.

The ACM found itself initially unprepared to reach out to the rural workers, the very black peasantry that Hector was to write about so often. In 1969, ACM cadre from clerical to construction workers and the underemployed helped rural workers cut sugarcane on Sundays; in the following years, others sought to unionize airline workers and bank clerks. None of these efforts were particularly successful. But the ACM and Hector proved themselves positively brilliant at leading ongoing struggles and at holding high the banner of Pan-African internationalism.

There was another reason why the ACM attracted so much support. The opposition to Bird had been sufficient to bring George Walter to power, under an evolving coalition always on the verge of destroying itself with internal squabbling—as it did after 1976, deposing Walter as hopelessly corrupt. (Walter, finally cleared, formed the next major opposition party, the United People's Movement, whose descendent United People's Party would invite in Hector and his supporters.) Only in 1971 did the Bird machine face defeat at the polls. The most promising activity took place outside of the electoral nonevents and the parliamentary structure. Responding to public restlessness, the ruling ALP introduced a Public Order Act, for easy access to martial law; Walter's government, once in power, repealed it as promised but substituted a Newspaper Act with the same repressive intent on the press. The following Bird governments, repealing the Newspaper Act in turn, reintroduced public order acts even more severe. The merry-go-round went round and round.[82]

What was a radical to do? The PAC, before its forced dissolution, offered a view closer to the Vere Bird of 1951 than any before or after, but also clearly inspired by James: "We are making it emphatically clear here and now that we are not affiliated to any party and are not seeking affiliation. . . . We are related to a much more glorious struggle and view politics—particularly in its present form—as a restrictive and narrow system which is as far removed from the needs of the struggling, suffering black masses as the earth is from the heavens."[83] This perspective contained, as Henry said, a different way of looking at the very idea of nationhood. A few years later, in the early 1970s, the ACM localized itself, in a sense, as the Antigua-Caribbean Liberation Movement (notably dropping Mother Africa and adding the Caribbean), setting itself as a movement rather than a party, with the long-range vision of regional unity. It was outside the system but not outside the nation.

Henry, as the key academic observer, was to say later that the ACM and its successors would have done better to focus their discussions of James's texts on the tactical *Party Politics in the West Indies* than on the nearly insurrectionary *Facing Reality*, which dwelt upon a reality (or hope) of fully industrial societies rather than a backward island order. But this was a retrospective judgment. In the days of continuing African revolutions, the Black Panthers in the United States, and the Vietnamese revolution against the most powerful military machine in the world, the sense closer to home grew that the moment for Caribbean unity had to be coming around again.

Hector himself observed that the resurgent energy and will for islanders to come together was hobbled, even before the Grenadian tragedy, by internal divisions and outward betrayals whose perverse logic would become more obvious with the collapse of the Eastern Bloc and the effective shift of China to the capitalist path. A section of the young radicals—more among expatriate intellectuals in Canada and the United States than among West Indians at home—had looked to China for revolutionary world leadership. Maoism, more formally known as "antirevisionism," carried the banner for the pre–Popular Front Communist parties, uncompromising, unliberal, and uninterested in internal democracy. The movement for a New Communist Party (NCP) lasted less than a decade as a real force, but swept away many white New Leftists and a larger proportion of the cadre of Puerto Ricans, Chicanos, Asian Americans, and African Americans on the campuses and in some unions.

When that movement effectively crashed, by the end of the 1970s, it could be seen to have left behind the wreckage of solidarity movements. In all-important Angola, for example, the Maoists (following China) for a time supported one of Africa's worst mass murderers, Jonas Savimbi, who shifted effortlessly into becoming the CIA's chief client in the Southern Cone. Worse for the Caribbean Left by far, though, was the Maoist rage at Castro and the Cuban Communist Party as a preposterously "main enemy" of Third World liberation. Pan-African meetings were disrupted, friendships rended with what one can only assume to be the assistance of CIA agents. And all this in the name of one form of state capitalism over another.

The Russians assuredly added their own poison to the mixture. Just when the young Grenadian Revolution brought Caribbean radicals together and Walter Rodney was challenging the Burnham regime, when the fate of the Jamaican leadership of Manley had not yet been decided— at that moment, the Soviet Union made it known that the time "was not ripe" for its supporters to move swiftly toward regional unity. Why it acted as it did, pushing the Cubans and Jagan's PPP away from the unity effort, remains unclear. Perhaps the focus upon Africa and retaining footholds in Asia against Chinese influence had been viewed as a matter of available resources. More likely, the Russians decided not to challenge the Americans on their home grounds (so to speak) in hopes that the Americans would give them a free pass on their own borders like Afghanistan—a fundamental misreading of U.S. intent. Like the stingy Russian support lent to Salvador Allende in 1972 as he faced the all-out counteroffensive of the CIA, Nelson Rockefeller, and Henry Kissinger, the Russians fought shy. For all their grand talk, they had left radicals in the lurch again.

No wonder Hector and his circle, but especially Hector himself, looked at *Facing Reality*, James's otherwise obscure 1957 document written in the aftermath of the Hungarian Revolution, for insight into process as well as a goal. It was the most syndicalistic or anarchistic treatise of length that James was ever to write. In the shadow of the Hungarian Workers' Councils, James envisioned the capacity and even the readiness of working people to take destiny into their own hands—if only they could rid themselves of the bureaucracy.

CHAPTER FOUR

The Great Moment Passed By

T he assassination of Walter Rodney in Guyana in 1979 following decades of turmoil there, Michael Manley's halted experiment in Jamaica of the 1970s, the coup in and subsequent invasion of Grenada, and the demoralization of the Caribbean Left to follow can all be seen as the context of Hector's own life and struggles. They are, at any rate, intimate to the struggles of unionists in Trinidad, interracial egalitarians in Guyana, and the suppression of Liberation Theology, along with the defeat of the Central American wave of revolution and the political-labor mobilization in Hector's own Antigua.

One event, so brief and yet so remarkable that it continues to puzzle scholars (to say nothing of its participants) thirty-some years later, dramatized all this, years before Maurice Bishop and his followers took power in Grenada. At the carnival in Trinidad in 1970, radicalized University of West Indies (UWI) students cheered as calypso bands held up pictures of H. Rap Brown and Stokely Carmichael and lofted the hated images of King Sugar and "white devils." The "black bourgeoisie" (in Trinidad, as in Jamaica, more likely to be brown) grew more nervous by the day, when student demonstrations and a Black Power march brought a rebellion in the army sent to quell them. Under different circumstances, it would have been a revolutionary situation. Proof of Pan-Africanism and of the vital role of Caribbean students abroad could be seen in the incipient cause for demonstration: Canadian authorities rushing sit-ins for Black Studies at Sir George Williams University in Toronto. It was, for young people back in the home islands but especially in Trinidad, the counterpart of the Kent State/Jackson State killings of students during the massive protests against Richard Nixon's invasion of Cambodia. Reacting in solidarity, they had lit the fuse of a Trinidad restless of promises made by another Williams, their own "Doctor" Eric, slipping downward from the pedestal that held him during the late colonial era.[1]

Counting on the enmity of East Indians to Black Power, Williams declared a state of emergency and brought in U.S. troops against his own people. Only a blockade of rebels from leaving the Chaguarmas Peninsula that he himself had marched on only a decade earlier, demanding the removal of U.S. troops, ended the threat. Then things died away so quickly that the moment seemed never to have existed at all. How had Williams survived? James liked to say, "just three letters, O-I-L."

The mutual mistrust between the students and the Trinidadian army, making combined actions impossible, was in a sense a demonstration of the weakness of the New Left Caribbean politics drawn closest to James and the hopes for a nearly spontaneous overthrow of neocolonialism. Out of the energy of 1970, matching Black Power and disillusionment with independence, came forum groups in the Windward Islands similar to Abeng; the left-wing newspapers *Tapia* and *Moko* published shortly in Trinidad, *Amandla* in Belize, and *Ratoon* in Guyana, all roughly similar to the *Outlet* and the Antigua-Caribbean Liberation Movement (ACLM). All were relatively short-lived, from intellectual formations that had difficulty setting down the institutional roots and commercial contacts needed for long-term survival. They also lacked Tim Hector, no small factor in the Antiguan Left's tenacity.

The difficulties suffered by these groups in making sustained contacts with working-class constituencies were exemplified by the best case. The support of the United Labour Front (ULF) by the Oilfield Workers Trade Union's (OWTU) in 1973 was followed four years later by a split and by leader George Weekes's participation in the coalition National Alliance for Reconstruction (NAR) government. With Bukka Rennie at the helm, the oil-field workers' paper, the *Vanguard*, remained in some respects quite a revolutionary paper as well as the practical-minded organ of the union.

But here things practically came to a halt in the radical politics of Trinidad and Tobago, and only partly because the sharp rise of oil prices in 1973–74 brought Williams and respite. A vogue in the themes of "vanguard" politics, with Trinidadian Maoists and Moscow-leaning Marxist-Leninists, seemed to turn Left politics backward.[2] The connections between Jamaican bauxite workers and the Workers Party of Jamaica (WJP) also marked a return to cold war terms, the Russian anti-imperialist camp envisioned against the Americans, with the People's National Party (PNP) inevitably defending the latter notwithstanding Richard Nixon, the Vietnam War, and the assorted corporate aims in Jamaica. A misalliance of Marxists and Rastafarians offered a parallel and more important example of black nationalism halted before its aspirations could be realized.

Walter Rodney's articulation of the connections in *Grounding with My Brothers* and many speeches and articles made sense, as far as possible, of the Rastas' rejection of "politricks" based on their own class experience, their struggle to initiate an African sensibility and pride to every gesture of collective self-including the right of children to attend school, groomed in their own fashion. He also spearheaded the encouragement by male intellectuals for Caribbean women's advance into selfhood.

In a later era when the Afro, Rasta braids, and cornrows could only be seen as style statements, it was easily forgotten what challenges such shifts in sensibilities first posed, a veritable reversal of the collective self-rejection that had marked the entire slave and postslave experience. The abandonment of the internalized color standards by which light was right (or as right as can be) and black, with the exception of black with plenty of money, was wrong for social status or marriage, intertwined with these impulses. So did the adoption of African names and dress. The rapid spread of Rastafarianism across the Afro-Caribbean, and the anxiety-filled response of various authorities, none prepared to use the energy of these young people rather than denying it, was a popular theme of Caribbean singers like Black Stalin, Jimmy Cliff (himself utterly opposed to the use of drugs), and a host of others.[3]

The dynamic tension could not be sustained. The seizure of the Rasta symbols and large expanses of Jamaican agricultural space by U.S. whites under the cover of the Ethiopian Zion Coptic Church, actually growing vast quantities of marijuana, offered a painful reminder of neocolonialism under new colors, and the extension of the tourist (drug as well as sex) economy in place of any self-sustaining possibility.

If the Trinidadian near-insurrection of 1970 had seemed to open an era, Walter Rodney's assassination, so heart-breaking to James, Hector, and others across the Pan-African movement, seemed in retrospect to have slammed it shut. Perhaps the possibility that the region could come out from under the vicelike American grip was never realistic, when so-called regional training institutes conducted by such scarcely disguised Central Intelligence Agency (CIA) outlets as the AFL-CIO's American Institute for Free Labor Development (AIFLD) and the Caribbean Congress of Labor operated openly in Barbados's "Unity House."[4] Then again, American capitalism and its global reach might flag, as seemed apparent during much of the later 1970s and again in the early years of Reaganism, offering new prospects for real independence.

Hector later dwelled repeatedly upon his own mid-1960s insistence that Rodney go back to Guyana. Perhaps he felt a degree of guilt, although it was five years before the assassination. But perhaps it was because that telephone argument was the passionate exchange of two figures who might easily have exchanged roles, had each been born in the other's place. Hector was prone to speculate that Rodney returning to Guyana before 1974 might have created a different conjunction of forces there, obverting the assassination. Perhaps, though it is unlikely.

Rodney's Guyana

Hector heard the dreaded news of Rodney's assassination from Conrad Luke, waking him up from bed. "Numbed for once overwhelmed by this mountain tide of Barbarism," he suddenly recalled Guyanese poet Martin Carter's lines, "This I have learnt/today a speck/tomorrow a hero . . . all are involved/all are consumed," and added, "I felt consumed," having considered political assassination as something that happened in the Spanish-speaking Caribbean but not in his own sector. And indeed, it had been most rare, even in societies where the lower classes had been brutalized by centuries of poverty and lack of opportunity, and where the political violence in Jamaica (consuming no leaders) shocked the region.[5]

Hector and Rodney had boldly agreed to set out on a project, far-reaching in scope. They sought to recuperate the Caribbean Federation, beginning with a definitive response to the challenge of Sir Arthur Lewis to grasp how (in Lewis's words) "these highly intelligent men, all devoted to federation, [came] to make so many errors in so short a period."[6] The two radical youngsters were to divide the task between themselves, Rodney examining the role of the individual in history and in the Caribbean, Hector specifically destroying the myths of islandhood, including the crucial one hurled by Trinidad and Jamaica that the big islands would inevitably beggar themselves for the sake of the small. (James had put the matter more simply: the islands had been joined only through London, but for them to be joined with each other meant that they directed their own collective economy, removing outside control; that, they would not risk doing.)[7] The story of disintegration would thus be told fully, accurately. But Hector had begged off, postponed the project, overmodestly considering the role of any two intellectuals, as intellectuals, to be insufficiently pressing. "I confess now, too, that he was right and I was dead wrong. As wrong as wrong can be." Without grasping the underlying trends, the causes of fearful retrogression could not be traced or understood.[8]

Rodney, working on his own and drawing greatly from James (but also from DuBois and E. P. Thompson), had, at any rate, seen the clearest, understandably given his circumstance among self-proclaimed socialists, that the new elite with no real basis in production had made themselves a political class and had to remain in power so as to exist and flourish. Official corruption was practically mandatory in order to build a lasting machine and to rationalize the sorry fact that "economic growth" did not seem to benefit the working classes, or even the merchants out of government. Nor did it truly repatriate national wealth from the foreign investors, who cut their own corrupt deals with the government. Political leaders increasingly turned toward the most conservative elements, those who had opposed independence, for loyal support, thrusting aside the tested radicals for all the most obvious reasons.[9]

For these reasons, Rodney ruled out the alliance with Jagan that, Hector insisted, might have made the decisive difference. He had other reasons as well. A regional gathering of Latin American and Caribbean Communist parties, few as the latter were, had closed with a declaration urging Communists to support regimes expressing solidarity with the anti-imperialist struggle. It was a familiar position, echoing the Popular Front of the 1930s and the armed struggle against fascism in the 1940s, allowing Communists to support the presumably progressive sector of the local bourgeoisie. Even Jagan seemed to submit, when Havana and Moscow analyzed Guyana as led by two progressive anti-imperialist parties, one of them dominant. (The open hand of friendship did no good; Burnham had no intention of a serious dialogue with Jagan or anyone else who might threaten his power.) At the risk of appearing "ultraleftist" in the eyes of radicals in the region and elsewhere, Rodney insisted that the masses were ready for greater changes. Pseudo-socialism, whatever it international identifications, was only an obstacle.[10]

Having hog-tied Jagan for the moment, Burnham saw the return of Rodney as a special menace. The Association for Social and Cultural Relations with Independent Africa (ASCIRA) and its outstanding leader, Eusi Kwayana, mobilized public support when Burnham attempted to prevent Rodney from accepting a position at the University of Guyana. Rodney also affirmed his alliance with the Guyanese New Left Ratoon group and even sat down to discuss prospects with Jagan. Drawing conclusions from Fanon's *Wretched of the Earth*, he argued that the petite-bourgeoisie (as a class, not as any specific ethnic identity) was strangling transformation; it was a thesis that James had argued, in the deepest philosophical terms, long before Fanon set pen to paper.[11]

Burnham, as various observers (but Andrew Salkey the most perceptive) noted, was more clever than Jagan, admired by the Guyanese for his brilliance if they could not entirely grasp the dark side to his capacity to maneuver. Once secured in power with CIA assistance, he bought time restructuring state machinery, exerting precise power of privileges, sometimes individual by individual as the FBI had done in 1950s America, even denying professionals the permits to work and travel as a political choice. Then he proceeded to clamp down on those Afro-Caribbean radicals, Pan-Africans, and black trade unionists who might create a separate power base. By the middle 1970s, his police would search the homes of political opponents on a regular basis. Kidnappings, shootings, restrictions on importation of newsprint for opposition newspapers, and violent break-ups of street and hall meetings provided backups for the normal sort of ballot-stuffing seen from Chicago to Argentina. That Burnham accompanied all this with declarations of anti-imperialism while insisting that Jagan and the People's Progressive Party (PPP) were part of the global Communist movement (and, more to the point, if Jagan were to return to power, West Indians would be badly punished) all demonstrated Burnham's perverse brilliance. No Caribbean leader, not even Castro, held a society with more power in his own hands, amid continued unrest.[12]

Thus the Working People's Alliance (WPA), founded in 1975, provided Rodney with the organizational collective energy, political and intellectual, to grapple with the tasks at hand. Led by himself and Eusi Kwayana, it sought to break down the racialism of Guyanese politics, to distance its vision of socialism from identification with any existing state (even Cuba, but most especially the Soviet Union, which provided real benefits to the People's National Congress [PNC] and to the WJP). Writing as its foremost thinker, Rodney was clearest on issues of democracy: no socialism could come into existence without the participation of ordinary people, more than going to the ballot box, more than simply the right to protest and express themselves. Censorship had no place, not even for a revolutionary government (like Maurice Bishop's).

Rodney also emphasized self-empowerment, himself leading study classes that emphasized independent thinking instead of slogans. And he emphasized links to working-class life, establishing connections with the bauxite workers, giving study classes, staying with miners' families. In both these directions, Rodney was the James that James himself could not be—but he was also the Hector, in a situation more complex but also more promising than one-party Antigua.

The crunch came to Burnham with his determination to change the Guyanese constitution without resort to a referendum. The PPP, WPA, and political, citizens', labor, religious, and other civic organizations formed an alliance but could not overcome the power of Burnham. A paltry 15 percent at most had bothered to vote, while Burnham was fully prepared to use force against Afro-Caribbeans as well as others. The linkage of Burnham's circles with the People's Temple and the Jonestown tragedy of 1978 underscored the corruption, even as the U.S. government expressed its collective horror and declined to condemn Burnham himself.

The spread of strikes among bauxite and government workers, along with an election boycott in 1979, prompted a growing sense of crisis. Rodney declared that a revolutionary situation was close; Jagan, always the parliamentarist, warned against premature action and, in effect, against Rodney as adventurist. A crowd burned down PNC headquarters, and Burnham responded by arresting the WPA leaders, who used their bail period before the trial to beseech large crowds. The WPA made a great point of its rotating leadership, Rodney adamantly refusing, despite his high intellectual status, to be exalted as another Jagan, Manley, or Burnham.

The prime minister's continued perverse brilliance was on display as he urged support for Maurice Bishop and had his army train the New Jewel cadre (some of whom, no doubt, would shoot Bishop three years later). Burnham also refrained from attacking Jagan in more than words while his thugs began a reign of terror against Rodney's supporters in 1979. In the pamphlet *People's Power, No Dictatorship*, Rodney assailed the "dictatorship" that has "reduced us all to such a level that the situation can be described only in terms befitting filth, pollution and excrement."[13] Words do not break bones. But Rodney's and the WPA's growing appeal to Afro-Caribbeans sick of Burnham was genuinely threatening. Repeated threats and arrests prompted James, from Washington, D.C., where he was teaching, to issue dire warnings, telling Rodney's comrades to protect the man against assassination. The warnings were in vain for several reasons that a grief-stricken James shortly elucidated.

First, he wrote, Rodney had not "studied the taking of power," had not grasped that the weapons to take power already existed—in the hands of the police and army, military forces that had to be won over or at least thoroughly demoralized. A seizure of power could also take place successfully only when the masses themselves were ready. The Guyanese, in James's assessment, were not. That very unreadiness, he asserted (and on good evidence), prompted Rodney, with a martial spirit, to become reckless enough to take chances; he was not going to ask anyone to do what he himself would not do.[14] His final mistake was his credulous trust in the lumpen proletariat, one of them in particular, a Burnham agent and ex-soldier in whom Rodney typically saw unrealized potential. The true potential lay in convincing Rodney to use a walkie-talkie containing a small bomb, setting off a blast that instantly killed Walter and wounded his brother, Donald.

Whether CIA involvement was direct or indirect may never be known. His assassin was flown secretly to French Guiana, and Burnham meanwhile declared Rodney either was on his way to blow up a jail or had committed suicide. A crowd of thirty-five thousand marched in Georgetown, and laments could be heard around the world. Decades later, Rodney would be posthumously awarded the highest honors of the Guyanese state. The harm, however, had been done.[15]

Social Democracy Manley-Style

"Prince of the Pauper's Struggle," Hector called Michael Manley, casting him more personally than observers from near or far normally could, rating him among contemporary Caribbean leaders only with Castro, among world figures with Nyerere and Willy Brandt.[16] It was a curious pantheon, but Manley and Willy Brandt, at least, had something important in common: they were the two great figures that the revived Socialist International—made up mostly of Scandinavian parties in power and others mostly out of power—could boast during the late cold war–era crisis. Practically discredited in Europe but still vital in Asia, Africa, and parts of Latin America, especially Cuba, Communists were transformed into a contradictory global combination of East Bloc bureaucratic rule and support network for Third World movements. They backed movements loyal to Russia, sometimes altogether repressive groups and leaders, but sometimes (as in South Africa and Vietnam) the best forces on hand.

Socialists meanwhile maintained their own ambivalence. In shunning communism, they often became the whipped curs of American domination. But an array of issues and prospects had revived them, absorbing parts of a collapsed New Left in the United States, France, Germany, and scattered other parts of the world. They could win elections at least, work with unions, provide detailed policy statements and programs, and make themselves ready for a role in a further deflated capitalism that might come.

Michael Manley was their singular champion. The vice president of the Socialist International, he led that movement from a past of paternalism at best—and support of U.S. aggression against the Third World at worst—into supporting the African National Congress (ANC) against apartheid. He led it not passively, with empty sympathy, but actively in world forums, and with money. Likewise in Angola, likewise in Zimbabwe, likewise in Zaire, likewise in so many other places where black people in particular were desperately trying to wrest their freedom from colonial and neocolonial hands, the Socialist International, with all its weaknesses, made a difference.

Manley was carrying a burden that Hector described with intense sympathy, the nonrevolutionary socialist who sincerely believed that the common mass would rise to rule.[17] Son of the most famous sculptor as well as the most famous politician and sportsman in Jamaica, he had rejected the boarding school life, studied in Britain but dropped out of college after a year, searching for himself and finding clues in Beethoven more than in politics or economics. He could write with equal fluency on boxing and cricket, painting and science. He was also, according to Hector, the most cultivated person ever to devote himself to Caribbean labor.[18]

Manley was therefore something almost new in political leaders of the region: a masterful literary figure. True, Eric Williams was a masterful historian and true scholar. But Manley, whose volumes on cricket history could stand the test even of James's *Beyond a Boundary* (or Hilary Beckels's most scholarly treatises), conducted masterful overviews of economic development and projects for changes that, with different global conditions, he might have carried out. His *Politics of Change* (1972) can be read

therefore as a nationalist manifesto, bringing the middle class and working class together with the most farsighted of capitalists to decolonialize
the country, ease the widening gaps between rich and poor, and contribute
to a democratic globalism.

Perhaps there was never a chance that the Jamaican industrialists
would stay with him or that the middle class could not be scared off in
the usual Red-baiting fashion even when Manley's proposals and activities
were modest and unthreatening. The accomplishments of Manley's first
years in office were, considering the long-delayed improvements in social
services, simply tremendous. Women gained equal pay for equal work,
with a significant maternity leave (and the old bastardy laws eased out);
education, including school food programs, was drastically improved;
some idle lands were transferred to the poor; housing was provided on a
scale never previously imagined let alone built; adult education accelerated; and the bauxite levy was dramatically increased, gaining Manley's
government the resources to promote its other programs.

But with the vigorous assistance of the U.S. State Department and
the CIA, the U.S. press and its followers abroad, the "threat of socialism" (more absurdly, the "threat of communism") remained the bogey
to terrify the Jamaican rich and middle classes, as always. Moreover, the
"brain drain" hit more dramatically in Jamaica than anywhere else in
the region, save Puerto Rico. The light-skinned Jamaican professionals, empowered by the change of U.S. immigration policies in 1965 and
welcomed by a booming community of relatives in Queens, New York;
Hartford, Connecticut; Toronto; and other places, lit out for a better
living. Had they not wanted to leave anyway, they were terrified by something more real than the threat of communism: the reality of violence,
perhaps stoked by the CIA, certainly worsened by the drug trade, but
also acted out directly, for political gain, by the Jamaica Labour Party
(JLP), including officials at its highest levels. It could not be forgotten
that the more moderate Norman Manley's promotion of the West Indies
Federal Labour Party, as a vehicle of regional integration, had been sav-
agely and successfully attacked by Alexander Bustamante less than fifteen
years earlier. Bustamante was gone, but the JLP had never changed its
stripes.

Michael Manley answered outrage with a warning to his own members not to strike back and successfully swept the December 1976 elections. Now the fat was in the fire, along with the treasury, and in accommodating to the International Monetary Fund (IMF) as he felt he had to do, the prime minister doomed himself at home. He therefore bought time, sympathetic observers would claim, so as to conduct the great work he had lately undertaken abroad. It was the final historical moment of the Non-Aligned Movement begun with such great hopes (and against which Washington plotted so continuously) at the Bandung Conference in 1955 in his father's time. Michael Manley made himself almost a one-man bridge between those nonaligned nations and the Socialist International's leading Scandinavian parties. He meanwhile maintained closer relations with the Cuban government as a point of regional pride and dignity, despite the continuous denunciations at home and most especially in Washington.

But fresh assaults by the JLP made the country almost ungovernable, and Manley's day was suddenly over as the Reagan era ramped up with a massive military invasion of Central America. Manley's return to power in the 1989 elections found him virtually prostrate to IMF demands—much as Cheddi Jagan a few years later—while striving to defend the near accomplishments of land reform and worker participation. He as much as admitted that so many more, like access of the world press to the nonwealthy, had been halted and reversed by the powerful. Neoliberalism had soon shown its failure, and the JLP's Edward Seaga departed a hated political symbol of Jamaica's shame and its defeat. But Michael Manley had tried. In his own defense on a crucial point, Manley had written in 1992 that the "New International Economic Order" that he had so highly valued had been killed by the determination of Ronald Reagan and his handlers to end any cooperative relation of global North and South.[19]

From Hector's point of view, Michael Manley was a Caribbean personality par excellence, the well-rounded, modest, fluent intellectual and dedicated public servant. After him, the same PNP would dominate politics again and again, mainly in the person of P. J. Patterson. No matter. For the era, the best moments were really over.

Grenadian Catastrophe

When an elderly C.L.R. James, living in London, first heard the news of the coup against Maurice Bishop, Bishop's assassination, and the invasion of U.S. Marines, he could not believe his ears. He thought perhaps the news was a false report, in tune with so many others from Washington (and elsewhere) in those days, as well as before, during and after the cold war. Sad to say, it was all too true, if filtered inevitably through ideological lenses. Hector frequently thereafter sought to depict the murderous coup supported by Bernard Coard and (if more ambiguously) the WJP as proof positive of the Vanguard Party model's failure.[20] On the other hand, he steadily portrayed Bishop as a martyr for the region, and not only that: a fellow devotee of James.

Grenada's New Jewel Movement (NJM) and People's Revolutionary Government were important from another respect, fully appreciated by Hector. The Soviet Union was still very much a superpower, if a faltering one, and the State Department ideologues—far more than the Kremlin's planners—envisioned a Russian base on the little Caribbean island. Resistance to Washington's all-out control of the region that its troops had invaded so often since the mid-nineteenth century had the stamp of popular support, very high for Bishop and his government at the moment of the counterrevolution and even after. The fact that Bishop and his circle (including Coard, at an early point) were separated from the mass of the island's population by education and other advantages was only typical, as typical as the one-man nature of revolutionary symbolism.

Dating back to the cold war years and the intensification of peasant suffering, the radical temperament saw an all-island uprising in February 1951, with the torching of big estates and physical attacks upon the servants of the ruling class. Vere Bird's leadership had perhaps kept the same pattern from spreading in contemporary (but considerably more urbanized) Antigua, turning rage into labor politics. Not so in Grenada. Like St. Lucia, St. Vincent, and Dominica, among others, it lacked the terrain for sugar plantations. Cocoa planters, educated abroad, reputedly did not even understand the patois of their workers, who lived in something resembling the relations of European feudalism. The middle class was so tiny that the number of physicians or first-class lawyers could be counted on the fingers of both hands. Important decisions were made from London anyway.

The Second World War had lifted cocoa prices temporarily and brought the same kind of prosperity to Grenada as to Antigua: wage work for the Yankees, in this case the oil refineries of Aruba and Trinidad and the building of a U.S. base at Chaguarmas. Grenadian workers returning home—Trinidad actually prevented them from staying—found themselves unemployed and restless. Moreover, many had acquired the radical spirit of Trinidad and Tobago's oil-field workers, led by none other than Grenada-born Tubul Uriah "Buzz" Butler.

Enraged peasants did not think to appeal to T. A. Marryshaw, the one nationalist intellectual of regionwide reputation, but also the son of a light-skinned elite as distant from them as anyone can be on a small island. Instead, they chose one of their own: Eric Gairy, the son of a rural plantation-overseer, shop steward in the Aruba fields, and public defender of tenants deprived of traditional rights by a new British cocoa owner. This small victory (not so small: the $3,000 compensation to former tenants was a considerable amount of cash for these people) allowed Gairy to found the Grenada Manual and Mental Workers Union (GMMWU), leading the first islandwide strike, one that touched off the rioting.

British troops arrived by ship and occupied the capital, as so often in colonial history. Weakened by this time, however, the British desperately sought a compromise between the plantocracy and the workers, compelling a recognition of the GMMWU. Gairy's own Grenada United Labor Party overwhelmed all opposition in the first election with universal suffrage. This election set a new pattern in place for more than a quarter century: on the one side, terribly traditional planters who considered any resistance to their rule as "communistic" and as intolerable as one of their waiters sitting down to dinner with them; on the other side, Gairy, who spoke proudly if not knowledgably of "God, Marx and the British Empire" as the sources of his always-uncertain ideology.

Gairy had no driving interest in educating the masses and no plan to transform the economy. He sought mainly the consolidation of his personal machine, by way of minimizing the influence of civil servants who apparently stood in his way. The small-scale development of black capitalism, linked to government subsidies, was "crony capitalism," quid pro quo with his friends. Investigations into his actions brought down his government in 1962, for a short-lived middle-class substitute linked intimately to the planters. By 1967, with the empire further weakened, Gairy won again. But his "Land to the Landless" promises, never seriously attempted, did not satisfy, in part because rising costs of living had outstripped any gains made by ordinary Grenadians. Gairy sought to make book on the regional Black Power surge, but he feared its consequences so much that following the demonstrations in Trinidad, he declared on radio that he had secured his own army of toughs to defend law and order.

What Gairy most feared was readily apparent and, in retrospect, also irreversible. An increase in young educated people, in the current political climate, made possible a cross-class movement to transform society. A nurses' strike in late 1970 showed that it would be women along with men, often leading them. The chief factors that he feared were exemplified in three graduates of the Grenada School for Boys or the Presentation College, and education in the United States or United Kingdom from which they returned: Maurice Bishop, Kendrick Radix, and Bernard Coard.

Gairy precipitated the revolutionary "rehearsal" by rigging the elections of 1972, defeating the middle-class Grenada National Party, whose modest program belied (it would appear later) the young radicals in its ranks swept aside by Gairy's election machine. At this point the British essentially quit, washing their hands of the final stages of independence. In 1973, the Joint Endeavor for Welfare, Education and Liberation (JEWEL) merged with the Movement for Assemblies of the People (MAP) into the NJM. Its clear leader was Bishop, who had studied law in Britain. His fellow radicals were, with virtually no exception, the educated elite.[21]

Bishop, as Hector would recall, had been born in Aruba, son of a small businessman who had temporarily immigrated there and from which he returned as the head of a commission agency. Known as a brilliant student, Bishop was college president of the historical club, debate team, and student council and the school newspaper editor. He worked for the civil service after graduation for a year and then departed to Britain, where he took a law degree in 1966 and made a slight living as a tax surveyor. The influence of the civil rights movement, and his own service to the West Indian community in London providing free legal services, propelled him in the direction of an all-Caribbean nationhood. He was deeply influenced by the Black Power movement in the United States, by the Cuban experiment, by African events, and by the 1970 revolt in Trinidad. For Hector, the Movement for the Assemblies of the People was Maurice Bishop personified, but also the logical opposite of Gairy the buffoon, the brute, and toady to the British and the Americans in ensuring no rule from below would be possible.[22]

At any rate, the group around Bishop was at the very least a unique elite. The MAP had been deeply influenced by the Left in Trinidad (unlike Coard, who had spent his vital political time in Jamaica) and had a mixture of black nationalism and antibureaucratic politics heavily influenced by C.L.R. James. The "People's Trial" staged in January 1974 by JEWEL and MAP against a particularly haughty plantation owner brought some eight hundred Grenadians to his estate, where he had denied the historic rights of beach access to locals. A mobilization blocking the national airport a few months later, a Peoples Convention on Independence with almost a third of the island's population of fifty thousand in attendance, and a People's Congress with ten thousand on hand calling on Gairy to resign climaxed in a call for a general strike. Gairy reacted with rage, ordering an attack on NJM leaders, beating them (including a murderous attack on Bishop's father, seeking to defend women and children from a police assault), and then denying them medical access.

Some commentators were to suggest later that a successful revolution in 1974 would have made the later tragic events drastically less likely. It would be hard to say, given the determination of the United States to uproot any and all regional threats. But the inability of NJM to draw the island's trade unionists organically into the struggle, the anxiety of the middle classes that prompted urgings for negotiations (ruling out the radicals of NJM), and the capacity of the wily Gairy to meet supreme political challenges by declaring independence in February 1974 closed out the crisis by ending the strikes and business lockdowns.[23]

The revolutionaries essentially used Black Power, so successfully exploited by Gairy, against him more and more effectively from 1974 onward. But after the defeat of the strikes and mobilization, the over-throw of the social democratic (if nominally Communist-influenced) Allende regime in Chile, and the floundering of Manley's Jamaican experiment, the internal weaknesses of the Grenadian Left were interpreted as a lack of will and discipline, that is to say, of Leninism. The fears of "communism" by islanders (less than ten years earlier, a majority heavily favored remaining imperial subject.) intensified the feeling that ideological talk had to be kept secret, in the hands of something like a Central Committee. Because none of the future Grenadian leaders had anything like a deep background in Marxism, revolutionary vision often came down to "leadership," minus the nuance and long view of history that a C.L.R. James could have supplied. Ironically, Bernard Coard's return to Grenada as a would-be Leninist may have prompted a wise strategic decision (in the well-trod Communist strategy of revolutionary "stages") to support a new moderate opposition, the United Progressive Party (UPP). Notwithstanding irregularities, the Alliance did well, and Bishop emerged as its outstanding leader.

The Grenadian Revolution, its form hardly anticipated by the NJM, took place only a few weeks before the overthrow of the Somoza government in Nicaragua, and the timing may have been crucial. Jimmy Carter had only begun hardening his positions and retained a human rights rhetoric that held open the possibility for a different world picture than one present only a few years later. Gairy moved to arrest the opposition and personally took a plane to New York, leaving the dirty work to his followers. The NJM, carefully planning for this situation in advance, led a tiny force of forty-six against the military barracks. No one opposed them. But it was also true that the revolution had been carried out from above. Even in a tiny country, the size of the NJM was amazingly small: estimated at no more than fifty.

What to do in power? The response of ordinary Grenadians and of nationalist-minded Caribbean citizens, abroad in the United Kingdom, United States, and Canada, was jubilant. Gairy, egged on by the CIA, obviously wanted to return and rule. Small-scale terrorist actions succeeded only in intensifying Bishop's popularity. Repeatedly postponing elections proved to be a major error. But the election of Ronald Reagan clearly signaled Washington's intention to get rid of the NJM government one way or another.

The first years of any revolutionary government are bound to be confusing and contradictory, but NJM rule was unique for obvious reasons. Grenada could not introduce "socialism," not even as the larger, more modern version of Cuba had introduced state socialism. It had to improve living conditions rapidly, and actually did so through public works programs largely funded by the Soviet Union, Cuba, and Libya, but also by Canada and the United Kingdom. Child care, housing, and education reached goals all but unimaginable previously. A constitution was drafted by none other than that redoubtable veteran of the Jamaican Left, Richard Hart.²⁴ Yet the government—like so many others of different complexions in the region—hitched its real star to tourism and the creation of a new airport. With Reagan in the White House cursing the revolutionaries, tourists were not likely to flood the tiny Caribbean island farther away by air from Miami than practically any other.

On the other hand, Bishop's pronouncements were more democratic, more sweeping, and more akin to C.L.R. James's vision of a Caribbean government guided by the popular will than anything yet seen in a prime minister. Bishop's role in the region's Left likewise loomed as large as the island and its population was small. He expressed visions of self-rule and of a revived federation that a mixture of British paternal tradition, U.S. neocolonialism (growing stronger by the year, with the retreat of the British), and interracial conflicts had ruled out elsewhere. In practice, as Hart recalled later, the aspiration for mass participation in government brought results varying widely from general meetings at which broad decisions could be made, to constitutional protection of common thieves certain to be treated harshly in their own communities.

The terminal crisis was set off when Coard, as ideological center of the NJM, resigned in a pique at the overwhelming identification of the revolution with Bishop. Any vision of "joint leadership," with a sharing of political and administrative leadership, had thus failed. What we know for certain about the calamitous events to follow is that during Bishop's absence from the island on a state visit to Eastern Europe, the prime minister had resolved to go over the head of the party leadership (as Lenin and Mao had done at various stages) to the people themselves. Coard and the NJM's Central Committee inner circle set themselves to resist what they viewed as a sort of coup. Landing on the island (and although warned ahead of time by the Cubans), Bishop faced arrest. A crowd acting spontaneously freed him and marched on a garrison, where a platoon of soldiers apparently loyal to the Central Committee (meaning Bernard Coard, above all) recaptured him and put him and two others against a wall and shot them point blank. The evidence surrounding the event remains doubtful, all these years later, because so much CIA and U.S. military work went into obscuring it. But even so, the calamitous series of events was something that could never have happened to Castro—not even from Cuba's none-too-supportive Communist Party—emerging from the bush at the head of the army and placing his brother in charge of the military.[25]

Writing in the immediate aftermath, in one of the most solemn essays that he was ever to put on paper, Hector assayed the entire Greek-like tragedy. He recalled that when the crisis was about to erupt, "I hoped against hope, that he would survive, that he would triumph. . . . I knew for sure that if he triumphed over his political enemies . . . that Caribbean and maybe even world history would take a new and upward leap."[26] Bishop had sought to provide avenues for the masses to rule more directly, but he had been too much the lawyer and orator, too little the organizer, to see what had to be done, let alone how to do it. Instead, he stumbled.

Bishop had sought consensus of the party around the revised program of empowerment. Hector believed that Coard was determined to achieve a bureaucratic collectivism on the East Bloc model—a tendency that Hector had carefully noted at the Intellectual Workers Conference when a Jamaican representative of the WJP insisted upon the didactic rallying songs of his organization, rather than the popular works of Bob Marley and others as the "true" music of the island (and region). Novelist Earl Lovelace had risen to object, and the room grew tense. The following day, George Lamming gave a deliberate analysis of socialism and regional culture against the specter of Stalinism.

Soon after, Hector warned Bishop pointedly about the direction of the NJM. Bishop shrugged it off, unable to see the danger. If East (represented in the then-recent Russian suppression of Solidarity in Poland) and West had alike no intention of permitting the masses to take power, then "Grenada was David, minus slingshot, but firmly pitted against the Goliath," was the reality of global power politics. It had perhaps been too much to expect a socialistic experiment on a tiny island to succeed. Efforts at propaganda victories notwithstanding, both global superpowers were happy to see the Grenadian Revolution, and all that it would signify, destroyed.[27] As he wrote later, knowing that Samora Machel, heroic guerrilla leader and a founder of independent Mozamabique, had died in the same month as the Grenadian counterrevolution, "October, then, is the cruelest month for me."[28]

And not only for Hector, of course. Of all the Caribbean trade unionists that C.L.R. James admired, none had his heart so fully set on Grenada as George Weekes of Trinidad's OWTU. Weekes had personally addressed mass rallies in happier days of Grenada, had in some ways served almost as a father figure for Bishop and others of the next generation. He initiated a memorial service at the Anglican Cathedral in December 1983, attended by Hector and by many of Bishop's colleagues free to travel to Trinidad and Tobago. Weekes resigned his own office, taking retirement, just a year after the tragic events. His successors, above all David Abdullah as educational director of the OWTU, were able militants. But with that retirement, an era had nevertheless truly ended for the Caribbean Left, personally connected on one hand to the postwar years and on the other to the approaching twenty-first century.[29] "The equation on which transformation of Caribbean society hinges," Hector insisted, "is how to give power to the people, and by a process of mass political education ensure that power of the people in Council supplants the power of the old State." Nothing less could be revolutionary change, and nothing would change that equation.[30]

Other radicals close to Hector but more fortunate in family background or political circumstance played inside straights even as revolutionary prospects dimmed. Rosie Douglas, Hector's intimate friend from Canada days, had followed his own father and brother into the politics of Dominica. First forming the radical Popular Independence Committee in 1975 young Rosie defected to the family Labour Party in 1980. From there he could climb upward to power. George Odlum, older by almost a decade than Hector, found a similar home, if not a comfortable one, in the St. Lucian Labour Party, rising first to foreign minister in 1979. The youngest of these rising leaders, Ralph Gonsalves, was a natural for the Labour Party of St. Vincent and the Grenadians, rising like Douglas to prime minister but with the health to enjoy years of influence. Hector's island was not the poorest of these economically, but it had by far the most impoverished politics.

On Home Ground

From practically the day of his return, Hector's star was rising, shining all the way up toward the heavens. From Canada, he had been writing for the *Antigua Star* and the *Workers' Voice* stories about the civil rights movements in Yankeeland and even further, also about campus agitation, sometimes about Caribbean culture. When the project for a renewed Pan-African Congress movement fell through and Vere Bird expelled George Walter from the Antigua Trades and Labour Union (AT&LU)—hence, from the government and into a likely volatile opposition—Hector's decision and his life's plan, in effect, were set in place. In a large part of that plan, he married Arah Weekes, whom (inevitably on such a small island) he had known since youth and wooed from abroad. They set out together on a family life interrupted constantly by work and often by poverty but also marked with the greatest good fellowship and mutual admiration.

The conjunction of events was auspicious in several ways. Walter led the formation of the Antigua Workers Union, the first important independent (independent, that is, of the leading party) labor organization in the colony's history. The union soon formed its own political party, not only seeking a potential grasp for power but out of necessity to defend itself: the Progressive Labour Movement (PLM). Newly arrived, Hector was the hands-down choice for its chair and for editor of its newsletter, the *Trumpet*.

Here, perhaps, Hector was realizing the destiny waiting for him. No Antigua newspaper had to this point dared attack Bird's corruption directly. On other islands where the more numerous whites and Creoles had formed conservative parties and held to them, through decades of labor-oriented political domination, the conservative forces had been fretful but held economic influence as their trump card. In Antigua, they counted instead upon their own influence on Bird, who, notwithstanding both race and nationalist rhetoric, served their interests in one way or another, as the Americans consolidated their own role on the island.

The *Trumpet* blew a different tune. Each week the front page carried an attack on the Birds, carefully written by Hector, scrupulous as to facts—insiders, but people he had known all his life, gave him the dirty details for a journalistic assault upon wrongful authority. The news of the island and region filled out the picture. The *Trumpet* was not so different from the *Nation* under C.L.R. James's editorship nearly twenty years earlier, but it could be said as easily that it grew out of the newspaper experience of Hector in his youth, watching his aunts work in the office of the *Workers' Voice* and him writing precocious letters about Antiguan life and sport.

Donald "The Don" Halstead, one of Vere Bird's key aides in struggles against employers of the 1940s–50s, led workers away from the AT&LU and toward the AWU, to be headed by George Walter. When it became clear in 1970 that Walter would be real head of the AWU's arm, the PLM, Hector, as chair of the PLM, walked away. The Don stayed. As a parliamentarian, he helped put through social security legislation and labor codes—and the special powers of the government to intimidate any opposition. Like his old patron Bird and his new patron Walter, Halstead was the conservative who played radical but returned to form.[31]

But from the perspective of many Antiguans in 1970, Walter looked ever more likely to succeed Bird and inaugurate a new era for the island by defeating the Antiguan Labour Party (ALP) in the coming elections. The AWU had to strike for the union recognition that Bird would not otherwise grant them, bringing out a supporting crowd of ten thousand, an astonishing number on such an island, for a march in the rain. Bird's police teargassed them, and he declared martial law. This time repression was in vain, because the population would not accept the Bird way so easily anymore. In that moment of Black Power from the United States to the United Kingdom, Bird truly looked like a sell-out to the colonial masters. His answer could have been copied from American conservatives (and no few liberals): that journalist Hector, stirring up the workers, was a "Communist," a charge carried from government press to radio and television network year after year if not day after day virtually until Hector's death.

The charge was ludicrous. As Hector later recalled, his brush with Communists in Canada—likely the first he had ever met in the flesh— had left him strictly cold. They certainly wanted to support the struggles of colonial peoples; but they wanted to draw youngsters like himself into their struggles, their organizations, to do so. And worse, they idealized life in the Soviet Union and the Eastern Bloc that, to Hector, seemed a bad version of state authority, closer to the lives of workers in countries with state-owned enterprises, authoritarian police, and no freedom of the press. He could appreciate the plight of Cuban revolutionaries, only ninety miles from Florida; he did not hope to see the limitations of the Cuban experiment replicated elsewhere in the Caribbean.

Bird could not have denounced Hector as a "socialist," because that term had become so generic in the region and covered many of its most respectable politicians, however little their practice gave any meaning to the term. Neither Bird (with his background in reading British Marxist sources) nor his handlers were probably able to grasp what kind of socialist or revolutionary Hector had become. Paget Henry was to say much later that Hector, leading his group in a study of James's texts, would have done better to have followed the models in *Party Politics of the West Indies* rather than *Facing Reality*. [32] And yet, looking back at the middle 1970s, things are not so simple.

There was a deep sense in James—whose pamphlet *Any Cook Can Govern* (1954) was certainly the most militant defense by a Marxist of democratic practice in antiquity—that the smallness and intimacy of the societies in the Caribbean could make a modern recuperation of city-state democracy possible.[33] The Hungarian uprising and the role of the workers' councils for a few weeks (until Russian tanks had reasserted control) reaffirmed his belief that the representative state could, under the best circumstances of mass mobilization, be replaced by direct democracy.

The Paris Commune had accomplished it almost a century earlier, and Marx had declared that experiment the true face of socialism; Lenin had gone over the head of the Bolshevik Party to recognize the full value of the Soviets, pointing alike to the Paris Commune as the appropriate revolutionary precedent. James had, of course, been writing for decades about the role of industrial workers, sparse in most of the Caribbean. But the Vietnamese (and a reinterpretation of the Chinese Revolution, which he had previously shunned as the barbaric advance of Stalinism) had shown the role of peasants in modern history that he, too, had failed to grasp.[34]

The limit of representative government, then, was to be "the last hill that the people of the West Indies will have to climb." This was an altogether remarkable view, improbable at any time except during the continuing mobilization of the early independence years, accompanied by strong symptoms of weakness in U.S. hegemony worldwide. James expected that in the postindependence period, leaders like Williams (after 1961) would foster a sense of disappointment and disillusionment. But he believed that a surge of activity, triggered perhaps by global impulse or perhaps triggering the global impulse, would carry the masses beyond— or at least could.[35]

The uprisings of 1968 against the Birds seemed to demonstrate the point, even if no workers' institutions a la Hungary came forth. Shortly after being forced out of the Walter party in 1969, Hector drafted the Afro-Caribbean Movement (ACM) document *The Caribbean: Yesterday, Today and Tomorrow*. Drawing upon James and Williams, among others, he recalled the slave uprisings and their contemporary counterpart in Black Power, defined in strictly socialistic terms, the "cooperative and collective control of resources by the people." Hector's meetings with an aged George Weston, foremost champion of Antiguan popular expression in another day, brought him a sense of certainty, expressed in poetic terms: "I was then too Pan-African; he too African. We thought of each other." The ACM headquarters was quickly and significantly named Weston House.

True to Hector's expectations, the new Walter government would betray, proving that it was no different in substance from the Bird machine. A major strike by workers of the Public Utilities Authority (PUA) proved decisive because the PUA reached out to the ACM for assistance, tactics to publicity. Failures of the movement to organize successfully at the airport, the principal bank, and a number of other sites could be seen as a sidebar to the PUA militancy and its significance.

Meanwhile, a series of bomb blasts and cane field fires, although none serious, were evidently planted to destabilize and discredit the former opposition now in power. To hear of it on the Bird-owned radio station, the end of civilization was practically at hand. A mysterious "AFF" avowed, in anonymous leaflets, that the capital city of St. Johns would be destroyed by fire, on a certain date in September 1972. The police claimed that they could do nothing. None other than Jamaica Kincaid's much-written-about mother herself, Annie Drew, stepped in to lead a minimovement of Antiguan women to ferret out the bombers. In what could pass for a Dickens novel, Drew disguised herself as a one-legged man and hid under a culvert, in Hector's phrase, "in the dead of night, a culvert which would hardly admit a scurrying rabbit." She and the other women, in a society so dominated by men, identified the perpetrators, even if the arrests never went back to the source.[36]

The events of the following year, 1973, sweeping across half a dozen islands, reaffirmed the sense that the radicals could and would have to stand alone—because any neocolonial government and not just the Birds would feel the need to suppress mass mobilizations. Walter had been excellent at denouncing misrule, but in office just as much a misruler, with still less of a glorious past to rationalize his actions. The fact that a Pan-African movement could defy the ban and lead one of the most massive marches in Antiguan history seemed to prove the potency of the independent opposition.

African Liberation Day, the notion of an Africa Day March and celebrations did not begin in Antigua; certainly the idea was passed around in various reaches of the diaspora for years. But Hector personally had the determination and fortitude to carry it through, notwithstanding claims by the government (articulated by former ally Donald Halstead) that permission had been withdrawn. Capturing an emotional sentiment intimately related to ongoing guerrilla wars in Africa, and the highlighting of African National Congress (ANC) efforts in South Africa to overturn that shadow of slavery, the world's most prominent apartheid system, it turned into a huge cause célèbre. Calypsonian Swallow won the first of several crowns with his apt tune "March for Freedom," an inspiration heard across the English-speaking islands. All in all, it was the first time that Hector personally provided regional leadership of the Left, and it also richly illustrated the ways in which Afro-Caribbeanism highlighted global policies. The heat of the situation grew suddenly more vivid when Hector, on the way to Halstead's office, waved to a friend and by coincidence, a bomb suddenly went off. Hector was taken into custody for "signaling" the explosion—until the ludicrous charges were dropped.

By 1976, George Walter had discredited himself, and Bird, aging but still vigorous, was determined to make the only comeback he would ever need. From the moment of regaining power in 1976, set on holding power for the rest of his life, he steadily became more despotic. He used what amounted to his own personal radio station to assault all critics on a regular basis. But not so different from Burnham, if with considerably less poise and high-flown rhetoric, Bird also made a point of attending regional conferences, positioning himself as an experienced leader and voice of the people. Starkly unlike Burnham, Bird was unprepared for expression of the Black Power that had, without the phrase itself, lifted the Antiguan up from low circumstances.

Soon that Black Power movement, pitting itself against Bird, took on new strength and allies. James himself came to Antigua in 1977, the old man addressing the devotees on "the impending confrontation" and making little effort to hide that he meant locally as well as globally. It was an impulse felt strongly by his listeners, and as much by the government. A few years earlier he had praised fellow Trinidadian Stokely Carmichael; now he looked to Black Power among Afro-Caribbeans still on the islands.

The Youth Forces for Liberation (YFL), representing militant younger leaders from the streets, Black Panther–style, had regarded the ACM contemptuously as "bourgeois black nationalist." They now sought and achieved merger in 1979, and the Afro-Caribbean Movement became the ACLM, adding the regional emphasis that had already been evident.[37]

Henry has observed that in retrospect, at least, significant gaps could be seen between reality and the hopes of the Antiguan radicals. Most of the ACM had indeed been the classical petite-bourgeois of colonial and postcolonial culture, the teachers, white-collar workers, educated but underemployed intellectuals, and so on. Only darker color, political opportunity, and ideals (as articulated mainly by Hector) separated them from what other islanders were inclined to call the "brown people of the cities." By contrast, the YFL had been composed of working-class but also sub-working-class members who (like the Black Panthers or their rival League of Revolutionary Black Workers in Detroit) needed the faith in near-time revolutionary change in order to maintain members' enthusiasm. If water and oil could mix, they had to mix fast, and perhaps the millenarian rhetoric of near-time transformation was a way to convince themselves—not only intellectuals but lumpen proletarians—that the necessary forces had truly been assembled.

Hector, echoing James, might continue to insist that the direct intervention of the mass of workers, unemployed, women, and youth must of necessity produce a new and higher form of democracy. But some of the ACLM's intellectuals grew increasingly restless: the political unpopularity of the Walter regime, and of the Bird machine back in power, suggested contrarily that positions could be advanced, important power won through elections after all. The decisive defeat of a 1979 teachers' strike, viewed melodramatically during the heat of struggle as the beginning of an insurrection, brought the struggle back down to earth. Some teachers joined the movement while some YFL veterans pulled out, and the ACLM looked subtly different by 1980.

The ACLM's newest manifesto, *Towards a New Antigua*, articulated positions that were to remain in place, more or less, for the rest of Hector's life. Notwithstanding the regional hopes suddenly raised (however soon to be dashed) by the Bishop regime in Grenada and the Sandinistas' revolution in Nicaragua, Hector and his comrades sought to provide a realistic mixture of holding action and strategic reconsideration on their own island. This time, Hector sought a socialistic version of "civil society," a phrase that would shortly come into common use for different purposes, equating human rights in the former East Bloc with the restoration of property rights and corporate prerogatives.

Hector's dramatic appearance before the United Nations (UN) in October 1979 had foreshadowed this line of strategy. Invited by the chair of the UN Special Committee against Apartheid—a committee whose very existence had been bitterly opposed by the United States—his first effort was rebuffed by coincidence that spoke to troubled times, a threatened hijacking and the evacuation of the complex. But speak on the next day he did, arguing that people of color had made a central contribution to civilization (notably including Western civilization), that the success of anticolonialism in creating free states had suggested a new path for the world. The apartheid government of South Africa, aided by V. C. Bird, was continuing to commit the worst attacks upon human rights and human dignity. He told the world body how the Antiguan government, subservient with its parasitic members and their class all too eager to comply with any lucrative request, had played a dirty part in the bargain. After the speech, Hector was surrounded by delegates congratulating him, including representatives of the U.S. Congressional Black Caucus. It was a global moment for him—but he chose to make it a moment for the ACLM.[38]

By the early 1980s, the ACLM called for a Human Rights Commission in Antigua, including the widest sectors of the public; a code of anticorruption measures that would demand an accounting of funds gained and held by politicians and public servants; and the end to the commonplace of political corruption, firings, and assorted victimization based upon a worker's party affiliation. The project of a worker-controlled economy was now set back in favor of a cooperation-oriented national economy, and frankly admitted so ("ACLM is clear that what is required now in Antigua is not a socialist economy for which Antigua does not have the preconditions.")[39] Close observers of James's writings might suggest that *Party Politics in the West Indies* had come back again.

The ACLM was to move further along these lines. Proposing the modernization of the hotel industry, the restructuring of the peasant economy, and the creation of a new and different kind of tourism based in the middle class, the *Outlet* sought to appeal to those African Americans and others who had long chosen Barbados for a dignified, well-deserved vacation. The *Outlet* also had to fight for its right to exist: in 1982, a government file containing the paper's registration mysteriously disappeared, Hector along with three compatriots arrested "for printing and publishing without permission." Donald Halstead, yesterday's political opponent, swore to the witnessing of the registration, bringing Hector's crew back out of prison and onto the job.[40]

Alas, it was not and could not be enough to transform the politics of the island. Barely able to accommodate a two-party system, with constantly shifting alliances among the two equally neocolonial (if occasionally nationalist in rhetoric) parties, Antigua was not prepared for a third. The ACLM secured less than a 2 percent total in 1980 (echoing the failure of the James-inspired Workers and Farmers Party in Trinidad of 1965) and did not bother to contest the 1984 elections. Now it could only be the beating heart of morality in what was to be long-term opposition.

It was hardly understood outside the region, and often not inside, either, how the Reaganesque hardening of strategy and tactics for the region considered Vere Bird and "his" island as the ideal satellite. Even before Reagan's election, the U.S. State Department had considered Antigua a ready resource: the U.S. tracking station was well set and the longest runway of the region available for U.S. purposes exclusively, if it wished. Not that it was necessary to know anything about Antigua's history or culture in order to exploit its resources, human and natural. Robert Coram observes that when a consulate general was established in St. Johns in April 1980, the officials arriving got most of their background information from travel brochures. Other details hardly mattered to them. The establishment of a Voice of America relay station for propagandizing other islands more effectively was rather harder for the Birds to accept, but only because the United States offered to pay so little for the privilege.[41]

After the Grenadian coup and invasion, the State Department came to consider Antigua the necessary and the perfect spot both for monitoring Russian satellites and for the Sound and Surveillance System (SOSUS) on the unmarked naval base to track Russian subs. Money and construction poured in while the diplomatic mission remained so small and unimportant that, as Corum quips, there was no room on the island even for the paper trail of documents shipped off to Washington, and the charge d'affaires was changed so often that no real knowledge of island history or population was ever expected. Meanwhile, the base maintained (and remains) the only significant catch-basin on the island, sufficient to support its own water needs even during droughts, while the resorts and towns, lacking the necessary engineering, are forced to import water during the long dry season.

What did Antiguans get out of the deal? For a while there were construction jobs, then maintenance jobs. Workers at the base, government officials, and the some members of middle class ate and drank at the base for pleasure and prestige, at commissary prices far below island rates. Vere Bird and his henchman risked hiking up leasing fees and encroaching on unused U.S.-leased land, by one means or another; usually U.S. officials gave in, doubtless from a desire to palliate a cooperative crook. A seeming threat to close down the base (along with several others in the region) after the fall of the Eastern Bloc was abandoned or at least postponed for one large reason—the United States was uniquely free here to ignore any and all ecological restrictions, bombing, dredging, wiping out reefs, and killing fish (or bird) populations at will. Then again, Vere Bird wanted the Americans to stay, as a guarantee of his own power.

Thus commercial expansion of a particular sort continued, with an influx of sex trade workers from the Dominican Republic. The brothels were declared officially off-limits to sailors, because of the spread of virulent sexually transmitted diseases (STDs). That ban was cheerfully ignored, as sex became one of the island's largest businesses, rivaling resorts, drugs, and gambling. Visiting U.S. sailors on the half-dozen or so port calls during any given year were sure to contribute their share of everything but resort stays.[42] The expansion of the airport in 1985 using mostly foreign funds created another huge opportunity for corruption with U.S. complicity so huge that Hector dubbed the son, Vere Jr., "Vere Airport Bird."

Perhaps the most interesting wrinkle in all this was the growing visibility and special role of Hector's childhood friend Lester Bird, the only legally trained and, for that reason among others, the most important of Vere Sr.'s scions. In the early 1970s, working at the *Antigua Star*, Hector had offered Lester one of his first useful jobs, navigating legally between rulers and ruled. By the early 1980s, Lester Bird had converted his nationalist positions into a posture: he denounced U.S. interference and control on various occasions but made sure that American delegations knew that what he wanted was not the expulsion of blessings-givers but more money. The extravagances that followed were extraordinary. None were more so than the Royal Antiguan Hotel, later the Ramada Renaissance, the first building taller than two stories on the island, constructed by imported Italians at great cost (largely underwritten by the Bird government) and then all but abandoned to deteriorate. Built over one of the prime sites of a pre-Columbian village, it was perhaps cursed. The islanders themselves and their collective history, not Lester or the other Birds, paid the price.

And it was not only the people of Antigua who suffered. Most of the island's mangrove swamps and coral reefs were destroyed during the hotel expansion of the 1980s. An expansive duck sanctuary became a solid waste dump. Sand was mined illegally, but without hindrance, for construction, and refuse dumped at will. The brief appearance of a Green Party during elections of the 1990s prompted Hector's approval, but the effort to prevent the sale of substantial properties with ecological resources—especially on the little island of Barbuda—was met with silence or denials at harm done.[43]

So what was to be done? The Caribbean-wide revolution was over, at least for the time being—and in reality for the rest of Hector's life. Two of his closest friends, Rosie Douglas and Ralph Gonsalves, would ascend to prime ministerships in Dominica and St. Vincent (and the Grenadines) by moving toward the near-center Left, while maintaining their spiritual ties with Pan-Africanism and a kind of Caribbean social democracy.[44] Hector was the unluckiest, according to usual calculations, because the Antiguan Labour Party was too corrupt to be reconstructed by an idealist but also because Hector had come from no alternative family dynasty. One of his great remaining tasks, then, was to keep hope alive while others of his generation on other islands struggled to govern, and like fellow editor George Odlum of St. Lucia, to keep a socialistic press alive as well.[45]

Meanwhile, the task at hand had become muckraking. With all the zesty journalism of assorted daily Caribbean newspapers, none did it better than the *Outlet*. And yet it would be false to portray Hector as a mere muckraker. He was to recall, at the centennial celebration of C.L.R. James at Trinidad's UWI campus in 2001, that early on, during the 1970s, the master had asked him whether he expected to overturn the government by revealing the dirty secrets of corruption. He had answered, no, but it was nevertheless the responsibility of the press to do so—and James had responded, yes, it was an important nonrevolutionary task.[46] What Hector stressed, again and again, was the larger historical picture. Bird and those around him had set out specific ideas and a general vision for development beyond the limits of colonialism, and then they repudiated their own rules, the legacy that they had created. Tourism, to take an obvious example, was to serve development, and not the other way around; controlling shares were to be kept on the island, and where possible, according to a 1946 resolution of the rising nationalist movement, ownership was to be held in common. Under Bird's actual leadership, all was turned upside down, tourist dollars flowing so little to islanders that taxes were required to pay for the cost of their collective upkeep in utilities, taxes, and water supplies. The father of the nation, Hector quipped, thus made himself the father of dam-nation.[47]

What had been evident before the temporary loss of power in 1971 had become burningly evident on the regaining of power. The dramatic jailing of Hector once again in 1986, this time in a blatant attempt to close down the *Outlet's* exposure of the airport scam, drove home the realization that the eclipse of one Bird for another, the second being Hector's childhood chum Lester Bird, was not going to alter anything important. The system ruled, as it did everywhere in the region.

Of terror, Antigua had known some during the recent period, usually nothing more than scare tactics by the government. Of horror, it saw a rising of drug crimes and other actions scarcely recognizable in earlier eras except when committed against blacks by whites and their lackeys. But the new times were ugly, uglier than Hector could guess. In October 1989, Hector had left his farm behind to go to work, his wife, Arah, alone with the former inmate that they had resolved to help rehabilitate. Instead, Arah was murdered in a crime that shocked the whole island and beyond, all those who knew of her work as a leading figure in Caribbean women's emancipation. Never, to this point, had a Caribbean feminist been cut down so. Hector dwelled on the tragedy in a personal hell, even after his later happy remarriage; no doubt he felt responsible in some way. He also knew that the senseless violence reflected a society out of control.

Tragedy and After

One of the chief (but to politically sympathetic doubters, least persuasive) claims of the older Marxism was that successful revolution was a "science" rather than an art, or a combination of circumstances, shrewd strategy, and the willingness by masses of people to lose everything in the effort. Bernard Coard and others conspiring against Maurice Bishop drew exactly the wrong conclusion from political disappointments in the region, that Marxist-Leninist ideology, "heavy music" (stern discipline), guidance of events from above, and the early use of physical force (weapons) offered the solution to the constrained social democracy of Michael Manley in particular.

C.L.R. James insisted, through his later life, that the Vanguard Party was wholly inappropriate for the advanced industrial countries. Indeed, he considered himself a consistent Leninist who saw Lenin as the leader repeatedly willing to go over the head of the party, first to the Soviets (or workers councils) in 1917 and then, in his last days, to the citizenry being crushed by the bureaucracy. For James, as for racist anti-Communists, Lenin was in effect a Third World leader ("scratch a Russian and you find Tartar") trying to release the energies of the masses to complete the huge tasks in building a cooperative society. James could still believe, without inconsistency, that as Trotsky had argued, this task was impossible short of the revolution spreading worldwide. But he had added the crucial proviso, alien to Trotsky and, until the Vietnam era, to the rest of the world's Trotskyists, that the revolutionary movements of peasants of the South, rather than workers of the North, might be the trigger for global transformation. He utterly mistrusted Communists everywhere to do this task—except in Asia, where the Vietnamese Communists were clearly leading a people's revolution of David against the American Goliath. In this respect he, too, was catching up to events, coming to conclusions that the activists of Tim Hector's generation took for granted.

But the imperial "center" did, with much difficulty and the spilling oceans of blood along with the destruction of rain forests in the process, hold after all. No doubt failures of nerve, like downright betrayal of purpose in Grenada, had played a large role. The whole character of "African socialism" had proved other, and hugely less, than James and his comrades had envisioned when the pace of anticolonialism suddenly picked up after the Second World War.

This realization came home most dramatically, probably for the first time, as Padmore, James, and Nkrumah prepared the Pan-African Congress of 1945, and quickly learned that non-Communist socialists (especially but not only the British Labour Party) had no intention of opposing the advancement of American hegemony in the cold war world.[48] The ways in which Padmore himself served as mere adviser to Nkrumah in the liberated Ghana, distrusted and kept from further influence by jealous power-holders of the Convention People's Party (CPP), might have served as a warning to James entering a similar relationship with Eric Williams. But the aging revolutionaries took the chances that they had and did the best that they could under favorable circumstances do so.

The final disillusionment might have come as the Sixth Pan-African Congress approached in 1974, because James was at his height as Pan-African eminence grise, well into his seventies and in health none too good, nevertheless shuttling from the United States to Britain to assorted sites in Africa. The "call" that he issued for Americans in particular, but for West Indians and any others who read the call, carried a clear and (to old observers of James) familiar message. More than a quarter century earlier, a little pamphlet called *The Invading Socialist Society* had emphasized the message that socialists needed to differentiate mere nationalization, a change of bosses, from socialist transformation.[49] Here, James emphasized that political independence meant nothing when the same corporations still dominated the economy. The social *relations* of production remained crucial, as they had indeed been for Marx.

Two weeks before the Congress would open, announcements appeared that only heads of state and those specially invited by states would be invited to intend. The hosts might as well have inscribed "No C.L.R. James Politics Invited" over the reception rooms, because his entourage—most notably the young radicals of the Caribbean—had effectively been banned.[50] As he observed, the emptied Congress left nothing behind. Nor was there a Seventh Congress, as he had hoped. The odds had been too great against a success that the new ruling strata of the Third World did not want. Nkrumah had, as Hector insisted, "placed Garvey's Black Star in the firmament," but it was up to the diasporans as well as Africans to "light the Black Star all over Africa and the Caribbean" with the empowerment of ordinary people. "This is our mission now," he concluded portentously, "and we can either fulfill it or betray it."[51]

CHAPTER FIVE

Beyond Tragedy

So don't cry for me
Don't cry for me
My work on earth is done
I am now at a better place
Don't cry for me.
Tell all Antiguans

So sang Destroyer Sr. in the calypso tents of July 2003, in what the *Outlet* described as the "dramatic monologue" of the fallen hero speaking to the nation. It was, the paper added, "one of the best composed songs" in the history of the two-island nation.[1] Prime Minister Ralph Gonsalves of St. Vincent and the Grenadines—now the last surviving of the four Afro-Caribbean socialist comrades George Odlum, Rosie Douglas, Hector, and himself—declared Tim "the best Prime Minister that Antigua never had."[2] He might have added that with Hector's passing, the effort of the 1960s–80s cohort to stitch the Anglophone Caribbean islands together in a democratic, egalitarian regional body had ended. That task remained for future generations.

Solace over the fallen hero's death was a hard message to accept, even after a pregnant further nine months had passed. Prime Minister Lester Bird, at the bier, had rightly said that a piece of Antigua had died with Tim.[3] As Hector himself might have predicted, the artists of the island had been among the first to give sense to what intellectual tributes could barely capture.

In 1985, returned to home and office after a week's imprisonment, Hector had reflected that "I shall stick to my views, with or without power, confident that in my time, or after my time," West Indians would arrive in their own way "at the view, that to overcome authoritarian state power, that power needs to be decentralized and placed in their control," and with de-centralization, "social ownership and control of the economy."[4] His refusal to join the Lester Bird government might weaken into a willingness to act as a partner under certain circumstances; but his larger vision never altered a whit. It had been set in place long before.

In the precursive shadow of another tragedy, the Caribbean Conference of Intellectual Workers had convened at the National Convention Centre at Grand Anse, St. George's, in late November 1982.[5] The newspapers in the United States and abroad were already full of the wild claims from State Department and Central Intelligence Agency (CIA) sources that the building of a new airport runway was actually some kind of subversive scheme by the ruling New Jewel Movement (NJM) and its leader, Maurice Bishop, to fly subversion into the American Lake. No Yankee invasion could possibly be resisted.

But for the moment, a certain optimism remained alive on the bright, sunny horizon. The global collapse of international opposition to U.S. policies was, seemingly, far away despite the evident languishing of East European societies. Polish Solidarity, it sometimes seemed, might bring dramatic change East and West. The Iranians had, meanwhile, thrown out their shah and his American henchmen. Above all, the Vietnamese victory against the military powerhouse of the world was less than a decade in the past. Further, the U.S. economy had only begun to recover from the oil crisis, and Ronald Reagan appeared at that moment of antinuclear protest and economic stagnation none too secure for reelection in 1984.

Thus the regionwide committee met: delegates from more than half a dozen islands, including George Lamming, Trinidadian labor leader David Abdullah, feminist scholar Merle Hodge, journalist Rickey Singh, and Hector. Prime Minister Bishop, just back from a Caribbean Community and Common Market (CARICOM) meeting, addressed them on the urgency of the issue. He said, in part, "Today, no corner of the earth is safe from the creeping ravages of the Coca-Cola culture," with the Caribbean as a veritable "laboratory" for its conquest of all. True Caribbean culture, he insisted, had been "developed in limbo, unrecognized, unrecorded or at best viewed with contempt." Black Power, following Negritude and variants thereof, had irrevocably changed the intellectual climate by rejecting secondhand and second-rate culture, helping Grenadians to begin their own "flowering of the arts," a creativity from poetry to dance.[6]

Tim Hector did not dwell later upon the tragedy of this conference (it met a second and last time in 1984 in Trinidad, after the Grenadian catastrophe, strengthened by the addition of Earl Lovelace and George Beckford, nevertheless at the point of dissolution), but its central concerns were ever his. Speculating on why Caribbean literature was unique, the trained literary scholar once more observed that, for him as a boy, books had "substituted for the biological brothers and sisters I never had," recalling the early beginnings of an intellectual life during which he read the standard classics again and again, struggling to understand West Indian life's contrasts to supposed ideal conditions and personalities. One thing was certain and decisive: Afro-Caribbeans had begun their collective lives as chattel, robbed of almost everything by the rigidities as well as the cruelties of plantation life. If the early British novel concerned itself with "the fashionable men and women whom comfort could not bless with sense," the very character of this protagonist did not, could not, exist among the Caribbean masses.

The peasantry here was the bottom line, and among Hector's favorite lines of his friend Guyanese poet Martin Carter was that almost unanswerable question "What new fevers arise to reverse the crawl/Our islands make towards their spiritual extinction?" Energy cursed (if also to some degree blessed) with "fever" necessarily destructive but also self-destructive to a large degree, it could break out of reification as among few other peoples of the world, with spectacular mass-based "carnivals of mass creativity, in song, dance and mas." This story, so close to home—he could remember his own college schoolmates telling him—was simply not worth telling, so much less interesting than the dynamic American imports. "With or without fever we could not and did not look at that which dominated us for centuries," he lamented. When Hector moved his cultural weather eye toward Michael Smith, the dub poet dead at twenty-nine from gunfire, leaving behind the chiseled poetic cry, "Me Cyann Believe It," Hector saw the present judged both poetically and politically.[7]

Gordon Rohlehr, at the same Grenadian cultural congress, had perfectly described poet Carter's constant paradox, in which the "avowal of faith and the reality of betrayal" are both "part of a fixed pattern." If cryptic, in that the image "does not quite correspond to the idea which it seeks to convey," it is necessarily so, in a reality itself that seems so elusive through centuries of displacement, slavery, and bondage, not to mention the climate's sudden and often violent turns, blistering heat to pouring rain, drought to flood and back. This society has been as indifferent to the poet as nature to the peasant and so, in Caliban's insight borrowed from Carter's phrase, "Accursed, I curse."[8] The age of artistic existentialism was hardly confined to the Caribbean. But here, as Hector observed, meaning was not precisely "lost." It had never been gained by the overwhelmingly Creole middle class, emphatically including the philistines that C.L.R. James had critiqued in his parting comments on Trinidad.

Hector's feelings about cricket were as strong as his views of formal literary output, of course, and he seemed at times to reach an antidote here. We have seen how much of his leisure he devoted to organizing regional teams, with all the detailed effort that the associated tasks demanded. He would have been happier in a revolutionary government, one imagines, as minister of sport than any other post. Near the end of his life, he was remembering the longest-lived of all Antiguan cricketers, Eustace "Tuss" Matthew. Brother of a man who married one of Hector's aunts, Tuss was close enough to respond (in Hector's tenth year) to unfavorable comparisons to a more famous player with the modest, "This boy, knows his cricket." High praise, indeed. A grown-up Hector captured Tuss more accurately as well as more charitably: master at his own stroke, a fine dancer ("in the style of Nipsy Russell") who carried grace onto the pitch, speaking (Hector claimed) pure Hemingwayesque English, Matthew received no trace of official honor at home. "Our value system did not and does not include our own, except as long service by the mediocre."[9]

Creativity could never be altogether stilled, even when unrewarded (especially at home). It was the remarkable theory of Hector that the conditions making possible an Emanuel Kant later produced such West

Indians as Garvey, Martí, Padmore, Fanon, James, Hubert Harrison, Claude McKay, Leon Dumas, and, of course, Walter Rodney. The impossibility of the ruling class governing the local economy, the collapsing old society and the inability of a new society to replace it had prompted the wide, philosophic expression of its outstanding sons and daughters, nearly all of them necessarily wandering abroad.[10]

How was this creativity to be reconciled with the constant and deepening economic gloom? A published collection of talks by Caribbean heads of state from 1973 to 1999 had opened and closed with a familiar sense of crisis. The first blush of independence tempered by realization that the most promising plan for regional unity, the federation movement, had already failed. A gnawing fear by the mid-1970s that oil crisis meant only disaster (except, perhaps, for oil-rich Trinidad, caught up in other severe problems). The Reagan administration lashed out at Central America during the 1980s, and the Soviet collapse left behind less perceived need for the United States to buy the region off with economic support. Finally, the global integration of the 1990s, marked by North American Free Trade Agreement (NAFTA) and the World Trade Organization, threatened to divide the region against itself worse than ever. As the dream of post-colonial federation had been crushed at its outset by a mixture of petty jealousies and a failure to convince the black majority that the brown and white classes would not have the most to gain, so the Caribbean Free Trade Association (CARIFTA), founded in 1958, and CARICOM, founded in 1973, have stumbled over familiar interisland conflicts. But they also failed under the cloud of the larger gloomy sense that *any* regional development strategy is doomed to failure. Once the world's greatest wealth producer, robbed of nearly everything created, it remained the backwater that it had become in the middle of the nineteenth century.[11]

Despite a determined optimism and some notable advances, outmigration of the young to the United States, United Kingdom, and Canada was the Caribbean export product that counted most. Thanks to growing remissions, it was the import product as well, one more proof of the tenacious dependency. The failure of Fabian socialism left the English-language Caribbean more easily tolerated than Marxist Cuba but with the same absent sources of revenue and the same sense of drift. (Cubans at least believed that something would change for better or worse with the departure of Fidel Castro; others in the Caribbean had no such point of perspective.) Most educated and uneducated populations alike responded with repulsion at the bullying and brute force considered the essence of the new "Bush Doctrine."

But what could they do, dependent upon U.S. tourists, increasingly limited but still important foreign aid, and formal goodwill that could turn vicious at some unexpected moment? As a sympathetic regional observer comments, the "what began as a definitely pro-labour working class commitment of the Left movement in the 1940s, had by the late 1980s developed into a clearly pro-capitalist programmatic stance," a pragmatic reconstitution that demanded compliance as the price of political survival.[12] Here and there resistance could be seen, more in election programs (still more in election speeches) than in the administration of government. And of course it was more nationalist than social democratic, although the struggle against whites holding on to power generated moments of expectation and "Black Is Beautiful" cultural expression hitherto held back on nominally conservative islands like Barbados.[13]

Perhaps less consciously, they had chosen, in effect, to wait it out. As time passed, casual violence grew more common, medical systems reeled from citizens with HIV, and the old subsidies of the Commonwealth continued to disappear. Many a small tragedy was hidden within this large tragedy. Thus dedicated labor-socialists and Caribbean nationalists like St. Lucia's George Odlum, long revered for the integrity of their politics and journalism, ended political careers, driven from power in their own party governments, providing a lamentable punctuation upon an era.[14] It was no more lamentable, of course, than those who stayed in power and carried out policies of social and cultural impoverishment dictated by the International Monetary Fund (IMF).

The Culture Critique

Another way to look at all this is through the eyes of Jamesean cultural commentary, prompting some of the most wide-ranging and least "orthodox" of Hector's many journalistic vectors. This analysis requires a turn back to the basics of James's contributions on the dialogue about Third World societies and empire, modernism, and postmodernism that has consumed literary scholars of the African diaspora for several decades. One of the best of them (and most keenly sympathetic toward James), Timothy Brennan, properly warns that the "cosmopolos" that has grown up in place of the earlier total domination of imperial values is most likely to be a global multiculture with unchanged power relations.[15] "Civil society" has been steadily redefined over the 1990s not just as restored property rights but as acceptance of U.S. hegemony. Or it fails to rise to civic requirements and must be viewed as an archaic form of society ("Old Europe"), if not a species of outright tyranny. As Hector put it in regional terms, a hapless Caribbean, after decades of pointless arguments over differences (or perhaps just egos) dividing it from itself, had finally come to common terms—American market values backed by American military threats. Post-9/11 State Department talk of a "transition" in Cuba with a "timetable" set by Washington only seemed more alarming because these hegemonic Republicans were evidently ruthless and reckless beyond the various presidencies since the Bay of Pigs.

This growing American threat to basic Caribbean culture occupied Hector's attention in the final years of his life, no doubt because of the accelerating pace of cultural penetration that threatened such standards as cricket and calypso with American sports and music instantly and permanently available via satellite. The deeper subjects of Caribbean destiny had been on Hector's mind since his teen years, clarified and intensified by his engagement with C.L.R. James in the middle 1960s.

It may be recalled that James and Hector both experienced the colonial version of the British public school education, rich in positives as well as negatives. Both were lovers of Shakespeare, capable and downright eager to quote from memory and to lecture on the social significance of the Bard's work. Hector had been teaching Shakespeare when he was fired. James, in the same years, had been preparing a manuscript on Shakespeare—it would have been his final fresh and full volume—before he apparently gave up the task as beyond his mental and physical powers.[16]

Hector, like James generations earlier, was imbued with regional sport even while working out a view of Shakespeare for the educated colonials. For a mature James, to tell a familiar tale once more here, the vibrancy of the calypso tent and the quarrels in the barracks of kept women were as much a part of Caribbean culture as, say, the notable sculpture of Edna Manley. The subsoil of what Caribbean peoples were and could do made them and their contribution unique.

James was one of the very first to articulate the notion that the twin horrors, the extermination of original inhabitants and the transportation of slaves from Africa, had compelled West Indians to create something for themselves. Part of the West in key ways, but with the unique cultural baggage or "tools" of African societies, they were situated to offer fresh perspectives, fresh opportunities for liberation. Brennan keenly sees dialectical reversals in this line of thought. Considered to be nothing (and not only by whites but also by regional writers like Naipaul), they were everything modern. Written off for centuries as hopelessly backward, they had in Haiti leaped out of historical obscurity, drawing upon their own internal resources to show others the way forward. More than any other activist anywhere, and more than the multinational literary critics who made James's legacy their own during the 1990s, Hector rendered these Jamesean dialectics his own.

And there was something more to the James critique that not even James seemed to grasp fully. The "Black European," as the young emigrant to England called himself, had discovered during his fourteen-year sojourn in the United States more about the role of black culture within modern society than he could have discovered either in the insular island culture or the nearly all-white Britain (and notwithstanding his engagement with fellow pioneer anti-imperialists set on freeing Africa). James's unfinished and perhaps unfinishable volume on American culture neatly reversed the valence of contemporary intellectuals' scorn for mass society by suggesting a way out, a route that relied heavily upon what was unique in American popular life, that is, black participation. Without failing to point to the scarcely concealed resentment and anxieties of the masses (also without conceding the levels of white racism that were evident to other observers), James thus elucidated a unique dialectic decades before academics and others caught up with it.[17]

Some of James's views were bound up with his critique of communism and his attempt to demonstrate his hatred of state tyranny hidden in pseudo-Marxist rhetoric. *Mariners, Renegades and Castaways*, the only substantial section published in his lifetime, viewed Ahab as the Stalinist tyrant, Ishmael unable to choose that multicultured (but mostly black) mass of working men fearless and indestructible except by common disaster. But beneath all this was a view of black culture within mass culture, a way to return to the Caribbean that he began to show in the coverage of culture in the *Nation* under his editorship. By going away, he had been able to come back changed. Since youth, he had been devoted to cricket and cricketers. Now he could see them within the scope of world culture, as he proved in *Beyond a Boundary* (1962), a book that many nonradicals and even left-wing sports devotees would regard as far and away his finest.

Hector drew upon this impetus, adding to it new significance from the emphasis that James had placed upon women's liberation and especially black women's self-affirmation since at least the middle 1960s.[18] Only James's stature and age had kept him from taking great heat for defying the rage of some black male writers at the appearance of *The Color Purple*, intensified by the film. He insisted, into distant old age, that such artistic expressions and the fuss they kicked up were a sign of vitality as well as serious art being made by people of color. Hector himself argued, in turn, that the treatment of women in the Caribbean as objects for sex and child bearing was one of the great obstacles to cultural and economic development. But more than that, he insisted that women had exerted more influence than they had been given credit for doing, and that to understand their historical roles was decisive evidence of cultural advance. He had special reasons to do so with Arah Hector close at hand, not an academic intellectual or a writer as, say, Merle Hodge, but a grassroots organizer who by the 1980s frequently spoke on Caribbean women's liberation in Antigua and other islands. If anything, he made the relevant points more often after her murder. Arah had no doubt taught him so at close range. But he made theory of it and that was one of his signal triumphs, both politically and intellectually.

He had equally national if not as intimate reasons with Jamaica Kincaid, the pride of the island for whom he argued, a little strongly but not without reason, the achievement of creating in mother and daughter new historic characters. James had often proclaimed that such creation was the stroke of the master novelist, able to capture thereby the leading social dynamic of the day within the personality of the individual.

In one of his finest and most revealing essays, Hector insisted (as he had no doubt taught youngsters, in his schoolroom days) that the Industrial Revolution, by creating a new class of owners, brought about the novel, with all the complications of proper behavior, courtship, parentage, and so on developed in its pages (and the improper ones as well, naturally). No such class existed in the Caribbean, as the tiny minority of rich whites would ape the European aristocracy, and the nonwhite middle class (almost equally small) struggled to maintain respectability. Drawing upon European (and American) models, Caribbean writers of the later twentieth century had enormous difficulty depicting themselves, their own class. They had somehow to create a humanism out of the "thinghood" of slavery's long shadow. It was a dilemma for which Kincaid had the answer: "without being surrealist [she] would change the narrative of the novel, juxtaposing . . . events in Antigua against events in the metropole, and not unlike Eisenstein in the movies with parallel shots as part of his narrative strategy."[19]

Thereby, "a new novel emerged." It was a bold claim perhaps undercut by the fact that the acclaimed writer for the *New Yorker* had her main audience in the metropole and not at home. Annie Drew, the mother in Kincaid's vivid literary explorations, exemplified the simple but overwhelming reality that "the poor have only their children," spending their lives seeing to the safety and development of their brood with all the attention and skill that another family could give to budding lawyers, businesspeople, professionals, police, and even criminals. Tragically, mother's devotion was not enough for the men-children of the novelist's family, and Hector could testify that he personally had been unable to help one of Kincaid's brothers—because he could not bring himself to keep someone arrested for rape from being fairly tried and punished, as a matter of public safety. But it was enough for mother and daughter, depicted in *Annie John* as well as two such people had been depicted any-where in world literature.[20]

In *My Brother*, Kincaid had tightened the screws of critique upon Caribbean manhood, and Hector said frankly that "if not her best, prob-ably the one that touches me most" because Kincaid wrote of existence and essence, and "dispossession and the intensifying marginalization of countries has [*sic*] robbed existence of all essence here." It was a severe volume because Kincaid's very real brother, left behind in Antigua, had nothing to do with his life but seek pleasure, obviously from the sexual favors of women and (Kincaid learned to her great surprise) from men as well. One of the growing number of people with HIV, he fell into self-denial after some small successes of treatment, continuing to enjoy and brag about his conquests even knowing that he was spreading death. The very routineness of the cruelty, the collective and individual self-hatred, seems to Hector to point up the urgent need of "ending our national dis-possession, ending our responsibility for nothing, that we will unlock the creative passions lock in us, which will create a community."[21]

James had prepared his disciples' thinking, here as elsewhere, by stressing early and often the cultural figures of the region who had made their way in the world—Alexander Dumas, St. John Perse, Aime Cesaire, Frantz Fanon, and Alejo Carpentier, to name just a few. If Lamming and Naipaul (before James turned sharply against the latter) had seemed to him to represent a new "international" phase of Caribbean culture, then the following literary generation, including Earl Lovelace and Michael Anthony, offered up a kind of nationalness new in its self-confidence.[22] James, always eager for new voices, immediately adopted Kincaid, but he barely tapped the newest emerging literature of Caribbean writers before old age and death overtook him.[23]

For Hector, Jamaica Kincaid would inevitably be special. She was his real-life counterpart in interesting ways. Not that she was a joiner of movements—to say the least—but hers was a voice entirely Caribbean, entirely Antiguan despite or because of the distance assumed from a most un-Caribbean, cold, and almost homogeneously white Vermont, USA. Kincaid, in Hector's apotheosis, presents a perfectly modern way of look-ing at Caribbean life, but also another logic outside the predatory one of the Antiguan developers and island consumers alike who think nothing of destroying avian breeding grounds for a dump, or replacing mediocre colonial institutions (like the schools or the public library, closest to Kincaid's heart) with still worse ones. They bore a heavy responsibility for the sad state of Antiguan young people at large, bereft of any kind of positive self-identity, Americanized into being second-class African Americans with high rates of incarceration and HIV but low rates of self-cultivation.[24]

Kincaid, for all her literary qualities, also had a definite historical view. She was and is unrelentingly critical of neocolonialism's rotten fruits, seemingly poisoned in the bud by the centuries-old extermination of Indians, slavery of Africans, and stubborn definitions of whites (colonists and more recent tourists alike) by which blacks are children if not dangerous creatures outside all reason. The very perversity of the iron-willed little girl in Kincaid's memory-tales, her unwillingness to yield herself to the collapse of Antiguan society but likewise unwilling to look at it in the Naipaulesque fashion as a burlesque imitation of Europeanness, would inevitably seem to Hector as marking the courage of the best that his own island culture had to give.

The question went squarely to the building blocks of language. That savants of French-speaking islands like Edouard Glissant have discussed Creole language and its importance more often and more effectively than have "native" English speakers like James and Hector is obvious and perhaps inevitable. Their Creole is no more French than Cape Verdean Creole is Portuguese, and speakers from either language who lack the other could fail to understand a single sentence of the other, while Caribbean English might best be seen as a simultaneous contraction and expansion, distanced mainly by speed of delivery and by subtle elements of diction diverted from the official tongue.

James spoke "BBC English," except when affecting a phrase, and as the schoolmaster's son, had presumably always done so. Hector, especially when speaking quickly, fell or rose more readily into the idioms and phraseology of Antigua's and the region's own. Then, suddenly, like dub poet Linton Kwasi Johnson being challenged by James himself to pronounce "Shakespeare" in the only way possible, Hector would drop into the Queen's standard. As Glissant urged, the duality had always been a multilingualism unaccepted by colonial authorities and their appointees, containing within itself all the rich possibilities of multilingualism from below. Threatened increasingly with extinction because of its formally subliterary nature, patois survives and even thrives because it is ineradicable from popular life. Like Yiddish (before the Holocaust and the compulsory Hebraicization of Jewish culture in Israel), cursed by assimilators and exclusionary nationalists alike as "jargon," a "mongrel" tongue, it carries the untranslatable.[25]

Linguistics also inevitably complicated and implicated the issue of federation. The earlier failure, as Glissant observes, basically demoted hopes for unity among the Anglophones to the cultural sphere. But if it marked a definite loss, this was not precisely a demotion because the positive cultural potential had been there all along, thanks both to common origins and to the many interconnections between islands. If the restraints of "nonhistory" (historical absence of common political nationality, thanks to colonial manipulations, but also to a paucity of resources to drawn upon) posed formidable and even perhaps ultimately impossible challenges, nonetheless the "passion of intellectuals can become a potential for transformation when it is carried forward by the will of the people".[26] That is, to return to the analogy to Jews of the prestate period: the popular belief that Jewish cultural identity within a global cooperative society contained the only real hope for true attainment finds it parallel here. Caribbean federation has always demanded and still demands a restructured world society. The old linkage of Pan-Africanism with socialism may or may not be a necessary condition. But some kind of democratic globalism, no longer dependent upon IMF and corporate rule backed up by militarism and environmental exploitation, almost certainly must be.

Hector had a passion, almost an obsession, to trace the cultural roots back to slavery and on through the slow but remarkable rise of sports, music, and carnival to the identity of Caribbeanness and even Antiguaness. To recall for readers his early training in the subject, he turned to a conversation with his grandfather in 1960. He had at the time given himself an imaginative identity: Dedan Kimathi, the last of the Mau Mau leaders captured in Kenya. And he was afire with reports of the Sharpsville

Massacre. So he told his grandfather that he was sick of hearing what white scholars had to say. The old man shot back at him, "What do you know about Black Consciousness?"

The proof that grandfather had much to teach and young Tim much to learn lay in an unlikely place, with the most famous of all native Antiguans, vaudevillian and lyricist/composer Bert Williams. The lyricist and vocalist of the hit "Nobody," making himself an entertainment giant (and a favorite writer whose work would be borrowed by whites) at the turn of the twentieth century, Williams had performed his own play, "In Dahomy," in Buckingham Palace for the Queen in 1903. He was then just twenty-eight. Known widely as the "Son of Laughter," Williams costarred in the Ziegfeld Follies, becoming its best-paid actor. Also the first black actor to join Equity (in 1920), he appeared with Eubie Blake in the (silent) film version of the path-breaking black Broadway hit *Shuffle Along*, among five film appearances (he directed the forgotten *Natural Born Gambler* himself). Williams was also hailed for his role in Eugene O'Neill's famous theatrical drama *The Emperor Jones* (Paul Robeson was to play the part in a disappointing film), and he lasted forty weeks in a Broadway revue of his own creation. Amid the black miniboom on the "Great White Way" that he had done so much personally to create, Bert Williams died of pneumonia while starring in a play written for him, literally collapsing on stage. Decades later, *Variety* was to rank Williams third among the ten leading comic actors in American popular theater.

There was a part of the remarkable race-and-entertainment story that reached no American (or other) historical treatment. Bert Williams's family had moved California during his childhood. But it was often claimed, at least in Antigua, that he had self-consciously copied the remembered mannerisms of Antiguan men illiterate and apparently shiftless, nonetheless armored with their own philosophy of life. As related to young Tim by his grandfather, this first black director on stage and in films had come from a particular district of the island (Sweetes) long famous for storytelling. If Shakespeare had written for the "men in the pit," the ordinary theatergoers of his age, Williams had thus self-consciously embodied the ordinary Afro-Caribbean. Williams's blackface routines, Hector insisted, had like the gestures of the court jester in *King Lear* used irony to poke fun at the mighty and to establish his own character. Williams had not spoken only for Antigua, of course, or for his own black skin, but for the region and its potentialities, suppressed but never destroyed.[27]

Hector had little more to say on acting in stage or film, perhaps because the entertainment pages of the *Outlet* were so filled with personality studies of black celebrities, generally reprinted either from U.K. or U.S. newspapers. He assayed more often in sport (even more heavily covered in the *Outlet's* back pages, often in great detail), such as boxing, where Hector had his current favorites or, more usually, his memories of what this or that black boxer had meant to him decades earlier.

When it came to cricket, Hector's writing was virtually endless. It was also, more perhaps than in any other sphere of knowledge except philosophy and politics, consciously within the footprints of his great mentor. James had campaigned long before Hector, during the 1920s, years before Marxist politics, for a black captain of the Caribbean team. He had returned to cricket reporting in the early 1950s, upon his expulsion from the United States, that is, his forced return to the United Kingdom. He did radio play-by-play for cricket matches, unrecorded and now lost, during his extended stay in Trinidad of 1959–60. He then became the wise old philosopher of the sport, a talking head on BBC test matches, when he returned to London in old age. Indeed, it was as a cricket personality, not a Marxist or even a West Indian, that the ordinary British fans knew the face and the distinct patter of the self-avowed revolutionist. (American networks would never have permitted such a left-wing tyro precious airtime, and if English "fair play" ever really existed, this must be a good example.)

That James had laid it all out in *Beyond a Boundary*, to that time the finest history of cricket, continued to say volumes to the fan, from British county cricket to the far reaches of Pakistan, Australia, and of course the British Caribbean. No one but James was situated to relate Garfield Sobers to Willie Mays, athletes of the ancient Greek games to modern Caribbean athletes, and to understand the sweeping importance of Afro-diasporic development in their play. No one, in other words, had observed cricket as the microcosm or playing field of a comprehensive world system of thought.

To Hector, the cricket enthusiast, team organizer, and theorist, the dramatic and often saddening sagas of Brian Lara, Sir Viv Richards, and Antigua's own Richie Richardson understandably took on the dimensions of Greek tragedy. These were the giants who went forth, representing the region's hopes, and despite some stunning performances, eventually saw their side go down not merely in defeat but in disgrace and virtual disintegration, mirroring the fate of the region in so many different ways.

It had seemed so much more hopeful during Hector's own apex of regional influence. He insisted that the 1984–85 regional side had been the finest of all in test matches since the British in 1948, quite a claim. In the years immediately following, Viv Richards had captained more successful test sides than any previous West Indian. Then the great days fled. The bowling grew decidedly inferior, the wicket-keeping "pedestrian." Richie Richardson, another genius bowler, never had the proper opportunity to advance the side "without restraint" (as *Wisden's* put it in 1992). Brian Lara brought his world-class talent to teams so divided internally that Richards had been dropped along with others, the best batsmen. As batting gave way, opposing teams pressed the advantage, and defense had no chance to hold on properly. The crisis only worsened during Hector's final decade, and the cricket fan suffered keenly at the losses piled on, one after another. Daily papers gave more column inches, but no regional publication, it is safe to say, covered them as frankly and insightfully as the *Outlet*. Its staff sports columnist for many years was Adlai Carrot, one of Hector's closest comrades.[28]

To be fair, an ongoing crisis in cricket affected even England's play. Toward the end of the fading twentieth century, hours (in some cases, days) were cut from county matches and test matches, out of a sense that sports fans—television fans in particular—would no longer interrupt domestic daily schedules for such devotions. The cricket hard core remained as hard as before, but it constituted a smaller and aging part of a population assaulted by competition from televised world soccer, and American baseball, basketball, and football. Even that old favorite British favorite of tennis was now more dynamic for Afro-Caribbean fans, thanks to the Williams sisters (a black/female as well a sports phenomenon heavily featured in the *Outlet* sports pages) as was golf, to a considerably lesser extent, thanks to Tiger Woods.

But Hector had his point and held to it. The collapse of hopes for a successful federation, the paucity of combined resources for a regional cricket side, was costing the West Indies dearly. Posing his views against an admired feminist critic of cricket (something new and fascinating to Hector), Christine Cummings, Hector insisted that the improvement of cricket did not need to wait for successful federation:

> The relationship between politics and economics, on the one hand, and culture on the other, while organic, is not that deterministic or mechanistic. Cricket can lead a regeneration, if it overcomes the adversary relationship between Board and Players, perpetuated by West Indian intellectuals who persist in seeing the Board as a pillar of reactionary, planter class thought. . . . It will take above all the revival of cup cricket in each and every territory, in democratic self-organization and with the clubs, as new inclusive models for civil society. Such clubs must employ the experience of past players as organizers, guides and motivators, upholding the fundaments of team commitment above the "I am in it for me" which is the globalizing trend.[29]

It would be hard to put the appeal for Caribbean unity-through-teamwork in a tighter nutshell or one more quietly socialistic.

Music found him likewise, this time with his own unique island story to tell. In most areas of black music, specifically jazz, Hector was content to describe his own highly subjective reactions to one jazz musician or another whose work he had found transcendent, as performances of Beethoven had been to his trained ear as well. Beyond these musings, the *Outlet* treated black musicians mainly as celebrities, role models or otherwise.

Only in one area of music did he extend himself early and often: the steel band. Travelers in the region sometimes point to the Antiguan steel bands as among the finest anywhere. Deprived of so much, they could see in the music a world of expression otherwise denied.

Thus he insisted that an Antiguan sailor, coming back from the Second World War by way of Trinidad, had brought home the one totally new musical instrument created in the entire twentieth century. Perhaps he meant the only absolutely *new* instrument of widespread popularity, inasmuch as world pop alone has introduced many new versions of old instruments. But the point is well taken. Even the argument for an Antiguan contribution makes some logical sense, because the very absence of bamboo meant the nonappearance of the "tambu bamboo" so popular (notwithstanding the ban of the authorities) in Trinidad of the late nineteenth and early twentieth centuries. Instead, Antiguans had invented their own "iron bands," banging bits of iron and steel together especially at Christmas gatherings, thus a metallic precursor to the steel band.

At any rate, thanks to that very Antiguan sailor Buster Carty, national pan had commenced in 1945 or so. Unlike earlier phases of Caribbean musical folk culture, nearly all of them essentially rural, pan was an urban phenomenon of the black working class. (It is fascinating to contrast signature tunes with the bands that played them: "Mary Had a Little Lamb" and "The Lord's Prayer" were delivered by bands like Brute Force and Lord Blackshirt: respectable themes, dread self-identities.)[30] Little Antigua, with so little else to claim for itself, saw the first recorded steel band tune, became the first island where steel bands spread across the territory, and remained for decades the only one where steel band calypsos were played in and out of season, at any time. New tunes brought imitations, adaptations, and marches through towns, frequently unnerving whites and middle-class blacks as well.

Repeating the old tricks of the planters, the black petite-bourgeoisie had literally set dogs upon the musicians and upon the crowds following them. Then a legislative measure banned the steel bands entirely—a measure aimed in particular at Hells Gate and Red Army, both notorious for their crypto-political militancy. The Steelband Association responded with a Charter of Rights, handed to Bird and thence to the colonial governor, who sagely dismissed the intended repressive measure. The musicians basked in their victory, drawing the logical conclusion of expressing their own powers, and the *Steel Band Herald*, published from 1949, was the most socialistic of island newspapers. Representing the extreme Left of Bird's following, the *Herald* congealed extended discussions (from conversations among musicians and writers prior to publication, Hector claimed, in his own family's household, a sort of gathering spot) on various social issues. "The steelband radicalized the radicals, and were themselves radicalized by the radicals," Hector recorded. It was a dynamic process between culture and politics that contained the ideal of a self-generating, all-encompassing democracy.

When George Walter took office and vigorously promoted the bands, showering them with patronage, the dye of a different hue was cast. Quickly, the vigor of the bands declined, in the setting sun of expectations for what independence could bring. "When the radicals accommodated the old colonial status quo of foreign ownership and local dispossession," Hector concluded, "the steelbands did likewise." And yet, as a spontaneous expression of self-understanding, pan had flourished, and Hector believed that its glory could and would come again, leading the region toward political-economic unity rather than trailing behind the politicians.[31]

Tim and the Devil?

Meanwhile, time was running out for Hector. Even before his heart condition was diagnosed as dangerous in 2001, he had begun to reconsider his options. Friends reported, after his death, that the leader had regarded the seven years of disciplined relation to the United Progressive Party (UPP) as the most frustrating of his life. He desperately needed more freedom to operate. The collapse of the regional Left during the 1990s also prompted him to look outward in a different way, imagining (to sympathetic journalist Robert Coram) that the *Outlet* could become the regionwide weekly that its small readership among the intelligentsia of various islands already promised, in a limited way.[32]

At the end of the 1980s, amid the physical and mental collapse of the patriarch, the floodgates of corruption had meanwhile opened wider than ever before—something hitherto considered well-nigh impossible for observers of Antiguan politics. Antigua had never been a stranger to international intrigue, of course. But with Reaganites ruling the American roost, restrictions seemed to be lifted on "greed is good," from Wall Street and the *New Republic* to St. Johns and the Bird-friendly local press. The "Nassau Understanding" of CARICOM leaders in 1984, in retrospect, anticipated the acceptance of continued U.S. domination, both economic and political, by a region haplessly seeking to adjust to the economic "adjustment crisis" with privatization and health and educational cutbacks in the making.[33] In Antigua itself, drug transport via U.S. Air Force facilities, winked at as the CIA had winked at friendly French heroin dealers since the beginning of the cold war and continued to do so in Southeast Asia, was a natural counterpart to moral as well as economic corruption. So was the global operation of retired (but still definitely connected) Israeli officials, intimate to the Iran-Contra transfer of funds.

Lester Bird, the most energetic of the four Bird scions by a long margin and the only one ever personally close to Hector, set up the most memorable of the deals with an American living in Antigua. A close contact of perennial Israeli leader Shimon Peres, this Israeli expatriate had already been charged with profiteering in the Indonesian shipbuilding industry. In seeking a new base of operations, he shifted to Antigua, where the Birds sold him three-quarters of the government refinery without so much as an act of parliament. The promised refinery, touted to bring native jobs, never actually opened. But the financier quickly took over all fuel-oil sales on the island, with a significant jump in prices. By the middle 1980s, he had cleverly linked himself with the Bechtel Group, widely known for its hand-in-hand operation with CIA officials, in a global deal that would have brought Israeli profiteers a reputed $65 million, including a large chunk to Peres's own Labor Party.

The deal fell through for various reasons, and while the financier satisfied himself with operating the local Swiss American Bank, Vere Bird Jr. engaged a still more notorious Israeli: Maurice Saftari. Thrown out of Jamaica for financial manipulations, Saftari was miraculously appointed the "Special Advisor on Aviation" on his new favorite island and the managing director of the imaginatively titled Antigua and Barbuda Airways International. No planes, of course, ever flew. Meanwhile, Saftari bought hundreds of acres of land at bargain-basement rates and set out to create an export farm of melons, a commodity demanding large amounts of water in thirsting Antigua, water acquired cheaply by siphoning off some from a government reservoir—and then refusing to pay the utility bill. Saftari soon ruined himself by taking more than $1 million from the

Overseas Private Investment Corporation of the United States, meanwhile gathering monies from the Swiss American Bank among others, with no serious prospect of repayment. Deeply in debt, he fled the island and yet somehow managed to keep making payments to the Birds.

Compared to these operations, the creation of a string of brothels—their Dominican sex workers known popularly as "Daughters of Santo Domingo"—connected with New York's Gambino crime family; the unimpeded role of U.S. military personnel in the regional cocaine trade; and the continuing controversy about the airport (Hector took to calling its chief promoter and beneficiary "Runway" aka Vere Bird) were merely typical. Like the Birds' protection of international swindler Robert Vesco, long on the run from U.S. (and other) authorities, it was an old story made new only by the depth and the shamelessness of scandal.

What nevertheless made these scandals special, in a way, was the ceaseless and unintimidated reportage of the *Outlet*. Raising a cry echoed by mounting international criticism not so different from the ways in which the little Christic Institute had set off the Iran-Contra investigations by a decidedly nervous U.S. Congress, Hector threatened to bring the whole mess down and the highest officials with it. Ronald Reagan got off the hook largely thanks to the congressional Democrats' unwillingness to look too deep, lest they expose their own role in global intrigue and also seriously damage the CIA that they, too, depended upon. The Bird family escaped for similar reasons, but not without serious wounding.

In a Contra-like episode, the home of the oppositionist Rev. Neville Brodie was firebombed, his family barely escaping with their lives. The Bird machine suggested that Brodie might have been involved in a subversive destabilization of the government and set alight his own house for publicity purposes. Unlike Washington, where sentences for lying to Congress were commuted and conspirators slithered into neoconservative think tanks virtually untouched, "patriots" ready to reemerge in new high-level conspiracies a decade later, Antigua saw a Queen's Privy judgment against Antigua's Public Order Act. The act had been used in an earlier attempt to shut the *Outlet* down and shut Hector up, but it could not be used this time. At least the continued public shaming of corruption was assured.

The Birds, notwithstanding the handlers and protectors to be found all the way from Jerusalem to Washington, had become a laughing stock. The moment had come, or at least many thought so, for a shift in Antiguan life and a shift of direction for Hector. Not long before the 1990 election, the idea of a legitimate, democratic if not socialistic opposition to the Bird machine seemed too tempting to resist. But Hector would only join his forces with the United National Democratic Party (UNDP) if he had enough influence in a new government to make a difference. UNDP officials refused; they had not intended that at all. The ALP triumphed in the polls again.

Years passed, and in 1995 the offer came again, this time to create a UPP with a legislative seat allotted to Hector in the opposition. As the foremost parliamentary figure of the new party, he would contest Bird family corruption on a day-to-day basis. But if the *Outlet* was to be the newspaper of record (while a foreign investor sunk capital into a daily for the Birds) for the opposition, Hector remained number two, with Baldwin Spencer as the shadow prime minister. Come the 1999 election, Baldwin pressed his advantage. During the familiar and inevitable Red-baiting against Hector, Spencer demanded that his ally and conscience step down. Hector did so willingly, a tribute to both the sense of loyalty and high purpose.

But he did not guess the full treachery of his new political partners, or why they hungered so for victory over the increasingly troubled ruling party. Like George Walter before them, Spencer and the UPP had never been so much interested in cleaning up Antigua as replacing the Birds in collecting the swag. While parliamentary debates offered volumes of hot air, money changed hands. It was, to be sure, in smaller amounts than given the Birds. But its presence revealed in the familiar pattern of trading upon public holdings and services. One last violent act serving the interests of the Birds seems to have driven Hector closer, momentarily, to his parliamentary allies. On the night of November 19, 1998, diesel oil was poured upon the equipment in the *Outlet* printery and set afire. For months the paper was printed in Barbados and shipped by air. Finally, the printery was reestablished, although the twice-per-week publication taken up in the middle 1990s was abandoned for weekly appearance. The *Outlet* had survived.

But by 2000 Hector could accept the political shenanigans of the anti-Bird faction no more. Exposés of the UPP in *Outlet* followed, and relations quickly reached the point of no return. Spencer actually chose the pretext for a break, soon after Hector accepted Lester Bird's offer to represent Antigua in regional cricket matters, doubtless anticipating that the UPP leader would take this act as proof of disloyalty. With the regional Left practically gone, his activity outside the island limited to the Martin Luther King International's occasional conferences of Pan-Africans, Hector looked to a different way of practicing his politics.

During the next several years, his last, forced "retirement" from regular politics allowed Hector to assume an ambivalent relationship with the Birds (especially his schoolmate and now prime minister, Lester) in all manner of cultural activities. Sports were especially important, because Hector represented Antigua regionally and internationally. He returned to ABS-TV from which he had been banned (in 1983) by the elder Bird, and returned with a vengeance: this time, he appeared frequently on many topics, as he did on ZDK-Radio, reporting on national issues, as if to recuperate the commentaries that he had heard from Trinidad stations as a growing boy. He challenged Commonwealth education policies' downward drift, mobilized Libyan money for sports administration in the region, and rightly claimed to have mobilized a CARICOM bail-out plan for the most distressed nations. All in all, a large accomplishment.[34]

It remained to be seen how great a personal price he paid for the necessary compromises. More than quarter century earlier, Walter Rodney's WPA had proposed a similar power-sharing condominium as an immediate response to the total crisis behind the racial conflict tearing Guyanese society asunder.[35] The offer had been rudely refused. Hector had never sought perks for himself in the usual island (or other political) fashion. But the proposed condominium with the hated Birds amazed and evidently troubled some readers of the *Outlet* and other political comrades young and old who had regarded Tim as the one uncompromising, uncorruptable political-intellectual figure on the island.[36] Hector had actually made overtures toward Lester when exposure of the Space Research Center had shaken the doddering elder Bird during the 1980s. That opportunity had been lost, and now something like it would need to be tried again, without a political machine or even powerful allies, if necessary. But Tim's death ended the prospect. It sent Lester into heights of poetic recitation that had not been seen (in him or Antiguan leaders) for decades, if ever. Meanwhile, the corruption continued shamelessly as the former opposition UPP actually took power in 2003 and soon began eroding the few institutions restraining official and unofficial rapacity.

In his last months, moved from Antigua to Cuba to the United States for treatment, and finally back to Antigua, Hector fell back upon his friends, his followers, and his personal consolations. Jennifer Dickenson Hector, bringing four daughters into his remarriage, gave Tim a home life otherwise impossible. At her insistence, he even abandoned his forty-year habit of heavy smoking. It came too late; life had already taken too much out of him.

Past and Future: Never Far Apart

The first scholarly survey of Caribbean historiography recalls that as recently as 1964, the priest described as "Grenada's living historian" looked back to the eighteenth century as the island's "happiest days," noting that its slaves, "generally speaking, according to the available evidence . . . were well-treated and happy."[37] By then, younger U.S. historians had already begun to become noticeably queasy about the standard formulations of admired oceanic scholar and leading textbook writer Samuel Eliot Morison, that Africans had been perfectly suited to bondage, mere children destined to be brought up by their white betters. In the Caribbean, the "white man's burden" of official scholarship and scholarly rhetoric lasted somewhat longer. Informally, within the circles of the powerful, it has never vanished. Black Power is a question, then, without any ready answer in the region, if anywhere; it cannot conquer and it cannot go away.[38]

Perhaps there was no wonder, as Jamaica Kincaid recorded about her childhood, that Antiguans of her generation (and after) inclined to describe slavery as something that happened yesterday. They were not hopelessly "out of history," as Naipaul would repeatedly describe them, but rather locked *into* a history in which victimization could easily justify casual criminality at the highest and lowest levels of society, wanton destruction of the environment, and constant thoughts of emigration. They were ill-treated and unhappy. Unless things greatly changed, they were destined to go on being ill-treated and unhappy, notwithstanding outbursts of collective rage and more constant consumerism in efforts at escape from themselves into the status of third-class Americans.

Hector's ceaseless, self-prescribed task pointed in an entirely different direction: a collective empowerment, from primary education onward, that could bring Antiguans out of what Sylvia Winter had described in theoretical detail (some of it as obscure as the literary dialectics of Wilson Harris) as the imprinting, the internalization of the Otherness created by slavery. To do so would be not only a contribution to Antigua or even to the Caribbean, of course. Wilson Harris puts it brilliantly when he looks to the "misunderstood arts of the Caribbean" and says that the "true capacity of marginal and disadvantage cultures resides in their genius to tilt the field of civilization so that one may visualize boundaries of persuasion in new and unsuspected lights to realize a different apprehension of reality." This new or renewed apprehension meant a renewal of language, a "different reading of texts of reality."[39] No scholar or intellectual, no one regional journalist, had probed the "hidden arts" more voraciously, or continued so insistently to repeat that there was renewal possible, even at hand. It didn't happen in Hector's foreshortened lifetime, but there was time yet for it to happen.

Hector continued, at any rate, to insist that the idea of socialism had been done its most irreparable harm by claims made on behalf of a state capitalism that continued to squeeze its needed surpluses from the hands and brains of workers and peasants. Sounding very much like C.L.R. James, he explained patiently:

> Socialism is not nationalization. Socialism is not a vanguard party in power. Socialism is not the commanding heights of the economy brought under state control. Socialism is not state decrees. Socialism is not "benefits" for the masses. Socialism is the independent creative spirit of the mass of the population given the room and the opportunity to create new institutions at work, for the reorganization of production in the interests of the majority of the toilers and so

creating popular democratic organs of self-management and therefore a new culture.[40]

The content was universal, of course, if the form that it took in Hector's mind and life was Pan-African, Caribbean, and Antiguan. The vision had shaped his being.

It was a commonplace quickly rendered a banality, after the fall of the Eastern Bloc, that sweeping visions of world change were now irrelevant, the idea of a classless society or of transformation from below, made by working people themselves, probably worse than irrelevant. The proper role of intellectuals had now become mainly "local," assisting some reform movement with neither global nor seriously egalitarian aspirations. "Reform" itself had been transformed from spreading the accumulated wealth of society downward to concentrating it at the top, and "reformed" economies were said to be those most eagerly inviting a takeover by international corporate interests. In this world, the test of democracy was an election formality accompanied by supine acceptance; military invasions would be required to bring benighted nations into the twenty-first century. Terrorist threats aside, anyone south of the U.S. border would easily recognize Gunboat Diplomacy, gone worldwide, as something old and familiar.

Surely no intellectual, no radical could be more "local" than Tim Hector. But far from exhausted or reconciled to neoliberal or neoconservative strategies, he had renewed the visions of both Pan-Africanism and Marxism, ever moving toward newer possibilities while not neglecting the meaning of the familiar tragedies. As the crisis of neocolonialism continued to fester, as the economies of the world's great powers raced forward more recklessly on every front, with ecological horrors and quintessential finance capital, the urgency for sweeping solutions outside the logic of the market and military yearned no less than it had in days of optimism.

In small but significant ways, even without the much-deserved recognition, Hector's efforts continued to pay off for Antiguans. Late in 2003, the Antigua and Barbuda Trade Union Congress (ABTUC) was born, fruit of a decades-long effort to bring union leaders of various sectors together. Political leaders from the ALP camp had nixed the Mayday marches, which from the historic 1951 event led by Vere Bird himself through 1967 had been a high point in Antiguan working-class self-recognition. The rebellious Antiguan Workers Union, fiercely promoted by Hector, had never since been able to convince their rivals to join them in a moment of common cause. May 3, 2004, marked a new day made possible by the collapse of the Bird machine. As the *Outlet* noted, the event started with a small turnout, "as if the workers were waiting else-where to [make] sure that the leaders were indeed keeping to their word." Then the crowd swelled, followed at last by the march. Prime Minister Spencer Baldwin promised government support, although it remained very much to be seen, as conditions worsened in many ways and hotel workers were forced into "leaves," aka payless "vacations."[41]

Likewise, some measure of freedom of the press seemed to have been won, albeit a victory inevitably precarious. It might be remembered that at the apex of Maurice Bishop's Grenadian rule and U.S. pressure (before the coup and invasion by U.S. Marines), the opposition paper there had been shut down after virtually inviting U.S. intervention. Hector had insisted that under no circumstances, not even these, could such repression be accepted as proper. When in May 2004 an award for excel-lence in journalism and annual scholarship were jointly announced by a minister of state, the named prize and fellowship were to be for Samuel Fergie Derrick, late publisher of the *Daily Observer*. The *Observer* had endorsed Spencer Baldwin in the crucial recent election, dumping the ALP. The real advocate of free press, through trials and tribulations of burned and otherwise destroyed printing presses, arrests, and jailings for more than thirty years, had been the unhonored Hector. Still, the Antiguan press was indeed freer now. Hector would not have insisted upon honors in any case; the result, the advance of freedom, for him always trumped egotistic advances.[42] Lamentably, his *Outlet* would not live on to enjoy that freedom. His presence, his ability to get funding, even loans when necessary, had been decisive. The paper drew its last breath in 2005.

The *Crusader*, long published by George Odlum in St. Lucia, had already passed with its editor in 2003, and the Anglophone Caribbean socialistic media, the outright Pan-Caribbean and Pan-African voice of the region, had now been stilled. It was a curious footnote of the eulogists to the fallen heroes that the Martin Luther King International, funded by Momar Khadaffi for the purposes of bringing together Pan-Africans in Libya and elsewhere for conferences, had not only lost its leading lights in three of the "four musketeers" but also disappeared as the wily Libyan leader sought reconciliation or at least stronger economic ties with the West.[43]

Hector did not live to see, and interpret in his shrewd and generous way, the further twists and turns of Caribbean history. Only a few years after a group of distinguished regional scholars had glumly predicted that the twenty-first century likely saw only a return to nineteenth-century subjugation—this time to two competing blocs (one Western European, the other North American)—the blundered invasion of Iraq seriously undercut global confidence in U.S. leadership.[44] The consequences not only emboldened an Islamic militancy but, closer to home, encouraged a variety of socialistic and egalitarian opposition forces from the South. And there were smaller but no less important regional signs.

Conservation groups in Trinidad and Tobago, for instance, had saved major ecosystems rife with unique species: the freshwater Nariva and the western district's Caroni Swamp and Bird Sanctuary. Locals, along with Earthwatch volunteers, have made Trinidad and Tobago the second-largest nesting colony of leatherback turtles in the world. Projects proposed by Prime Minister Patrick Manning under such elusive titles as "Eco-Roadway" (actually intended to bring a major thoroughfare through a crucial forest, opening it to large-scale developers and the more usual poachers) remain to be fought. But there is hope in this new, green internationalism.[45] We can be sure that no one would have welcomed it more than Tim.

By the time another bold regional leader, Hugo Chavez, invited Caribbean leaders in 2005 to share Venezuelan oil at reduced prices, China was bidding to play a large role in what might become a very different bloc in global power struggles. At the very least, new options seemed to open for Caribbean maneuver. If the United States continually stumbled in global misadventures or simply failed to keep pace economically, if one Latin American nation after another turned leftward in elections, could the Caribbean be far behind? And what would it mean now, decades past independence? One can only be sure that the judgment of the *Outlet*'s editor is being missed and will continue to be missed.

Did he mean, Robert Coram innocently asked him in the early 1990s, to be "remembered as a newspaperman rather than a politician?" "Hector laughed. 'I want to be remembered as a human being.' "[46] And so he certainly shall certainly, one of the most interesting human beings that the islands have produced, one of those idealists of the twentieth century whose vision is so desperately needed for the increasingly dangerous era to follow.

Afterword

TIM HECTOR, HUMANIST, POLITICAL VALUES,
AND NATIONAL RECONSTRUCTION

—EUSI KWAYANA

Tim Hector was born in the same year as Walter Rodney and died of natural causes and those caused mainly by unnatural, human-made stress, twenty-two years after his colleague, comrade, and contemporary had fallen at the hand of an assassin in the employ of the state. It is almost laughable to add that I was born in the same year as Malcolm X, 1925.

The birth of Tim Hector and Walter Rodney in two different Caribbean countries in the same years seems to suggest some intelligence in areas of life of which we know nothing. The fact that they have now both been removed, however, suggests the opposite. I have written a small book on the activity and influence of Walter Rodney's life and work in Guyana, and I now wish to treat Tim Hector as a Caribbean person striving to see the Caribbean working people placed in the borders of a real nation with real dignity and presence in the modern world. The details of his Antigua-Barbuda activities will not receive equal emphasis here. I have learned details of their long collaboration in the Caribbean cause primarily from Hector's writings. Individuals even in a movement are fully entitled to set in motion what they know to be necessary for further stages of a revolution without conveying such plans to their own movements, which are preoccupied with more than they can handle on the domestic scene, as was surely the case with Guyana. At a proper time, they would pass information on to their colleagues or to those of their colleagues who were so placed as to contribute.

There are areas of political discourse that a new generation may wish to conduct entirely within its own generation, especially when these areas are of longer-term importance. Older political generations should not be uneasy about this, as they enjoyed the same privilege in regard to later or unborn generations, whose future they were for good or ill helping to determine. This remark is offered by way of explanation of the limits of older generations being able to pass fair judgment on later ones. Especially among younger generations, much political communication and synergy take place in the midst of social relations that are not labeled "political." This becomes very clear in reading Tim Hector's tributes to notable artists, cricketers, and political figures whom he knew personally outside of public activity and formations. In these spheres, for example, people think aloud more freely than they normally would at a formal forum, where such thinking might lead to confusion. When Rodney said to me as we were alone driving from one place to another, "That's why I can never be a full-time politician," he was expressing something deeply felt, which he let slip and might not have considered useful to declare in a formal meeting.

When Paul Buhle asked me to write something about the relations between Walter Rodney and Tim Hector, he was asking me about an area of experience that never would have concerned me unless some dramatic incident had been reported. It is a kind of generational sovereignty that is an important part of my philosophy and remains so in spite of the fact that Buxton Friendship, under my very nose, became an armed camp of dozens of youth and child soldiers who thought that they had found a way to quick freedom.

My own view of Tim Hector can be expressed in one piece of intelligence, also of a nonpublic though not secret nature. In 2000, the Jubilee 2000 invited me to London to speak at a tribute to the late president Julius K. Nyerere of Tanzania. I was genuinely puzzled by the invitation. I had not been about London since about 1965 and had never had more than a minute's conversation with President Nyerere.

My concern increased when I was told that I was to speak for the Caribbean. My response was that my choice of such a person would be Tim Hector of Antigua-Barbuda. I argued that he knew much better than I the pulse of the Caribbean, especially of the younger generations, that he was very well informed, and that his view would be more relevant to the future. I did not add that he was better educated by a long way and that he, unlike me, kept up an interactive and, from his side, intelligent dialogue with every new tendency that emerged either in political economy or in world affairs. The whole idea of Caribbean endeavors as action on the human stage was his, whether in politics, art, sport, or philosophy exemplified in sports, especially cricket, including the unbroken stream of Caribbean contribution.

In a more intensive way than C.L.R. James, his admitted mentor, Hector—whether he knew it or not—had a particular specialization and facility. He delighted in selecting a Caribbean actor on the scene in some department of life and establishing the place of that person in global activity and totality. This is one way in which he strove to make the Caribbean a nation and to explain to the world the components of its genius and distinctiveness. For him, Caribbean characters were not merely outstanding Caribbean people but outstanding people from the Caribbean, and he often clarified that he was talking globally. Anything less is akin to the way women of distinction are described as being not distinguished people but outstanding women, until the assertion is corrected.

A person of marked personal qualities, I learned from Shakespearean critics, often has the defect of those very virtues. C.L.R. James and Tim Hector, both bright stars in the firmament, capable of illuminating analysis, shared one defect. They could sometimes extend their practice to unfamiliar areas and escape with credibility.

Tim Hector was an analytical activist thinker. That is short for an analytical, activist intellectual. Certainly he was not alone responsible for his massive output in all these areas. As a political pioneer of the Jamesian Left within a Canadian university, he probably stood alone at first. At home in Antigua, he had the understanding, skill, and empathy of Arah, his wife and comrade, and of a number of gifted colleagues who, with him, cofounded and nurtured the Antigua-Caribbean Liberation Movement

(ACLM), to become the organizer and voice of the powerless in Antigua-Barbuda, especially of the young people.

Hector was libertarian, and it seems that he became more and more libertarian as he matured—not libertarian in the sense of a liberal without an ideology, if that is possible, but a person who did not fear discussion, debate, open argument about issues in the common tongue. He did not fear "the open word."

From him, we learn that his mother was a "shadow in the heat . . . a very present help" to the family in trouble. And the Hectors and the ACLM family also had their share of troubles. There is no question, however, that he was the one whose point was most likely received as leader, even though he never ran a Stalinist organization.

Those who have seen and heard the ACLM in St. Johns realize that it constituted a popular political and cultural attitude, rather than a major political force. This attitude comprised wellsprings of culture of class, of self-reliance, of self-respect, of hostility to dependence and, most of all, a keenness of the sense of being Antiguan. The ACLM membership and following were well informed on the rest of the Caribbean and the so-called Third World, because they were concerned.

Despite Hector's and the ACLM's labors, the ACLM entry into the national electoral politics was never rewarding in terms of seats won. This tended to discourage and worry elements of the ACLM, including Tim Hector. It was of course less the fault of the ACLM than the fault of the circumstances and especially of the social and political structure. Part of the negative results of the party system in countries like Guyana is real but cannot be demonstrated in a simple experiment.

The working of the system and the way it reorders life are such that political office comes to be seen by the people and the office holders as a form of property to which certain castes are entitled. The social majority tends to assign roles to activists and organizations in the political arena.

The idealism of the New Left in most places in the Caribbean has then been, in a sense, its own electoral undoing. Part of the reality is that the public perceives that these are a new breed of people who believe in their country and in us and do not have to be rewarded to do their duty, since their duties are imposed by conviction and conscience. But there are other responses in a complex of responses. Many of the general public see the established and establishment parties as part of a corrupting process called "politricks" and feel silently that those not already involved in its machinations will be better out of it. Add to these subjective and unspoken responses the more traditional ones: "Leh Bird (a)lone," or "leh Burnham lone."

The whole idea of a person merely being of quality "among Third World artists" or for the Caribbean or for Southeast Asia was an affront to Tim Hector. Of course, there were those actors and workers who were outstanding on a domestic basis only. Beyond that, however, it was his self-appointed task to show the Caribbean's contribution and sometimes Antigua's to the whole fund of human accomplishments. Since it was not readily admitted by others, he would proclaim it and tell it on the mountain, tell it on Mount Outlet. This is one of the reasons I preferred him to myself as a Caribbean spokesperson for the Caribbean at Jubilee 2000's celebration of Julius K. Nyerere in London.

It is in this sense that Hector wrote of Wilfredo Lam as "without doubt the most celebrated painter produced in the Caribbean," but then adds "from whom the great Picasso learned not a little about line as about composition." Of C.L.R. James, he writes similarly, "James is the most important revolutionary thinker of the 20th century." To make such a claim for a black man is to make a large claim. The whole idea of Western civilization was to prove that black men are no important part of history. Hegel, the all-important Western philosopher with the arrogance of ignorance, had after all asserted that Africa was "no important part of world history."

Hector summoned Paul Buhle as witness, and Buhle testified, "I make no pretence to a definitive statement, because the richness of James's life and the trajectory of his influence will require a large collective scholarship barely under way"—one of the highest tributes that can be made to any writer. Hector might have been slightly misinformed about some episode that he chooses for comment, but his comment was fair. He did not seem to be troubled by the multijealousies that afflict the political personnel of the Caribbean, that is, of politics in a small population.

It was 1962 when I first knew Antigua. My friends H. H. Nicholson (cofounder of African Society for Racial Equality) and his wife, Marguerite, had invited me to Tortola. There was I, landing in Antigua an unknown, for a connection to St. Thomas. A taxi driver and I spotted each other—as it was not a crowded flight from North America—or I might have gone unnoticed. He asked me where I wanted to go. I had picked up some tracts at the airport, and I told him, "Let us try Beachcomber". He asked, "You gon' try that?" I said, "Well, I don't know the place, and I don't want to waste your time." The taxi driver said, "Come, I will take to a place where you will be with your own people and feel good. Is a nice little place." I welcomed the offer. He took me to a cottage where the woman of the house readily welcomed me and said it would be $5 a night. I was relieved—I had on me the full bounty of $20 and cannot now say with certainty whether it was Guyana or U.S. currency, probably U.S. obtained for my departure. But the change left me some money with which I could manage until the next day, when I would find my way to the airport. I may have arranged the trip with the same taxi driver. Why would I not?

In the time we spent together, the taxi driver gave me a full analysis of the politics of the place, at a time when general elections were pending. Next morning, a free day, I went down into the streets and continued my exploration. There was a strike that crippled the city. George Walter, who was leading the opposition party in the elections, also led the union. At the union headquarters, I picked up a program of an annual conference of the Antigua Trade Union with its motions from various branches. It seemed very democratic. The prime minister and also the former head of the union was Vere Cornwall Bird. I found that the union had considerable power over the government. The motions, which I do not have by me, seemed to be more than appealing for government action.

To my astonishment, I found that Antigua-Barbuda, allowing for the governor and the Colonial Office's overlordship, was in domestic reality a one-party state and had been for fourteen years. The Antigua Labor Party (ALP) during all that time was the only party to win elections in the whole of Antigua-Barbuda. The ministers were all officials of the union. At the time, I knew nothing about Bird's socialist traditions, but what I was seeing was control of the legislative assemblies by the majority of working people of the state.

The same Vere Cornwall Bird seven times ordered or condoned Hector's arrest and imprisonment, pursued his family, and acted to deprive the Hectors of their means of livelihood. Yet it was Tim Hector, more than any writer, including Eric Williams and Gordon K. Lewis, who placed before us Bird's true legacy for Caribbean society in general and for African descendants in particular.

Hector also asserts what I, as a full-time political activist in Guyana, did not know. As the first act of statehood in 1967, it was Bird, the man without degrees, who started the Caribbean along the road to reclaiming its resources.

Hector records the Bird government's buying back of thirty-three thousand acres of land from the sugar plantation syndicate as the first act of statehood: the new status between colony and independent country accorded to Antigua-Barbuda. And he concludes, "Nevertheless Bird had changed Antigua and Barbuda from a plantation society, underwhelmed by disease and poverty, to a modern consumer society overwhelmed by alien production and alien accumulation of foreign debt. He goes into the historical beyond to be with his ancestors as the tallest figure in our 367-year history. It is his by right. Unchallengeable."

The ACLM had become part of the United Progressive Party (UPP), with Baldwin Spencer as its leader. When I finally got to Antigua again in 2002, I could not see Tim because of routines brought on by his illness. I met some of the old ACLM leaders, and they expressed disenchantment with his political behavior. Tim had been appointed to the Senate on the recommendation of the UPP. There, he could give the country the benefit of his political maturity in domestic as well as in foreign affairs. There was to be an international conference, which the Antigua government would attend. At some point and for some reason, the UPP instructed Hector not to attend this conference, as, in effect, an adviser to the Bird government. I could not learn from Tim whether he had been warned. However, Tim chose to attend the conference or meeting at the request of the Bird government, but now, of course, the government of Bird.

The UPP withdrew Tim Hector as senator, and the party seemed to regard him as now softening to the Bird government. The indignation

I heard on this score was deep. It was then that I tried to defend Tim as perhaps being in the same country where the meeting was to take place and deciding on national grounds to help Antigua—not to be wanting for quality representation if he could help it. I was informed by his former colleagues that he had been warned not to attend. Hence his withdrawal from the Senate was justified. The UPP also did not like Tim's negative response to the young woman who claimed to have knowledge of misconduct on the part of a member of the political directorate.

Clearly both Tim Hector and the UPP have a measure of right in their attitudes. Perhaps Hector was not sufficiently respectful of Baldwin Spencer and the UPP, and in fact we do not know his response to them. It might have been dismissive of the ban as too narrow. Then we have to take into consideration Hector's alleged friendship with Bird. It is a civilized thing that Guyana, a small nation, has also enjoyed for half a century this kind of friendship between opposed political sides or main actors. We, too, have had engagements, relations of tolerance, and efforts to outwit by engagement.

Tim was doubtless faced with the resolution that in foreign policy it was the wholeness of Antigua that was at stake and not Bird's party. His former colleagues saw it as a breach of discipline and perhaps giving aid to the political rival, not this day's enemy. In a time of dissatisfaction among the people, this gesture toward the ALP could make UPP supporters feel unsafe, even threatened. The government should have taken the public into its confidence, made known the scope of the meeting, and declared why it wanted nongovernmental help. It should have been written to the leader of the opposition, explaining why Tim Hector's help would make a difference.

We get a glimpse of the stresses in Hector's 2000 essay on Caribbean culture. He had been extolling the art of Bert Williams, a consummate artist of Antigua-Barbuda, and revealed his aim to promote in Williams's memory and for posterity the establishment of a Bert Williams Room as a Millennium Project in Antigua Park. He dreamed how it would inspire later generations. And in a strange apostrophe, he added, "Was the hope drunk? Or is it dead? At any rate, were I to proceed on the mission, the mean and petty would say I am in collaboration."

Analyses of the Caribbean have too long ignored the forces at work, even when these very forces result in action. Tim Hector thus passes on to Baldwin Spencer the UPP's official response to globalization in our times. The response is no different from Hector's familiar stated ideas of policy, and those of C.L.R. James long since, and it sums up the wealth of Hector's contribution to the necessities of any Caribbean future, however unrealized in our time. It is clear and profound:

> Baldwin Spencer and the UPP declared for a national economy, based on worker and popular share-holding, joint ventures in the manufacturing sector, local ownership and management of hotel and import sector so as to aid rapid capital the integration of such an economy in a wider Caribbean and Central American confederation. But, with the people in control of their base communities. This community development through elected community councils must have clearly defined and inalienable powers.
>
> Only a people so secure in their own communities can be integrated in a larger confederation of Caribbean and Central American states. Only such a regional state can create the space for economic and social development.

Appendix

ONE CARIBBEAN AS A ZONE OF PEACE

The following essay, published in the Outlet *issue of December 14, 2001, may be properly regarded as the fullest, most cogent elaboration of Hector's views during his final years. It sums up brilliantly his understanding of the environmental danger now facing the region as a manifestation of long-standing historical trends, and the need for a starkly different regional vision. The essay also illuminates Hector's urging of peaceful solutions and the opportunity as well as obligation that a longer life would have lent him for Caribbean leadership.*

P.B.

I am writing this from Havana where I am attending the tenth meeting of the Sao Paulo Forum to whose executive body I have just been elected.

The Sao Paulo Forum is a grouping of Latin American and Caribbean progressive forces, which began in Sao Paulo, Brazil, in 1990. The next forum was in Mexico City in 1991, then to Managua, Nicaragua, in 1992, Havana in 1993, Montevideo in 1995, El Salvador in 1996, Port Alegre in 1997, Mexico again in 1998, then Managua in 2000, and now Cuba again in 2001.

Since 1992 I have not attended because of my membership in UPP and not wishing to involve that party in controversies as to where and why I was meeting with the most progressive forces in the region and all sorts of backward conclusions drawn and spectres being raised by the ruling directorate as well as by backward elements within the UPP. Now that that phase [is done, and] my one compromise with anti-intellectualism, backwardness and reaction is over, I can now revel in being free of that suffocating straitjacket—though self-imposed.

Here at the Tenth Sao Paulo Forum a tremendous debate is taking place over globalisation and in particular the Free Trade Area of the Americas. Nothing of the kind goes on at home, as the reactionaries rule in government and Opposition alike. A debate that has seized hold on the world, drawing global protest, has met with nothing but silence at home. *Outlet* alone raises the issues of the new world order, or better, new World Disorder.

What has startled the rulers of the world, and even progressives, is the vitality of the movement, arising, in a manner of speaking, spontaneously in Seattle, Prague, Porto Alegre, Quebec, Gothenburg and Genoa, against what I call, the Dictatorship of the Market, as determined by the U.S. or the G8 governments, the OECD countries and the multinationals.

What has startled even me, [as I] wrote to my very dear friend and colleague Paul Buhle, after Seattle, is that the world has reached a new stage. Yes, what has startled even me and compelled me to write Paul Buhle is that in this new international movement "For a Different Globalisation"—as Seattle demonstrated—was the large amount of youths who have returned to political action, since the 60s, questioning and rejecting the existing capitalist world order. That this new movement among youth is global is all the more startling.

In truth the most varied forces have come together "For a Different or an Alternative Globalisation," in a new self-organised international movement. The mobilisations carried out during the different summits of international leaders and officials are a very clear sign of a new impulse among the peoples of the world. It gives cause to hope, and not just hope, but to work for a new future.

They, in their thousands and tens of thousands are not just against globalisation, not merely an anti-globalisation movement, but at Porto Alegre thousands of representatives of social, religious and political organisations met and promulgated their common support for an alternative globalisation. This is absolutely new in world history. Not since the Crusades, has the world seen the international like. Not even the single greatest movement of the twentieth century, the revolt of the formerly colonial, black and coloured countries which saw over a hundred new nations created matches this new movement.

Among the key proposals for an alternative globalisation, posed at Porto Alegre is the primacy of human development and survival over any other consideration, especially mega-profits. Further this new international movement declared its support for only a type of development that does not harm our environment, and, simultaneously, is carried out with respect for human rights and the principles of economic and social justice. They have called for the cancellation of the Third World's and the poorest countries public foreign debt. They have required compliance with the Kyoto Protocol, which U.S. President Bush unilaterally reneged on, and which sought to reduce the emission of contaminating gases and air pollution, with its devastating effects on world climate. They have advanced as well postulates relating to education and health care in the world.

On behalf of the Caribbean, the English-speaking Caribbean and speaking here in Havana for the English-speaking Caribbean, I have advanced in the memory of Maurice Bishop, Walter Rodney, Frantz Fanon, George Weekes, Rosie Douglas, C.L.R. James, George Padmore, and Ché Guevara that the Caribbean be declared a zone of peace by vote of the U.N. Security Council and the U.N. General Assembly.

This would mean the removal of all foreign military bases in the Caribbean in independent and dependent states, be it in Antigua, Guantanamo or Vieques, it would include Russian, French and American military bases and pacts. It would remind the world of one of the Caribbean's principal claims to distinction in the comity of nations, that though these islands and territorial states have been fought over, annexed and conquered by imperialist powers, Caribbean people have at no time fought a war among themselves. Though we are among the most rebellious peoples in the world, rebelling against the pernicious slave world order in which we began our history, the worst form of slavery known in history; and rebelling too against internal and external powers, the Caribbean people have never made war on each other, irrevocably committed to Peace. This makes the region unique. Therefore the Caribbean should be declared a Zone of Peace and be so regarded and respected by all.

Maurice Bishop, I remind, can claim paternity of the idea. The point is now to make the shadow into substance, the abstraction into reality, the word, flesh, and therefore dwelling amongst us.

The Caribbean as a Zone of Peace, must involve and include, international recognition that the ruthless extermination of the Indians (Tainos) throughout the Caribbean, constitutes a great crime against humanity. It was, in fact the first of the world's horrendous genocides. Moreover, and it is from then that the barbarian germ of genocide was planted in human consciousness and the foul contagion has spread to all continents, as rulers and dominant races and tribes have adopted political positions, aided and abetted by religion, to the right of Genghis Khan and Alexander the Great. Therefore reparations must be paid for the genocide against the first peoples of the Caribbean, and their indigenous survivors must themselves administer self-determined programmes of affirmative action designed to bring them into the modern world, with due respect for their native language and culture. This, to be sure, is a first step in a really new world order: the redistribution of income.

Similarly, reparations must be paid by Euro-American powers for African slavery in the Caribbean as a condition of declaring the Caribbean a Zone of Peace. Such reparations must go to programmes of industrialisation, education, housing, health care, but primarily to women's development for their double oppression as slave, in colonial and patriarchal societies as well as oppression in the household, with priority to single mothers, themselves thrice oppressed—the third instance being the social arbitrariness imposed on them and their children.

One other point I made as a condition of the Caribbean as a Zone of Peace must be the immediate cessation of shipments of nuclear wastes and other hazardous waste through the Caribbean regional waters extending from the Bahamas to the Guyanas.

And finally to ensure the Caribbean as a Zone of Peace there must be an immediate cessation of foreign countries returning hardened criminals to the Caribbean to intensify crime. All such criminals who have lived abroad for more than ten consecutive years must not be returned or deposited to the Caribbean. The poor Caribbean ought not to be solving the criminal problems of the most advanced countries.

Fortunately, I recently chaired a meeting, which will bring progressive Caribbean forces together to agitate and struggle for One Caribbean as a Zone of Peace. It will include organisations and individuals, women's organisations, Trade Unions and Farmers' organisations. The founding meeting has been carded for March, 2002. As such it will signal to the world the Caribbean vision of itself for the new millennium and "For an Alternative Globalisation." It will bring the Caribbean centre stage in the new global movement of People.

I want now to show the form of globalisation, the reactionary and fundamentalist vision of globalisation proclaimed by neo-liberals or capitalists and their intellectual forces and statesmen.

According to this reactionary and fundamentalist vision of globalisation technological advances have unleashed forces independent of the control of humankind and nation states, as though the technological advances were a new divinity, whose omniscient and almighty decrees, brook no dissent from this supremely jealous and intolerant god. It is assumed from this that the global economy is in the hands of transnational agencies, as the human agency of the new planetary divinity. And in this new global village united only by informatics and by the speed of the means of transportation, economic transactions no longer take place in national or regional spaces but in planetary spaces. All independent of the will of people, controlled exclusively by the Divinity of the Market.

Consequently, decisions about the allocation of resources technological advances replacing labour, the distribution of income and specialised production in the various countries—the new division of production and labour—are taken outside national spaces and states, which, of course have no say. The New Divinity rules, allocates, displaces, downsizes, de-regulates, and let no damn dog bark!

In effect, countries no longer compete in the world market, but firms. And in that predatory world, only such firms will survive, exclusively because of their capacity (probably genetic, but definitely racial) to downsize and subordinate labour and exalt technology over humanity, with ever increasing concentrations of Capital. To such transnational or multi-national firms, national or regional loyalty will be transferred.

Naturally (or is it un-naturally?) these firms will be uprooted from national spaces, though backed by the greatest military might from space as well as on earth, and such global enterprises, powered by computer chips and other innovations would fly by themselves imposing its own order, as the divine magic of the global market decrees.

It is said therefore that this globalisation of our time and in our time is an absolutely new and unprecedented phenomenon, incomprehensible to mere non-corporate mortals, who, of necessity, with the end of history, must go along to get along. Or be damned to eternal exclusion, immiseration and pauperisation.

For, national or regional economies have lost all power. Sovereignty has lost all national or regional meaning. The only real Sovereignty would be the sovereignty of the Market, which is blind, deaf and dumb, but magical in its dispensation of favours on its chosen 20 per cent, but ruthlessly unmerciful in its disregard of the unfortunate 80 per cent.

I want to emphasise that this domination, this hegemony of 20 per cent over the other 80 per cent of this world can only take place if the 20 per cent, through collaborators, can inflame and sustain at red-hot heat of racism, ethnic division, party division, religious divisions, animosities between indigenous and immigrant peoples, with women in all categories subordinate, and with the immiseration of the whole, with children preyed upon as pornographic objects of hedonism let loose. An essential policy of the whole system will be trade union bureaucrats in company unions keeping the working classes divided for the political elites, and the dominance of Capital. Meanwhile, political parties, without ideology of any kind, except the dominant ideas of the dominant 20 per cent, will keep nations in subordination, in fee simple

I want to re-emphasise that there is nothing new in globalisation, while not contending that there is nothing new under the sun.

Let me prove the point with an immortal analysis of history and political economy.

As long ago as 1848 the great Karl Marx said: "The bourgeoisie had through the exploitation of the world market given a cosmopolitan character to production and consumption. . . . The bourgeoisie has by the rapid improvement of all instruments of production, by the immensely facilitated means of communication drawn all, even the most barbarism nations into [global] civilisation."

That capitalist globalising process then is nothing new. It only appears new in that consumption of the same news, the same TV, radio and newspaper presentations of the ruling elite, the same video games are more global, more cosmopolitan, if you prefer. And with the same global consumption pattern, the same atomised and dehumanised consciousness, turning us all into consuming zombies, measured only by the things we have, or do not have, all worshipping and paying homage to what is known as one of the lesser gods, namely, Standard of Living or Economic Growth. A regular diet of the most animal sex and the most horrific violence, laser violence as in sci-fi completes the picture of global civilisation, with its ever more brutal wars.

The truth is if we look at the last century we can see from 1900–1910, that monopoly capitalism then dominant in Great Britain—which in its grand delusion ruled over an empire on which "the sun would never set"—France, Germany, Holland, Belgium latterly in the U.S.A., and partially in Russia sought to escape their recurring economic crises by engaging in colonial domination.

No corner of the globe escaped the greed of these imperialist powers. Imperialist globalisation was born with colonial conquest. The crises of overproduction in these advanced countries pushed these imperialist countries to expand demand by drawing into their vortex, and getting "a more reasonable share," as it was said then, of the colonies.

Thus the First World War, which would gulp down the lives of some 10,000,000 people. Humanity had never before seen such staggering losses of human life. The brutality of the American Civil War at the end of the nineteenth century, a Civil War fought over slavery and in which slaves played a decisive role, laid the foundations, as well as the genocides in the Caribbean and U.S.A. lodged in the collective unconscious (to borrow from Karl Jung) of Euro-America, and too, the terrorism of slave society, which allowed a few planters to ceaselessly terrorise, by an admixture of terror and benevolence, the whole black race. In these cruel antecedents lie the new brutal regimes of terror, which dominate global civilisation.

Despite or because of the Russian Revolution of 1917, imperialist globalisation intensified in the 1920s and 1930s. It was intensified by the growing rivalry between the imperialist powers to lay hold of the markets and raw materials of the whole world. The world crisis of 1929, known as the Great Depression, was a crisis of overproduction in the industrialised countries, linked to financial collapse. The larger capitalist countries sought to get out from under this Depression by means of a Keynesian policy of public works and huge weapons programmes.

End result—the Second World War. In the course of which 50,000,000 people lost their lives. Barbarism had reached unprecedented heights. So, on the one hand there was the constant revolutions in production and on the other ever-increasing barbarism. Or both were a unity.

U.S. imperialism enriched itself at the start of the Second World War by selling goods and weapons to both "democratic" and "fascist" countries. The U.S. entered the Second World War late, with a view to avoiding the socialist revolution in France, Italy and Germany, which were halted by the advance of the Allied Forces and the Red Army. The U.S. also hoped to acquire the colonies of a weakened British Empire, not as outright colonial possessions, but their markets and their economies, just as it had acquired Cuba and the Philippines at the end of the Spanish-American war at the end of the nineteenth century.

Before, during and after the Second World War Stalin turned the Russian Revolution into its opposite, where the State ruthlessly exploited the working people, maintaining capitalist relations of production most rigidly. Barbarism triumphed over socialism. It was only a matter of time, before the new technocrats and party officials in the Soviet Union who "planned" production, substituting themselves for the working class, collapsed into private ownership of production, and outright capitalism in 1990. In the ensuing process production in the former Soviet Union stood at 57 per cent of what it was in 1990, and in the Ukraine fell to 39 per cent, while in Russia itself 60 per cent of the population receives an income—when they are paid at all—below subsistence level. Criminality has become endemic.

In the interim most Third World countries managed by titanic struggle to free themselves from colonial rule, by seeking first the political kingdom and hoping that all other things would be added. That hope, as in Shakespeare's *Macbeth* proved drunk. For, as in the economic kingdom the price of Third World raw materials and primary production, fell painfully low, as the cost of advanced countries manufactured goods increased many times, in spite of the expanded market. Thus sharply contradicting the very fundamental law of capitalism, that with increased demand, prices would fall. Not so at all. The truth is, prices were arbitrary to allow the industrialised countries a superior standard of living (as "proof" of their racial superiority) at the expense and impoverishment of the newly freed black and coloured formerly colonial countries. And above all to allow Capital to accumulate in fewer and fewer hands in the industrialised countries.

The new, formerly anti-colonial leaders merely took over the positions in the State left by the Colonisers; kept the Colonial State, virgina intacta, and proceeded to plunder the wealth of their countries, in association with the financial and corporate interests of the industrialised world. Whereas the bourgeoisie made their wealth by the corruption of industry and the environment, the new Third World elites, made theirs by state plunder and from the foreign public debt, given for infrastructure, and not industrialisation or agricultural transformation.

At another crisis of imperialist globalisation in the 1970s, the national elites in the Third World were forced or acquiesced into debit, in a huge way, for the construction of massive infrastructure, while they were offered, by various means, the opportunity to enrich themselves off this public foreign debts. The aim of globalisation was to preclude and prevent the creation of national industry agriculture and commerce based on the needs of the popular masses, and to ensure consumption of the over-production of the industrialised countries.

This resulted in the following conditions currently in the world; 15 per cent of the world's population lives in 28 developed countries sharing 77 per cent of world exports; 77 per cent of the world's population lives in 128 countries sharing 18 per cent of exports.

The United Nations' "Report on Human Development 2000" shows that the poorest 20 per cent of the world's population consume 5.4 per cent of global wealth, whereas the richest 20 per cent consume 48.3 per cent of this same global wealth.

World redistribution of income is a necessity of human survival on planet earth.

But let us make the picture even clearer. The President of the World Bank was forced to admit that 20 per cent of the planet control 80 per cent of the global economy.

This results in a picture in which 1.5 billion human beings survive on a monthly income of less than 30 U.S. dollars and it is estimated that by 2025 this figure will reach 2 billion. But, there are another 2.8 billion people living on less than US $60 a month. More than 600 million men and women are homeless. An African family consumes 20 per cent less today than twenty-five years ago.

65 per cent of the world today have never received a telephone call in their lives, in spite of increased means of communication in the global information revolution, and 40 per cent have no access to electricity.

The Caribbean and Latin America groans and strains on the way to its calvary, under the cross and yoke of an external debt which exceeds US $750 billion, dedicating 56 per cent of its revenue to servicing this gargantuan debt. Most of which debt went down the corrupt political beltway, or enriching multinational banks.

The more over-production becomes a menace to the industrialised countries the more they destroy, by various nice-sounding stratagems national production in Third World countries. So that both in the Second World—the former satellites of the Soviet Union—and in the Third World productive capacity is dwindling.

The current phase of globalisation, perhaps its last, is characterised by constant revolutions in the field of information technology, communications and transport, and simultaneously, the unprecedented concentration of capital in trans multinational corporations, which are in a mad rush to conglomerate even more for global hegemony, backed by the enormous armed power of an uni-polar world.

There interlocking forces represent current globalisation. First the big transnational corporations. Then the imperialist states, which protect and defend these concentrations of global capital. Thirdly the institutions dominated by these same states, such as the IMF, the World Bank, the World Trade Organisation. Through these, and lesser organisations like the OECD, imperialism mainly the U.S., imposes conditions on the governments of the dominated countries and dictate policies and laws, which they must enact, if they are not to be subject to sanctions, and if need be to wars of destabilisation or outright wars of aggression.

But there is a fourth and independent factor in the growing unity of the world, against the IMF, World Bank, WTO, environmental abuse and pollution of the world by the industrialised countries and the great income disparities of a world or global village organised to satisfy a small 20 per cent, at best, global elite.

One Caribbean as a Zone of Peace is a distinct and direct challenge to that militarised world order in greedy pursuit of more and more capital, at the expense of humanity, but in the name of anti-terrorism and sham democracy. Check it out!

Notes

Introduction: In the Sunlight, in the Shadow

1. Tim Hector, "Globalisation and Us," *Outlet*, 17 September, 1999, reprinted in "Tim Hector Anthology" issue of the *CLR James Journal* 8 (Winter 2000/2001), 117 (hereafter cited as Hector Anthology).
2. Gordon Lewis put it best: "The West Indian union leader . . . in general knows little more about the proletariat of his locals than a good sepoy colonel of 1856 would have known about the Indian village from which his recruits come." Gordon Lewis, "The Challenge of Independence in the British Caribbean," in *Caribbean Freedom: Economy and Society from Emancipation to the Present*, ed. Hilary Beckels and Vernene Shepherd (Princeton, N.J.: Marcus Weiner, 1996), 512.
3. Tim Hector, "Don't Cry for Me," *Outlet*, July 18, 2003.
4. Tim Hector, "The Past Dominates the Present," *Outlet*, September 26, 1987, reprinted in Tim Hector, *The World and Us* (n.p., n.d.), 155–56.
5. Kari Levitt and Lloyd Best, "Character of the Caribbean Economy" (1975), in Beckels and Shepherd, *Caribbean Freedom*, 405–20. This is not to say that Levitt and Best were wholly pessimistic, but their view was shadowed by a historically based realism.
6. James had, of course, been an early champion of Naipaul's writing, especially the marvelous *A House for Mister Biswas*, but James expressed personal disillusionment and exasperation at Naipaul's cynical turn; "On the Run" was payback. The imagined "Lebrun" was a Communist who wrote for East Bloc newspapers—the very opposite of James—but the old man with a small political circle was unmistakably James, "pure and principled," in a phrase that Naipaul uses to ridicule intellectual and political steadfastness as empty or even self-serving rhetoric, the "revolutionary without a revolution," ultimately a man who had made himself a Marxist so that, as an Afro-Caribbean, he could be "somebody." In the end, this Lebrun becomes an ideological aide-de-camp of African dictators, perhaps the most absurd of insults to throw at an intellectual who had been refused participation in the Sixth Pan-African Congress because of his contempt for official regimes. See

"On the Run," in V. S. Naipaul, *A Way in the World: A Novel* (New York: Knopf, 1994), 107–61.

7. Wilson Harris, "Judgment and Dream" (1989), in *The Radical Imagination: Lectures and Talks by Wilson Harris*, ed. Alan Riach and Mark Williams (Liege: Liege Language and Literature, 1992), 22. Special thanks to Harris for giving me this rare volume. Hector, for reasons never clear but probably as much for form as content, steadfastly preferred Naipaul to Harris, confounding the judgment of his comrades and this writer.

8. Thus a BBC radio staffer wrote the author that as the grandson of Antiguan activists, he grew up reading *Outlet* and, from abroad, savored the online version of Hector's essays because "the scope and depth . . . is of such quality that one is always left feeling . . . as if one has accompanied Tim on a grand journey. . . . Tim was a virtuoso the lines of which we may never see again." E-mail from Adrian Harewood, April 27, 2005. Thanks to Harewood for permission to reprint these lines.

9. Wilson Harris, "Continuity and Discontinuity," in *Selected Essays of Wilson Harris: The Unfinished Genius of the Imagination*, ed. Andrew Bundy (London: Routledge, 1999), 182–83.

10. Tim Hector, "My Grandmother in Time and Place and Luck," *Outlet*, August 30, 2002.

11. "Definitive Biography of CLR Urgently Required," *Outlet*, June 21, 2002.

12. Ibid.

13. Tim Hector, "Lying Flat On Our Backs," *Outlet*, May 25, 2001.

14. Paget Henry, "Flame That Burned Brightly," *Outlet*, December 13, 2002.

15. Tim Hector, "Antigua Vision—Caribbean Reality," *Outlet*, October 18, 2002.

16. Brian Meeks, "Introduction: On the Bump of a Revival," in *New Caribbean Thought: A Reader*, ed. Brian Meeks and Folke Lindahl (Kingston: University of West Indies [UWI] Press, 2001), viii–xviii.

17. Meeks, "Introduction," esp. xiii–xvi. He points to a number of essays in the volume, among them Hector's former student and my erstwhile collaborator on matters of C.L.R. James, Paget Henry.

18. Selwyn R. Cudjoe and William E. Cain, eds., *C.L.R. James: His Intellectual Legacies* (Amherst, Mass.: University of Massachusetts Press, 1995). This volume consists mostly of papers given at the C.L.R. James Memorial Conference in 1991 at Wellesley College, organized by the C.L.R. James Society, with especially ardent efforts by Black Studies chair Selwyn Cudjoe, a native Trinidadian and publisher of Caloloux Publications, which has published a series of books on mainly Trinidadian historical themes.

19. One of the most interesting is Nicole King, *C.L.R. James and Creolization: Circles of Influence* (Jackson: University Press of Mississippi, 2001).

20. James's Detroit disciple since the early 1940s, Glaberman had republished obscure pamphlets (or distributed them) since the 1960s and distributed many of them

exclusively until the collection of several volumes of collected essays, in the 1980s, by Allison and Busby. His last effort was *Marxism in Our Time: CLR James on Revolutionary Organization* (Jackson: University Press of Mississippi, 2000).

21. V. S. Naipaul, *A Way in the World*, offered a preview of the James presented in Farrukh Dhondy, *C.L.R. James: A Life* (New York: Pantheon, 2001).

22. Paul Buhle, ed., *C.L.R. James: His Life and Work* (London: Allison and Busby, 1986). Not to make too much of this, it was the first such scholarly work on James and included essays by great intellectual figures such as Wilson Harris, along with those who had studied James's life deeply and those whom he had influenced along the way. The original journal publication was *Urgent Tasks*, the organ of the Sojourner Truth Organization, itself a post–New Left mixture of Maoism and Jamesanism, destined like many such small organizations for an early demise. Like the rest of James's work published by Allison and Busby, the reprinting of *His Life and Work* in book form was the result of Margaret Busby's energy and loving attention.

23. Jim Murray's own unexpected and untimely death in 2003 effectively closed out the C.L.R. James Institute and reminded the eroded inner circle of old-timers how dependent upon specific individuals the activities of James's devotees really were, and are. Murray was not a particular an ally of Hector's, in the small conflicts that beset the circle; but his devotion to James never flagged. The assorted materials Murray collected are now in storage at Columbia University. Other collections of James's material, also limited in scope and contents, are held at the Oilfield Workers Trade Union headquarters in San Fernando, Trinidad, and at the UWI–St. Augustine, Trinidad.

24. Paul M. Buhle, *C.L.R. James: The Artist as Revolutionary* (London: Verso, 1988). I make no claim to its completeness; quite the contrary. Regrettably, the subsequent biographies, up to the present, have not pushed appreciably further in respect to his Caribbean background (and continuing connections) and his sojourn in the United Kingdom in the 1930s where James first traveled abroad, became a cricket reporter, a Trotskyist, and anticolonialist of note and wrote *The Black Jacobins* among other works. Though far from a best seller, *The Artist as Revolutionary* attracted considerable interest, thanks to Edward Said's review in the *Washington Post*, added interest in James (on his death) from National Public Radio, and for the British world, the BBC/Channel 4 documentary noted above, organized mainly by Tariq Ali.

25. Paget Henry and Paul Buhle, eds., *C.L.R. James's Caribbean* (Durham, N.C.: Duke University Press, 1992).

26. The journal owed greatly to Selwyn Cudjoe in the first year or two, later to the efforts of Brown University's Africana Department; but it has owed most to Paget Henry, who has nurtured it editorially and sold it personally, customer to customer, at Caribbean scholarly events. It is at present available via Africana Studies,

Brown University. Paget Henry and Tony Bogues have followed up the work on
James with international conferences on George Lamming and Sylvia Winter.

27. I wish to insert only a small claim for myself here: with a kind of ravenous intellectual hunger, I made the initial selection of the "Hector Anthology" of the
C.L.R. James Journal, 8 (Winter 2001). Paget Henry wrote the introduction. An
earlier Hector anthology, *Their World and Ours* (n.p., n.d.), was printed crudely
and received little circulation. It remains a collector's item: thanks to Paget Henry,
I have had it to work with on the present study.

28. Henry, "Flame That Burned Brightly."

Chapter 1: The Caribbean Context

1. Eric Williams, *From Columbus to Castro: The History of the Caribbean, 1492–1969*
(New York: Random House, 1970), a volume inspired by James's grand view and
on that point alone, never destined to be entirely outdated by more sophisticated
historical approaches. Sylvia Winter, however, added a crucial philosophical
dimension to the meaning of transition from aristocratic society to modern
capitalism, a transition so refracted in the Caribbean by the continuing aristocracy
of race. See Sylvia Winter, "Beyond the Categories of the Master Conception:
The Counterdoctrine of the Jamesian Poesis," in Henry and Buhle, *C.L.R. James's
Caribbean*, esp. 63–70. Kelvin Singh has restated the basic points admirably in
"Globalisation and the Caribbean: A Five Hundred Year Perspective," in *Caribbean
Survival and the Global Challenge*, ed. Ramesh Ramsaran (Kingston: Ian Randle,
2002), 18–29.

2. Tim Hector's remarks to the C.L.R. James Centennial Conference in UWI Trinidad,
2001, CD supplied me by Matthew Quest.

3. Tim Hector, "Free Paper Come! Free Paper Come!" *Outlet*, July 19, 2002.

4. Tim Hector, "The Triumph of 'Solitude' Is Part of the Black History Which Is in the
Future," *Outlet*, February 22, 2002. He comments on Bernard Moitt, *Women and
Slavery in the French Antilles, 1635–1848*.

5. Ibid.

6. See the essays in the "Women and Gender" section of Beckels and Shepherd,
Caribbean Freedom, 215–59.

7. One of the most memorable passages in James's semiautobiographical *Beyond a
Boundary* (1963) recalled that his grandfather, born in Barbados, agreeing to start
a plantation locomotive broken down in the time-crucial harvesting process, nevertheless insisted upon making the repairs in secret: as a black man, on point of
pride, he was not going to show the whites how to do it again. But James's early
learning of "culture" in the British school tradition predisposed him away from

African traces, perhaps because the more sophisticated literature on such was also slow to develop, perhaps because the narrative of "newness" in the Caribbean drove him ever back to a somewhat reductive position. In Naipaul's mocking version of James's family history in *A Way in the World*, a great-uncle is a mere lackey, the carriage-driver for Bajan white aristocrats, nostalgically looking backward to happy days of subservience: a reversal of the real history.

8. Rhoda E. Reddock, *Women, Labour and Politics in Trinidad and Tobago: A History* (London: Zed Books, 1994), esp. 11–46.

9. Williams, *From Columbus to Castro*, 153.

10. Ibid., 157.

11. Paget Henry, *Peripheral Capitalism and Underdevelopment in Antigua* (New Brunswick, N.J.: Transaction Books, 1985), 52.

12. What we can say of Williams's account is a thousand times more true of James's *Black Jacobins* (New York: Vintage, 1963): this is a volume not to be replaced, even as updated and occasionally challenged by an assortment of younger scholars.

13. Although ferocious anti-Stalinist James would not have easily admitted it, the return of the figure Spartacus from obscurity owed far less to the *Black Jacobins*, in which it was a passing reference, than to the novel and the film of that name, notable in part because novelist Howard Fast had written it while in prison for his refusal to testify to the House Un-American Activities Committee, and the spectacular 1960 film marked the return of one outstanding blacklistee (i.e., former Communist) screenwriter Dalton Trumbo from the blacklist. See Paul Buhle and Dave Wagner, *Hide in Plain Sight: The Hollywood Blacklistees in Film and Television, 1950–2002* (New York: Palgrave-McMillan, 2003), 173.

14. This view of the United States, in recent years once more sharply contested by the devotees of empire, was put forward most sharply by William Appleman Williams, *The Tragedy of American Diplomacy* (Cleveland: World, 1959). See my biography, *William Appleman Williams: The Tragedy of Empire* (New York: Routledge, 1995), cowritten by Edward Rice-Maximin, for the connecting points of Williams and James. Williams knew them well; James was not so clear-minded here, perhaps because Williams was so weak on the role of independent black movements.

15. C.L.R. James, "The Making of the Caribbean People," a 1965 speech in Montreal reprinted in *Spheres of Existence: Selected Writings* (London: Alison and Busby, 1980), 173–90. James quotes his own passages of 1938 to this effect and admits a sense of pride in saying it because "there were not many people thinking in those terms as far back as 1938. There are not enough who are thinking in those terms today" (184).

16. Werner Zips, *Black Rebels: African-Caribbean Freedom Fighters in Jamaica* (Princeton, N.J.: Markus Wiener, and Kingston: Ian Randle, 1999), translated by Shelley L. Frisch, makes grand claims for history and continuing traditions of the Maroons

of insular Accompong, in the Blue Mountains. If perhaps too grand, he neverthe-less recuperates what reggae singers sought to incorporate in their metaphorical histories of rebellion, but also what ethnologists of dance had discovered genera-tions earlier: a crucial sense of cultural autonomy and continuity.

17. Jay R. Mandle, *Persistent Underdevelopment: Change and Economic Modernization in the West Indies* (Amsterdam: Gordon and Breach, 1996), 49–50.

18. See W. K. Marshall, "Metayage in the Sugar Industry of the British Windward Islands, 1838–1865," 64–79; Rosamunde Renard, "Labour Relations in Martinique and Guadeloupe, 1848–1870," 80–92; Sidney Mintz, "The Origins of Reconsti-tuted Peasantries," 94–106; and O. Nigel Bolland, "Systems of Domination After Slavery: The Control of Land and Labour in the British West Indies After 1938," 107–23, all in Beckles and Shepherd, *Caribbean Freedom.*

19. The most concise view of these events is in William Appleman Williams, *Empire as a Way of Life* (New York: Oxford Press, 1980).

20. Harris thus hailed C.L.R. James but appealed for "an open state of consciousness" beyond the limits of Marxism, something analogous to magic realism. Wilson Harris, "Continuity and Discontinuity," in *Selected Essays of Wilson Harris: The Unfinished Genius of the Imagination,* ed. Andrew Bundy (London: Routledge, 1999), 180, 182.

21. A point strongly made by Kelvin Singh, *Race and Class Struggles in a Colonial State* (Kingston: UWI Press, 1994), 7.

22. O. Nigel Bolland, *The Politics of Labour in the British Caribbean* (Kingston: Ian Randle, 2001), 173–75, an epochal study.

23. Ibid., 178–79.

24. We know about these events mainly because of the careful work of Walter Rodney in *A History of the Guyanese Working People* (London: Heineman, 1981), 104, 154–59, 163–65.

25. Reddock, *Women, Labour Politics,* 100–103. See Alvin Magid, *Urban Nationalism: A Study of Political Development in Trinidad* (Gainesville: University Press of Florida, 1988), 105–54, on the historical background and consequences of the Water Riot.

26. Bukka Rennie, *History of the Working-Class in the Twentieth Century—Trinidad and Tobago* (Toronto: New Beginning Movement, 1974), 37. Thanks to Matthew Quest for making this book-length pamphlet available to me.

27. Ibid., 25–29.

28. Bolland, *Politics of Labour,* 195–205.

29. Ibid. After Bolland, we could include sections of Singh, *Race and Class*; a pamphlet by Richard Hart aimed at a popular audience, *Labour Rebellions of the 1930s in the British Caribbean Region Colonies* (London: Caribbean Labour Solidarity/Socialist History Society, 2002), is the last look by an actual participant in the struggles. Behind all these, the detailed treatments of the uprising in Ken Post, *Arise Ye*

Starvelings: The Jamaican Labour Rebellion of 1938 and Its Aftermath (The Hague: Martin Nijhoff, 1978), remains essential.

30. Perry Anderson offers his own, somewhat distanced, view of the disputes and their importance in *English Questions* (London: Verso, 1992), 17.

31. See, e.g., Harvey J. Kaye, *The British Marxist Historians* (Cambridge: Polity Press, 1984), esp. 223–49. I also want to acknowledge extended conversations with E. P. Thompson about a field of related subjects.

32. It is important to note that of the new generation of young Caribbean intellectuals, only Stuart Hall participated in the *New Left Review* circle and that he left it by the mid-1960s, landing in another milieu around the Centre for Contemporary Cultural Studies at Birmingham. The conversation therefore lacked a Caribbean dimension, although Robin Blackburn was to become one of the most distinguished English-language scholars of slavery. I want to acknowledge here Blackburn's participation with me (at my invitation) interviewing C.L.R James in the middle 1980s and also his eagerness to reach out to Thompson. By that time, the combatants had moved on, but also wished to bind old wounds.

33. Anderson, *English Questions*, 17.

34. Quoted in Perry Anderson, *Arguments within English Marxism* (London: Verso, 1980), 159–60. Thompson became more urgent in these arguments during the last decades of his life, as he returned to the study of Blake and finished a quasi-utopian socialist (or at least science fiction socialist) novel of his own.

35. Richard Hart, *Origin and Development of the Working Class in the English Speaking Caribbean Area—1897 to 1937* (London: Community Education Trust, [1986]), 6–7. Many thanks to Hart for this document.

36. Michael Anthony, *In the Heat of the Day* (London: Heineman, 1996).

37. The best account is in Singh, *Race and Class Struggles*, 20–36.

38. James's *Captain Cipriani* (Port of Spain, Trinidad: privately published, 1932), expanded as *The Case for West Indian Self-Government* (London: Hogarth Press, 1937), was the author's first nonfiction of note, and it captured in lovely strokes the public persona of Cipriani. Some passages are reprinted as an appendix to Henry and Buhle, *C.L.R. James's Caribbean*, 267–70. Singh, *Race and Class Struggles*, 131–57, offers the clearest account of Cipriani's stumble and fall.

39. See Joyce Moore Turner's "Biography" in *Richard B. Moore, Caribbean Militant in Harlem, Collective Writings 1920–1972*, ed. W. Burghart Turner and Joyce Moore Turner (London: Pluto Press, 1988), 19–53.

40. Robert Hill's introduction to the reprint edition of *The Crusader* contains the most incisive treatment of the ABB yet offered; Barbara Bair's contributions to the women's history of Garveyism are also fundamental. See *The Crusader* (New York: Garland, 1987); and Robert Hill and Barbara Bair, eds., *Marcus Garvey: Life and Lessons* (Berkeley: University of California Press, 1987).

41. That Domingo knew Richard Hart well and, in turn, Hart has become a major source of my own information and insight seem an almost unbelievable connection between region and the Marxist political tradition.

42. See Paul Buhle, *A Dreamer's Paradise Lost: Louis C. Fraina/Lewis Corey (1892–1953) and the Decline of Radicalism in the United States* (Atlantic Highlands, N.J.: Humanities Press, 1995). DeLeon's own origins in Curacao (born into a Sephardic family of a Dutch physician) intrigued me during my membership in the Socialist Labor Party during 1963–64; it was a Caribbean connection with the uncompromising, antiracist socialist most unique. DeLeon, an amateur scholar of anthropology, evolved a theory of socialism as a phase of civilization and provided the IWW, founded in 1905, with a grand vision of a future, stateless society. He was, in that sense, a Caribbean intellectual after all.

43. The alternatives to the Communist movement were bleak, for Afro-Caribbeans even more than for African Americans. Maida Springer, born in Panama, became political in the middle of the 1930s with the group of Communist Party oppositionists under Jay Lovestone, and she followed Lovestone into the CIA milieu of the AFL-CIO of the cold war years, virulently opposed to black nationalism or even anticolonialism under any but American hegemony. C.L.R. James, joining the Trotskyists in the United Kingdom, remained with them for a bit over a decade in the United States, without a single Caribbean comrade and precious few black ones at all. The Socialist Party, which boasted strong support for an interracial Southern Tenant Farmers Union, was all but dead after 1940 and had provided no haven for Caribbean radicals since the 1910s. A few of the ABB pioneers, like famed Afro-American nationalist "Mother" Audley Moore, spent careers drifting between the Communist Party and nationalist entities, frequently risking expulsion from the former, with loss of political contacts and support.

44. Richard Hart, *Rise and Organize: The Birth of the Workers and National Movements in Jamaica (1936–1939)* (London: Karia Press, 1989), 18–24. See also the classic treatment by Post, *Arise Ye Starvelings*.

45. Mandle, *Persistent Underdevelopment*, 51–52.

46. Kafra Kambon, *For Bread, Justice and Freedom: A Political Biography of George Weekes* (London: New Beacon Books, 1988), 11. Writing as pamphleteer-historian, Selwyn Cudjoe puts these developments somewhat differently, in *A Just and Moral Society* (Ithaca, N.Y., and Tacarigua, Trinidad-Tobago: Calaloux, 1984), 66–67.

47. Rennie, *History of the Working-Class*, 47–50. On Buzz Butler, see the interesting collection of documents and introduction in W. Richard Jacobs, ed., *Butler versus the King: Riots and Sedition in 1937*, with comments by George Weekes and Joe Young (Port of Spain: Key Caribbean, 1976).

48. Ibid., 50–54.

49. Ibid., 61–65.

50. Ibid., 65–68.

51. Ibid., 76–82.

52. Kambon, *For Bread, Justice and Freedom*, 14, 15.

53. The nature of Adrian Cola Rienzi and his associates' ideological commitments remains fascinating and unresolved. Richard Hart has kindly sent me an e-mail describing them as Marxists in the general sense, Rienzi's OWTU associate Ralph Mentor as having a framed picture of Stalin on his desk at the office, and Rupert Gittens, their counterpart on the Public Workers and Public Service Union, rumored to have been a member of the French Communist Party. Rienzi himself, studying in Britain to become a lawyer, may have been close to the Communist Party there. On the remarkable multicultural identity of Rienzi and his activities, Singh's text is a revelation. See Singh, *Race and Class Struggles*, esp. 133–34, 149–51, 207–13. Perhaps the most important point, however, is that whatever the sympathies of Rienzi and others in Trinidad, there was nothing to join; like their Jamaican counterpart, they remained a ginger group, and in that sense different from the British Communist Party, a relatively small but in some part definitely working-class organization with its own press and party structure, as well as a formidable intellectual cadre that was to include some of the outstanding scholars in the English-speaking world, E. P. Thompson, Christopher Hill, and Eric Hobsbawm among others.

54. Those testifying against Butler found themselves genuinely puzzled by the phrases that he used. Accuracy was not his strong point, but the use of often colorful language had the needed effect. See "Judge's Notes," in Jacobs, *Butler versus the King*, 34–36.

55. Ibid., 33–34.

56. Rennie, *History of the Working-Class*, 107–40.

57. W. Richard Jacobs, "After the Trial," in Jacobs, *Butler versus the King*, 181–85.

58. E-mail from Richard Hart.

59. Richard Hart, *Towards Decolonisation: Political, Labor and Economic Development in Jamaica 1938–1945* (Barbados/Jamaica/Trinidad and Tobago: Canoe Press, University of West Indies, 1999), 78.

60. Rennie, *History of the Working-Class*, 153–55, would argue that the leadership was so petite-bourgeois that it had no capacity to lead workers on another path but capitulated with the first American threats to its influence. He has a point.

61. Catherine Sunshine, *The Caribbean: Survival, Struggle and Sovereignty* (Washington, D.C.: Ecumenical Program for Interamerican Communication and Action, 1985), 108–9. It is notable that Maida Springer was the only woman in the AFL's delegation to WFTU in 1945; she would become George Meany's and Jay Lovestone's representative in parts of 1950s–60s Africa, representing the "American side" of business unionism in the cold war conflict and forming a close alliance with Kenya's Tom Mboya, the designated pro–United States potentate of African labor until the exposure of his ties and his subsequent assassination.

62. This view returned, in retrospect, during the upwelling of Pan-Caribbeanism. Bukka Rennie suggests that a potent revolutionary movement of the 1930s was quashed by petite-bourgeois corruption, not overwhelmed by colonial conditions, although he could also be read to suggest the latter. Rennie, *History of the Working-Class*, esp. 153–55.

63. Tim Hector, "The Cold War and Caribbean Nationhood," *Outlet*, April 22, 1988, reprinted in Hector, *The World and Us*, 438–53.

64. Hollis "Chalkdust" Liverpool, *Rituals of Power and Rebellion: The Carnival Tradition in Trinidad and Tobago, 1763–1962* (Chicago: Research Associates/School Times, 2001).

65. Ibid., 4–210.

66. Ibid., 213–350.

67. Ibid., 334.

68. Ibid., 353–488.

69. John Wickham, "Literature and Being Barbadian," in *Barbados: Thirty Years of Independence*, ed. Trevor A. Carmichael (Kingston: Ian Randle, 1996), 244.

70. See, e.g., Alison Donnell and Sarah Lawson Welsh, eds., *The Routledge Reader in Caribbean Literature* (London: Routledge, 1996), 108–113, for introductory material on this period.

Chapter 2: What Makes Antigua Different?

1. Richard Hart, *Labour Rebellions of the 1930s in the British Caribbean Region Colonies* (Balham, UK: Socialist History Society, 2002), 21.

2. Tim Hector, "Antigua's First Freedom Fighters," *Outlet*, February 14, 2003,

3. Ibid. Hector, here as often in his journalistic style, drew directly from the materials in front of him. In this essay, he used Barry Gaspar's recent book and colonial records (sent by a friend) in tandem, adding his own comments.

4. Henry, *Peripheral Capitalism*, 24–25.

5. Ibid., 28–35.

6. Ibid., 43–45.

7. Ibid., 44–46.

8. Ibid., 55–57.

9. The novel was *With Silent Tread*, by Friedas Cassin; it is described in Henry, *Peripheral Capitalism*, 59.

10. Tim Hector, "The Black Condition, Then and Now," *Outlet*, February 8, 2002. This essay was written for Black History Week.

11. Margo Jefferson, "Blackface Master Echoes in Hip-Hop," *New York Times*, October 13, 2004, offers a tribute to Williams on the occasion of a reissue of some of his work, but gives the Bahamas as his birthplace.

12. Hart, *Origin and Development of the Working Class*, 17.

13. Quoted in Henry, *Peripheral Capitalism*, 82.

14. According to many on the island, he likely had many more children out of wedlock. His sons were Vere Junior, Lester (future prime minister and a boyhood friend of Hector's), Ivor, and Roswald. His daughter, Hazel, is perhaps the most unusual Bird of all: a radio evangelist.

15. Tim Hector, "V. C. Bird, the Summation," *Outlet*, January 8, 1982, reprinted in Hector, *The World and Us*, 230–45. See also an essay by Lomarsh Roopnarine, "A Dual Legacy of Antigua's First Prime Minister, Vere Cornwall Bird (1909–1999)," *Revista/Review Interamericana* 30 [1999], at sg.inter.edu/revista-cisla/volume30/roopnarine.html

16. Quoted in by Hector, "Past Dominates the Present," 148–50.

17. Quoted in ibid., 155.

18. See Reddock, *Women, Labour and Politics*, 163–78, 240–49.

19. Hector calls the showing of the books "a masterpiece of book-keeping" by a trained bookkeeper, a comment that itself might be taken as ironical, since Bird had apparently proved himself so deft at rearranging details in "the books" prior to his union days. Hector, "Hail Bwana! Farewell Papa!" *Outlet*, July 9, 1999, reprinted in Hector Anthology, 28.

20. Howard A. Fergus, *Gallery Monserrat: Some Prominent People in Our History* (Kingston: Canoe Press, 1996), 136–39. Unlike Bird and Williams, "Maas Bob" did not lead the minination into independence; that fell to another leader of the MTLU, the more militant socialist William Henry Bramble, who is best remembered for bringing comprehensive electrification to the island of twelve thousand in 1963. The airport bears his name. Ibid., 131–35.

21. Henry, *Peripheral Capitalism*, 95–96.

22. Vincent A. Richards, "Decolonization in Antigua," in *The Newer Caribbean: Decolonization, Democracy and Development*, ed. Paget Henry and Carl Stone (Philadelphia: Institute for the Study of Human Issues, 1983), 26–29.

23. Hector, "Hail Bwana!"

24. *The Biggest Gun in the World* (1990) was written by Walter Bernstein, the last of the formerly blacklisted writers still actively working on scripts. Here, as demanded by drama, Bull comes across more quirkily positive than in real life.

25. "The Crisis in Education," *Outlet*, January 26, 1978.

26. Tim Hector, "The Unmaking and Making of Tim Hector," *Outlet*, December 6, 1996.

27. Tim Hector, "In Love and Revolution and in Time to Come," *Outlet*, April 13, 2001. James, in *Beyond a Boundary*, recalled being the "child at the window" in the first years of the century, confined by a stern, book-loving mother to books.

28. Hector, "My Grandmother."

29. Tim Hector, "A Thing or Two about Whores and Whites," *Outlet*, January 11, 2002.
30. Hector, "Unmaking and Making."
31. Tim Hector, "In Youth, of Cricket, Patronage and Rebellion," *Outlet*, July 6, 2001.
32. "Artists and Intellectuals Salute Him," *Outlet*, December 6, 1996.
33. David Abdullah, "Leonard 'Tim' Hector—a Caribbean Colossus," *Outlet*, November 29, 2002. Abdullah was one of the younger militant leaders of the OWTU succeeding James's friend George Weekes via the post of educational director of the union.
34. Hector, "Unmaking the Making."
35. Hector, "In Youth."
36. Tim Hector, "St. Michael's School: Reflections," *Outlet*, March 2, 2001. He ended this piece with the thought that he might yet return to teaching, craving to help the children but knowing that his removal from the political field would gladden the hearts of the island's political machine.
37. See Tim Hector, "Traitor to the Working People," *Outlet*, February 3, 1984.
38. Hector, "My Grandmother."
39. Valerie Harris-Coleman, "Profile: The Man—Sen. L. Tim Hector," *Outlet*, November 29, 1996.
40. See Bolland, *Politics of Labor*, 247–50. Walcott would have been too young to appreciate the strikes and riots firsthand, but the memories of them would have been strong, even for families that cloistered their children from lower-class experiences.
41. Bruce King, *Derek Walcott: A Caribbean Life* (Oxford: Oxford University Press, 2000), 16–20, 32–35.
42. Tim Hector, "Reflections on an Exile," *Outlet*, October 23, 1998.
43. Hector, "Unmaking and Making."
44. Hector, "My Grandmother."
45. Hector, "Unmaking and Making."
46. Ibid.

Chapter 3: Independence and Neocolonialism

1. A friendly critic of this book's manuscript observes, accurately, that the post–New Left socialistic movements in Holland and the Scandinavian countries would offer the nearest analogy. But within the United States, certainly the local progressive formations that took over some degree of municipal power from Burlington, Vermont, to Madison, Wisconsin, and to Berkeley and Santa Cruz, California, among other places, were also counterparts. In none, to my understanding, did the apocalyptic fever burn so brightly as in the Caribbean of the 1970s–80s; the painful realization that American power had emerged from crisis intact if not strengthened had the effect of dampening expectations. It is also fascinating that politicized reggae was

resoundingly popular among the politicized sectors of these U.S. cities, Jimmy Cliff's visits for a time constituting something like political rallies for the egalitarian or socialistic faithful.

2. Quoted in Selwyn R. Cudjoe, *Resistance and Caribbean Literature* (Athens: Ohio University Press, 1980), 184.

3. See ibid., 179–205, for an overview. Gratitude is expressed to Lamming for a conversation on this subject, and to Wilson Harris for exchange of letters on various related subjects.

4. Patricia Mohammed, "A Very Public Private Man: Trinidad's Eric Eustace Williams (1911–81)," in *Caribbean Charisma*, ed. Anton Allahar (Kingston: Ian Randle, 2001), 155.

5. Selwyn D. Ryan, *Race and Nationalism in Trinidad and Tobago: A Study of Decolonization in a Multiracial Society* (Toronto: University of Toronto Press, 1972), 361–68.

6. "Flying in the Face of God," *Outlet*, November 22, 1996.

7. Kirk Meighoo, *Politics in a Half Made Society: Trinidad and Tobago, 1925–2001* (Kingston: Ian Randall, 2003), is the fullest treatment of the political context of the Williams era. But Selwyn Cudjoe, in his annotated selection of Williams's writings, has the immanent critique, understanding the Doctor better than he understood himself.

8. B. W. Higman, *Writing West Indian Histories* (London: McMillan, 1999), 90–95. A conversation with George Lamming in 2004 reminded me that Williams would have chosen the scholarly road; the political road chose him.

9. "Flying in the Face of God."

10. Kambon, *For Bread, Justice and Freedom*, 36–37.

11. I wish also to acknowledge a telephone conversation with George Weekes, from James's flat in Brixton, in 1987, in which Weekes briefly and politely laid out his views, eagerly acknowledging his debt to James.

12. Cudjoe, *Just and Moral Society*, 68–71.

13. C.L.R. James, *Party Politics in the West Indies* (Port of Spain: Vedic Enterprises, 1962), 158–59.

14. Mohammed, "Very Public Private Man," 180–87.

15. James, *Party Politics*, 160.

16. This is a point made most vividly to me by George Lamming, in conversation.

17. C.L.R. James, "On Federation," in *At the Rendezvous of Victory: Selected Writings* (London: Allison and Busby, 1984), 91.

18. Ibid., 127.

19. James, *Party Politics*, 4.

20. Ibid., 160–61.

21. Ryan, *Race and Nationalism*, 408–15.

22. See Buhle, *Artist as Revolutionary*, 144–47.
23. Ivar Oxaal, *Black Intellectuals Come to Power: The Rise of Creole Nationalism in Trinidad and Tobago* (Cambridge, Mass.: Schenkman, 1968), 134.
24. C.L.R. James, *PNM Go Forward* (Port of Spain: privately published, 1960), excerpted in James, *Party Politics*, with other documents.
25. Kambon, *For Bread, Justice and Freedom*, 38–41.
26. James spent many pages, doubtless too many pages, detailing this campaign against him and Selma James in *Party Politics in the West Indies*; he was obviously hurt, more by Williams's refusal to defend him than by the slings and arrows of the petite-bourgeoisie. But it is his most curious volume, no doubt because it is composed of particular documents prepared tactically for different audiences. My gratitude goes to Paget Henry for this observation.
27. Lloyd Best saw this most vividly in the unwillingness of the PNM to place the rural (Indian) peoples on a par with the urban (black and other) population, thus ensuring and hardening the differences. Best, "Chauguramas to Slavery," *New World Quarterly*, 1965 cited in Ryan, *Race and Nationalism*, 481 n. 35.
28. Elizabeth Wallace, "The Break-Up of the British West Indies Federation" (1977), in Beckles and Shepherd, *Caribbean Freedom*, 455–75.
29. James, *Party Politics*, 162.
30. W. Andrew Axline, "From Carifa to Caricom: Deepening Caribbean Integration" (1979), in Beckles and Shepherd, *Caribbean Freedom*, 476–87, is a far too optimistic account.
31. Ibid., 338–39. In those days and well into the 1980s, the *Vanguard* might easily be regarded as one of the most revolutionary labor papers anywhere, revolutionary in the spirit of the old IWW rather than Communist or socialist outlets. When James dramatically returned to Trinidad in 1982, the OWTU hailed him in a banquet notable for its red flags and revolutionary salutations. It was his biggest welcome home until his dramatic funeral.
32. Tony Martin, whose works are a standard source for Garvey scholars, sums up the legacy cogently in "Marcus Garvey, the Caribbean, and the Struggle for Black Jamaican Nationhood" (1983), in Beckles and Shepherd, *Caribbean Freedom*, 359–69.
33. Tim Hector, "Martin Luther King, Not a Saint but a Revolutionary Socialist," *Outlet*, January 19, 2001.
34. Richard Hart, ed., *Documents on the Ouster of the 4-Hs from the People's National Party of Jamaica in 1952* (London: Caribbean Labour Solidarity, 2000), 2–3, 4, 6. Manley is quoted from the *PNP News Letter* of February–March 1952. The notorious "4-Hs" were Hart, Frank Hill, Ken Hill, and Arthur Henry. Special thanks to Hart for sending me this rare document.
35. One tragic consequence has recently been explored by Gerald Horne in his *Red Seas: Ferdinand Smith and the Radical Black Sailors in the United States and Jamaica* (New York: New York University Press, 2005), 232–57. Smith, who had left Jamaica

as a young man and become a Communist as well as the leading Afro-Caribbean in the National Maritime Union, was expelled from the United States to his homeland in the Joseph McCarthy era, but ferociously attacked by Bustamante as a threat to law and order, with no defense of free speech or activity from the Manley forces, reassuring the United States of their anticommunism.

36. Among others active in and around the YSL was Bertell Ollman, a young Marxist teaching at UWI and later effectively banned from speaking publicly. Thanks to Ollman for conversations and letters about these days.

37. Horace Campbell, *Rasta and Resistance, from Marcus Garvey to Walter Rodney* (Trenton, N.J.: Africa World Press, 1987), 86–87. More than a decade earlier, before illness struck her down, Marcus Garvey's ex-wife Amy Jacques Garvey worked within the PNP, stressing Pan-Africanism and receiving a polite hearing; Manley was not moved by her pleas, however. See Ula Yvette Taylor, *The Veiled Garvey: The Life and Times of Amy Jacques Garvey* (Chapel Hill: University of North Carolina Press, 2002), 198–99.

38. Ibid., 100–101.

39. Brian Meeks, *Narratives of Resistance: Jamaica, Trinidad, the Caribbean* (Kingston: UWI Press, 2000), 25–47.

40. Many thanks to Richard Hart for clarifying this point: Manley arranged the expulsion in March 1952 of the "4-Hs." The PFM was in a sense its unacknowledged successor: the PNP needed a left wing and had to reconstruct it after the real founders of the Left had been expelled.

41. Richard Hart has maintained an amazingly balanced view of the Manleys, their work, and its successes as well as failings. Thanks to Hart for sending me his position paper, "The Achievement of Independence in Jamaica," presented at the University of West of England, Bristol, December 4, 2002.

42. Meeks, *Narratives of Resistance*, 120–21.

43. A new dramatic telling of the Jagan story has been made by filmmaker Suzanne Wasserman, director of *Thunder in Guyana* (2005), a documentary mainly about Janet Jagan, released to highly positive reviews—more evidence that passions had cooled now that the seeming threat of communism had abated and the chief actors were dead or elderly.

44. Tim Hector, "Modern Martyr and Exemplar of the New Caribbean," *Outlet*, March 11, 1997, reprinted in Hector Anthology, 54–55.

45. Janet Jagan, "Dr. Cheddi Jagan, Founder of the People's Progressive Party, Father of the Guyanese Nation," www.jagan.org/biograph7.htm.

46. Richard Drayton, "Liberal Imperialism in British Guiana, 1953–64," paper prepared for the Cambridge Historical Society meeting of February 4, 2003, kindly sent me by Richard Hart. Drayton happens to be the son of the Guyanese Dr. Harry Drayton, a close associate of Hart's for many years and a founder of the University of Guyana.

47. See Cheddi Jagan, *The West on Trial: The Fight for Guyana's Freedom* (London: Michael Joseph, 1966). Arthur Schlesinger Jr. conceded the substance of these allegations in 1990, offering mild regrets.

48. Drayton, "Liberal Imperialism."

49. Hector thus recalls a preparatory meeting in Guyana for the Sixth Pan-African Congress in which a rising Afro-Caribbean activist ridiculed the senior socialist, making him out a fool for contesting rigged elections (and ignoring Jagan's response: "What was the alternative?"). Hector's own response was to rush to the bathroom and "for one of the few times in my life since a grown man, I cried . . . because my own Afro-Caribbean people . . . had conspired with the British and Americans to destabilize and ruin a fine man." Hector, "Modern Martyr," 52.

50. Ibid., 54.

51. Tim Hector, "Walter Rodney, Friend, Scholar and Caribbean Figure Extraordinary, Part 1" *Outlet*, June 23, 2000, reprinted in Hector Anthology, 59–67.

52. Ibid.

53. Rupert Charles Lewis, *Walter Rodney's Intellectual and Political Thought* (Detroit: Wayne State University Press/Press University of the West Indies, 1998), 1–19.

54. Ibid., 20–23.

55. Ibid., 36–46.

56. Ibid., 76.

57. C.L.R. James, "Rastafari at Home and Abroad," reprinted from *New Left Review* (1964) in James, *At the Rendezvous of Victory*, 164, 165.

58. Ibid., 165.

59. Paget Henry, unpublished memorial service tribute. Thanks to Henry for making this available to me.

60. Tim Hector, "Salute to the Maestro" (1981), reprinted in the *Outlet*, January 3, 2003.

61. Hector, "Unmaking and Making." The passage goes on to read, "Dear Paul Buhle remains my connection with the industrial world, and Cyril Ramaposa in South Africa, and a few others in between." It was Hector's Jamesean politics, maintained over the long haul, with some encouragement from myself along with many others.

62. David Scott, "The Archeology of Black Memory: An Interview with Robert A. Hill," *Small Axe*, no. 5 (March 1999): 103–4.

63. Recollections of Hector at the 2001 centennial conference for C.L.R. James at UWI, Trinidad; CD kindly made available to me by Matthew Quest.

64. Robin D. G. Kelley, "The World the Diaspora Made: C.L.R. James and the Politics of History," in *Rethinking C.L.R. James*, ed. Grant Farred (Cambridge, Mass.: Blackwell, 1996), 112–14.

65. Ibid.

66. The role of CIA operatives is especially well expressed by an uncritical biography of one of the AFL-CIO's most important black operatives, Maida Springer. See

Yvette Richards, "African and African-American Labor Leaders in the Struggle over International Affiliation," *International Journal of African Historical Studies* 31 (1998): 301–34. Springer's handler and financier was Irving Brown, the manipulator behind Jonas Savimbi and against the African National Congress. These "labor colleges" were far less successful than in the Caribbean. But lamentably, an elderly A. Philip Randolph and a younger Bayard Rustin energetically represented AFL-CIO and American corporate interests, reaching out to emerging African elites and rewarding those who supported U.S. positions.

67. Ibid., 118–19. This is not to suggest that James's judgments were flawless: as Kelley makes clear, he gave too much credit first to Nkrumah and then to Nyerere; he saw what he wanted to see in the redemption of Africa from the colonialists, in the case of Ghana (if not Tanzania) what the masses themselves had seen in the early days of the revolution and new regime.

68. Hector, "My Grandmother."

69. James's own comment in an interview with Stuart Hall, undated but apparently during the early 1980s, is printed in Farred, *Rethinking C.L.R. James*, 44.

70. Hector, "Walter Rodney," 62–63.

71. Ibid., 63.

72. Paget Henry, "The Caribbean Economic Tradition," in Henry and Buhle, *C.L.R. James's Caribbean*, 147–48.

73. Hector, "Unmaking and Making." Others in the Caribbean-Canadian group did belong to Communist organizations, and James was careful not to criticize them for it; they were to draw their own conclusions from discussion and further political practice.

74. David Hinds, "Tim Hector: An Example of Tenacity, Independence and Patriotism," posted November 16, 2002 on www.guyanapolitics.org, hector_tribute.html.

75. Hector, "Reflections on an Exile."

76. Conrad Luke, "Tim Hector: A Man for All Seasons," www.candw.ag/-jardinea/ffhtm/theprofil.htm.

77. Robert Coram, *Caribbean Time Bomb: The United States' Complicity in the Corruption of Antigua* (New York: William Morrow, 1993), 38–39.

78. Henry, *Peripheral Capitalism*, 155.

79. Tim Hector, "Antigua in Time and Place: Rise and Disgrace of the PLM," *Outlet*, November 18, 1976, reprinted in *The World and Us* (n.p., n.d.), 94–100.

80. See Henry, *Peripheral Capitalism*, 157.

81. Paget Henry, "The Antiguan Left," in Henry and Buhle, *C.L.R. James's Caribbean*, 239–41.

82. Henry, *Peripheral Capitalism*, 160.

83. Quoted in ibid., 162.

Chapter 4: The Great Moment Passed By

1. See, e.g., Ray Kiely, *The Politics of Labour and Development in Trinidad* (Kingston: UWI Press, 1996), 114–29, for an insightful, polemical account of the march, a small-scale soldiers' revolt, and the failures of the existing Left movements to prepare for the consequences of mass unrest.

2. Ibid., 338–39. Kiely, sharing an admiration for the OWTU and Weekes but devoting his analysis to the weakness and divisions of the various Marxist entities, offers a gloomy perspective in *The Politics of Labour and Development*, 129–51. As a unique sphere of sustained Marxist labor politics, the Trinidadian Left deserves more study, research, and interviews.

3. Campbell, *Rasta and Resistance*, 167–70.

4. See Evelyn Greaves, "Labour in Independence," in *Barbados: Thirty Years of Independence*, ed. Trevor A. Carmichael (Kingston: Ian Randle, 1996), 185–86. Thanks go also to Barbados Workers Union educational leader Robert ("Bobby") Morris for a conversation with me in Bridgetown in 1987 about the trajectory of C.L.R. James's influence. I deeply regret that I could not engage him in a major project of interviewing veterans of the late 1930s strike wave, then in their last days; by the time the scholarship of this and other islands was done on a considerable scale, twenty years later (and not at all in many places), the adult participants in those events were almost all gone, and researchers had to rely upon printed sources.

5. Tim Hector, "Walter Rodney Was Most Rare," *Outlet*, June 20, 1997, reprinted in Hector Anthology, 68–74; Lewis, *Walter Rodney's Intellectual and Political Thought*, 204–8.

6. Quoted in Hector, "Walter Rodney Was Most Rare," 72.

7. C.L.R. James, "A National Purpose for the Caribbean Peoples," a speech given to the West Indian Students' Association in Edinburgh in 1964 and printed in the last of the three selected works, *At the Rendezvous of Victory*, 155.

8. Hector, "Walter Rodney Was Most Rare," 74.

9. Hector, "Walter Rodney," 59–67.

10. Lewis, *Walter Rodney's Intellectual and Political Thought*, 212–14.

11. *Notes on Philosophy*, a lengthy document written when James was living in Nevada at the end of the 1940s, waiting for a divorce and attempting to gain U.S. citizenship, had been virtually unavailable until typed and mimeographed in the mid-1960s by James's Caribbean following in Canada. It was finally published as *Lenin and Philosophy* in 1978 by Allison and Busby, and he described it to me as his favorite work. Steeped in a reading of Hegel, it was also the least accessible of his writings, but one may assume that Rodney had familiarized himself with the document of the master, who argued that all the way back to the French Revolution and up the present, the petite-bourgeoisie, substituting itself for the working masses, had seized

state power, even nationalized commerce and industry as well as adopting revolutionary rhetoric, but for control over the working class. I acquired one of the few copies, in 1967, from Solidarity Bookshop in Chicago, connected with the IWW.

12. See Linden Lewis, "Linden Forbes Burnham (1923–85): Unraveling the Paradox of Post-colonial Charismatic Leadership in Guyana," in Allahar, *Caribbean Charisma*, 104–8.

13. Ibid., 235.

14. C.L.R. James, "Walter Rodney and the Question of Power," in *Walt Rodney—Revolutionary and Scholar: A Tribute*, ed. Edward Alpers and Pierre Michel Fontaine (Los Angeles: Center for Afro-American Studies and African Studies Center, University of California, 1981[?]), 125, 138, quoted in Lewis, *Walter Rodney*, 241–42.

15. Lewis, *Walter Rodney*, 243–48.

16. For a more intimate Caribbean view, see the special *Caribbean Quarterly* issue, vol. 47 (2001), especially the essays by Hilary Beckles and Anthony Bogues.

17. Tim Hector, "Manley in Power: The Trial and the Tribulation (Part II)," *Outlet*, March 18, 1997.

18. Tim Hector, "Michael Manley, Prince of the Pauper's Struggle, Part I," *Outlet*, March 14, 1997, reprinted in Hector Anthology, 33–39.

19. Michael Manley, "When Reagan Killed with a Smile," *Sunday Gleaner*, May 17, 1992, reprinted in Richard Hart, *Michael Manley: An Assessment and Tribute* (London: Caribbean Labour Solidarity, 1997), 21.

20. I do not wish to add my personal view to the controversy surrounding the coup, the assassination, the arrest of Coard among others, and the eventual trial and convictions; I only wish to note that Richard Hart has been an assiduous legal and moral supporter of Coard, arguing that the charges against him remain unproven in any legal sense. See Hart, *The Grenada Trial: A Travesty of Justice* (Kingston: privately published, 1996). He had demonstrated, at the least, that the Reaganites sought a pretext for invasion and would have invaded sooner or later in any case. The disorder provided them the perfect opportunity, one that they may very well have arranged. See also an early account that still has value: Manning Marable, *African and Caribbean Politics, from Kwame Nkrumah to Maurice Bishop* (London: Verso, 1987), 197–272.

21. Brian Meeks, *Caribbean Revolutions and Revolutionary Theory: An Assessment of Cuba, Nicaragua and Grenada* (Kingston: UWI Press, 1993), 133–45.

22. Tim Hector, "Maurice Bishop in Normal Grenada," *Outlet*, November 4, 1983.

23. Meeks, *Caribbean Revolutions*, 145–49.

24. Thanks to Richard Hart for recounting this to me, in his always generous way. He barely escaped the country and the fate that might have awaited him by slipping past the U.S. occupiers. Thereafter, he became a political savant and scholar of the Caribbean community in the United Kingdom.

25. Meeks, *Caribbean Revolutions*, 174–80. Thanks again to Richard Hart for sending his paper, "Grenada Update, an Assessment of the Revolution," typescript of a lecture delivered at UWI in 1984 and reproduced by the Jamaica Committee for the Defence of Human Rights in Grenada. See also Hart's introduction to *In Nobody's Backyard: Maurice Bishop's Speeches, 1979–1982: A Memorial Volume* (London: Zed Press, 1984), xi–xli.

26. Tim Hector, "Grenada, the Fall of a Revolution: Maurice Bishop, His Struggle, His Death and Its Significance," *Outlet*, October 28, 1983.

27. Ibid.

28. Tim Hector, "'To Make Themselves Masters of the Country'—250 years later," *Outlet*, November 7, 1986.

29. Kambon, *For Bread, Justice, and Freedom*, 317–9. I wish to acknowledge a conversation with Weekes, made from James's Brixton's apartment in 1987, touching on many matters.

30. Tim Hector, "Bishop and Machel—Men of Great Vision," *Outlet*, October 31, 1986.

31. "The Don Is Dead," *Outlet*, May 23, 2003. A lifelong personal friend of Hector's, Halstead assisted the ACLM several times in crucial legal issues; in the end, before his final illness, he had been part of the UPP opposition that failed to challenge Lester Bird successfully.

32. Henry, "C.L.R. James and the Antiguan Left," 226.

33. He made a special point of remarking this to me in 1980, as I interviewed him in Washington, D.C., about the region. See Paul Buhle and Jim Murray, "West Indies: Microcosm, an Interview of CLR James," in *Free Spirits: Annals of the Insurgent Imagination*, ed. Paul Buhle et al. (San Francisco: City Lights Books, 1982), 91–93. The interview was conducted at James's bedside, in Washington, D.C., in 1980, shortly before James would leave for his final stay in London.

34. As I can testify, this change of view prompted a major political division among the remnant of James's small U.S. following; a group statement along the lines of *Facing Reality*, to be titled "The Gathering Forces," was drafted, then postponed, and finally abandoned. I published a portion of it in a 1971 issue of *Radical America*. The older lieutenants of "Johnsonism," syndicalist in their bent, could not accept what they considered James's "Third Worldism" in general, and perhaps one can see the larger contradictions of Caribbean radical politics, especially its most leftward edges, mirrored here. Conversations with Matthew Quest have reminded me of this flickering controversy little known outside James's circles.

35. Henry, "C.L.R. James and the Antiguan Left," 251. I have relied on Henry's account throughout the following narrative of the ACM/ACLM's inner history.

36. Tim Hector, "The Matriarch of Matriarchs," *Outlet*, July 23, 1999, reprinted in *Hector Anthology*, 12–21.

37. Ibid., 242–43.

38. Recalled in Tim Hector, "Antigua at the United Nations," *Outlet*, October 10, 1980, reprinted in Hector, *The World and Us*, 113–23.
39. Hector, *The World and Us*, 243–54.
40. "The Don Is Dead."
41. Coram, *Caribbean Time Bomb*, 117–9.
42. Ibid., 120–34.
43. Ibid., 163–70. Coram is to be congratulated for an excellent summary of the problems.
44. Douglas was elected to the prime ministership in 2000, the same year that he succumbed, at the premature age of fifty-eight; Ralph Gonsalves barely lost in 1998, and his Unity Labour Party came to power in 2001, where it remains today, with Gonsalves himself occupying several cabinet posts along with the prime ministership.
45. There is a further parallel or disparallel: Odlum was St. Lucia's foreign minister from 1979 to 1981 and again from 1997 to 2001. He was dropped from the cabinet twice for his acerbic criticism of his own governing party's behavior.
46. Tim Hector, asked to comment briefly on his relationship with James in Canada and beyond, spoke from the floor at the symposium. The contents of the symposium have not yet been made available. Thanks go to Matthew Quest for loaning me a CD with this speech.
47. Tim Hector, "V. C. Bird, Renegade at Large," *Outlet*, December 23, 1981, reprinted in Hector, *The World and Us*, 213–29.
48. George Padmore's frustration is recorded in James Hooker, *Black Revolutionary: George Padmore's Path from Communism to Pan-Africanism* (New York: Praeger, 1967), 104–8.
49. C.L.R. James, *The Invading Socialist Society* (Detroit: Bewick Editions, 1976), reprinted from a mimeographed brochure of the Johnson-Forrest Tendency of 1947.
50. C.L.R. James, "Toward the Seventh: The Pan-African Congress," a speech delivered in 1976 at the First Congress of All African Writers in Dakar, Senegal, and at Federal City College in Washington, D.C., later that year, reprinted in *At the Rendezvous of Victory*, 245.
51. Hector, "Return to My Motherland," *Outlet*, June 12, 1987.

Chapter 5: Beyond Tragedy

1. Jerome Kaiseau, "No Easy Fight This Year," *Outlet*, July 11, 2003.
2. News release from *Antigua Sun*, November 21, 2002, quoted in cricket.caribbean. com/modules.php?.name.

3. Ibid. Bird added that a part of him had died as well, one more bit of the small island saga.

4. Tim Hector, "I Choose Prison Any Time, Rather Than Power Corruptly Used and Abused," *Outlet*, July 26, 1985, reprinted in Hector, *The World and Us*, 124–46.

5. I wish to thank George Lamming for traveling hours from one distant part of Barbados to another (via the capital, Bridgetown, and the change of buses) in 1987 to give me half a dozen pamphlets produced by this conference. For this and for the hours' discussion about James, I owe Lamming more than I can ever hope to repay. Nineteen years later, in Providence, Rhode Island, where Lamming was teaching at Brown University for a semester, we were to return to the same issues, after I took him to the grocery store on Saturdays to pick up his weekly provisions.

6. "Address by Cde. Maurice Bishop, Prime Minister of the People's Revolutionary Government at the Opening of the Caribbean Conference of Intellectual Workers" (Caribbean Congress of Intellectual Workers, n.p., n.d. [1982–84]), 1, 2, 23.

7. Tim Hector, "Why Is Our Literature So Different? Why?" *Outlet*, December 22, 2000.

8. "Gordon Rohlehr, The Poet and Citizen in a Degraded Community: Martin Carter's Poems of Affinity 1978–1980" (Caribbean Congress of Intellectual Workers, n.p., n.d. [1982–84]), 1–20.

9. Tim Hector, "Eustace Tuss Matthew—A Founding Father," *Outlet*, March 16, 2001.

10. Tim Hector, "Fan the Flame," *Outlet*, October 7, 2002.

11. Kenneth O. Hall, preface to *Integrate or Perish: Perspectives of Leaders of the Integration Movement, 1963–1999*, ed. Kenneth O. Hall (Mona: University of West Indies, 2000), iv. Needless to say, Hall's gloss was an attempt to make the situation seem more hopeful. See also Ian Boxill, *Ideology and Caribbean Integration* (Kingston: UWI Consortium Graduate School of Social Sciences, 1993), 40–48.

12. Perry Mars, *Ideology and Change: The Transformation of the Caribbean Left* (Detroit: Wayne State University Press, 1998), 151–52.

13. Hilary Beckels, "Independence and the Social Crisis of Nationalism in Barbados," in Beckels and Shepherd, *Caribbean Freedom*, 536–38. As a sometime visitor in the later 1980s, I can record the vitality of public debate and the sense that Bajans could choose to be a sort of Caribbean Sweden, with comprehensive education, health care, and so on. A decade later, would-be modernizers, believing in nothing so much as the global market, had triumphed at the expense of the humane vision. Beckels himself was often cast as a public pariah by the elite for stating his case on class and race.

14. Odlum's death in September 2003, two years after his fall from power and influence, offered a particularly sorrowful note; Hector greatly admired Odlum and his historic role, as did George Lamming, among others of the receding James circle, even when making criticisms. Odlum had been a founder of *Forum*, the

counterpart to Hector's ACLM. An October 3, 2003, issue of the *Outlet* had several essays devoted to Odlum. See also posting www. guyanacaribbeanpolitics.com/ memory_odlum.html

15. Timothy Brennan, *At Home in the World: Cosmopolitanism Now* (Cambridge, Mass.: Harvard University Press, 1997), 1, 4.

16. The full story, still more confused and tragic, can be told now: a series of chapters, given to publisher Lawrence Hill, was lost in 1979; James, who vowed that he would write them afresh, could not say how much had actually been finished. They were at any rate lost and have not turned up in any archive. Perhaps the fullest commentary is on a Caribbean-produced LP of 1972 in which King Lear's "the times are out of joint" is explored as the break-up of the old society and uncertainty of the new, as observed by Shakespeare through Lear's self-tortures. The philosophical nub, that kingship is too much for anyone to bear, was elucidated best if also briefly by Dave Wagner, "Philosophy and Culture," in Buhle, *C.L.R. James*, 203–5.

17. If one were forced to choose a single individual who has caught up, that would perforce be Robin D. G. Kelley, entirely self-conscious in his embrace of James's contributions; it would absolutely not be those who diluted the critiques with attacks on Pan-Africanism and black radicalism to advance themselves by drawing the support of cold war liberal doyens: the so-called Hanging Judge of recent black criticism, with flattery on his volumes from Arthur Schlesinger Jr. and Saul Bellow would be the perfect counterpoint. Walter Mosely, who has acknowledged no link with James, is arguably the literary figure closest to James's vision.

18. *A Woman's Place* (1952), a pamphlet written by Grace Lee and Selma James and published by James's group, was more than a decade ahead of the times and reflected his own views.

19. Hector, "Matriarch of Matriarchs."

20. Ibid.

21. Tim Hector, "Bare Dispossessed Man!" *Outlet*, November 21, 1997.

22. Noted, in an interview James gave in 1962, by Stefano Harney, *Nationalism and Identity: Culture and the Imagination in a Caribbean Diaspora* (Kingston: Zed Books, 1996), 33, 38–47.

23. See Selwyn Cudjoe, ed., *Caribbean Women Writers: Essays from the First International Conference* (Wellesley, Mass.: Calaloux Press, and Amherst: University of Massachusetts Press, 1990), a reconstruction of tradition very much in line with James's vision and Hector's interests, collected and overseen by the first president of the James Society.

24. See "Jamaica Kincaid and the Modernist Project," an interview with Selwyn Cudjoe, in Cudjoe, *Caribbean Women Writers*, 215–32, and the accompanying essay, Helen

Pyne Timothy, "Adolescent Rebellion and Gender Relations in *At the Bottom of the River* and *Annie John*," 233–42.

25. See Paul Buhle, *From the Lower East Side to Hollywood: Jews in American Popular Culture* (New York: Verso, 2004), 4–5, 20–22.

26. Edouard Glissant, *Caribbean Discourse: Selected Essays*, trans. J. Michael Dash (Charlottesville: Caraf Books/University of Virginia Press, 1989), 222–23.

27. Tim Hector, "In Salute to Curly Ambrose and Bert Williams," *Outlet*, September 15, 2000, reprinted in Hector Anthology, 98–100. Hector had urged a Bert Williams room in an island millennial project or even a school of performing arts in Antigua named after Williams. It didn't happen. See also Jefferson, "Blackface Master,"

28. Tim Hector, "Crisis in Cricket? Or Crisis in Society? Or, Both?" *Outlet*, April 2, 1999, reprinted in Hector Anthology, 101–4.

29. Ibid., 106–7.

30. Of the inspiration for Lord Blackshirt, nothing need be interpreted; Mussolini was "dread." Brute Force was more enigmatic, but an American noir film of that title also appeared in Hollywood after the Second World War, directed by young radical Jules Dassin, about prisoners who dream of being free. The director was put on the Blacklist a few years later. See Paul Buhle and Dave Wagner, *Radical Hollywood* (New York: New Press, 2002), 334–35.

31. Tim Hector, "The Steelband as Nationalism and Art," *Outlet*, July 21, 2000, reprinted in Hector Anthology, 108–15.

32. Coram, *Caribbean Time Bomb*, 258–59.

33. Hall, preface, xii.

34. Dorbrenne O'Marde, "Life and Death: The Basis for a New Caribbean Future," *Outlet*, January 3, 2003.

35. Eusi Kwayana had been the architect of this notion. See David Hinds, "Commentary—Power Sharing: Towards a New Political Culture," guyanapolitics.com/commentary/hinds/040701.html, posted May 17, 2002

36. Ibid. O'Marde reflected, "I have problems at time[s] with things I cannot name," pointing to the ambiguous nature of the relationship between former friends and former enemies, Lester and Hector.

37. Quoted in B. W. Higham, *Writing West Indian Histories* (London: McMillan, 1999), 156.

38. See the eloquent comments by Rex Nettleford, "Race, Identity and Independence in Jamaica" (1972), in Beckels and Shepherd, *Caribbean Freedom*, 519–27.

39. Harris, "Continuity and Discontinuity," 182–83.

40. Tim Hector, "Socialism—To Be or Not to Be," *Outlet*, April 12, 1985, reprinted in Hector, *The World and Us*, 524–30.

41. "Workers Rally for a New Beginning," *Outlet*, May 7, 2004.

42. Corthwright Marshall, "Fan the Flame: The Long Road to Press Freedom in Antigua and Barbuda," *Outlet*, May 21, 2004.

43. Colin James, "Antiguan Journalist, Tim Hector, Dies," *Jamaica Observer* online, November 13, 2002, at jamaicaobserver.com.

44. The pessimism is rife in Ramsaran, *Caribbean Survival.*

45. McKenzie Funk, "Treasure Island," *Audubon Monthly* 107 (July–August 2005), 62–69

46. Coram, *Caribbean Time Bomb*, 259.

Index